WITHDRAWN
FROM STOCK

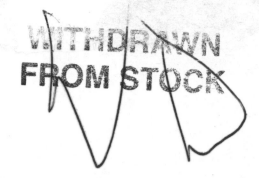

Complete Book of Women's Running

D0348294

RUNNER'S WORLD®

Complete Book of Women's Running

Get Started, Stay Motivated and Run with Confidence

DAGNY SCOTT BARRIOS

RODALE

796.42/ 3883650

This edition first published 2008 by Rodale
an imprint of Pan Macmillan Ltd
Pan Macmillan, 20 New Wharf Road, London N1 9RR
Basingstoke and Oxford
Associated companies throughout the world
www.panmacmillan.com

ISBN 978-1-905744-25-1

Copyright © 2008 by Dagny Scott Barrios

The right of Dagny Scott Barrios to be identified as the author of this work has been asserted by
her in accordance with the Copyright, Designs and Patents Act 1988.

All rights reserved. No part of this publication may be reproduced, stored in or introduced into a
retrieval system, or transmitted, in any form, or by any means (electronic, mechanical,
photocopying, recording or otherwise) without the prior written permission of the publisher.
Any person who does any unauthorized act in relation to this publication may be liable to
criminal prosecution and civil claims for damages.

1 3 5 7 9 8 6 4 2

A CIP catalogue record for this book is available from the British Library.

Book design by Susan Eugster
Cover design by Katie Tooke
Book photography by Mitch Mandel/Rodale Images

Printed and bound in Great Britain by Mackays of Chatham plc, Chatham, Kent

This book is sold subject to the condition that it shall not, by way of trade or otherwise, be lent,
re-sold, hired out, or otherwise circulated without the publisher's prior consent in any form of
binding or cover other than that in which it is published and without a similar condition
including this condition being imposed on the subsequent purchaser.

Notice

The information in this book is meant to supplement, not replace, proper exercise training. All
forms of exercise pose some inherent risks. The editor and publisher advise readers to take full
responsibility for their safety and know their limits. Before practising the exercises in this book,
be sure that your equipment is well maintained, and do not take risks beyond your level of
experience, aptitude, training and fitness. The exercise and dietary programmes in this book are
not intended as a substitute for any exercise routine or dietary regime that may have been
prescribed by your doctor. As with all exercise programmes, you should get your doctor's
approval before beginning.

Mention of specific companies, organizations or authorities in this book does not imply
endorsement by the publisher, nor does mention of specific companies, organizations or
authorities in the book imply that they endorse the book.

Visit **www.panmacmillan.com** to read more about all our books and to buy them. You will also
find features, author interviews and news of any author events, and you can sign up for
e-newsletters so that you're always first to hear about our new releases.

RODALE
LIVE YOUR WHOLE LIFE™

We inspire and enable people to improve their lives and the world around them

Contents

Acknowledgments

AMONG THE NUMEROUS LIFE-ENHANCING ASPECTS OF RUNNING, the people you meet are near the top of the list. Over the years, I've been lucky to get to know many of the wonderful runners, coaches, physicians and leaders in this sport. Dozens of these people have graciously assisted in the creation of this book, offering their time and knowledge.

First and foremost among them is Maureen Roben – runner, coach, mother and overall delightful spirit. Never without a smile and a laugh, Maureen is a force of nature who has quietly given back to the sport for years with her Women's Running Camps. She served as the sounding board for this book and helped to devise its workout schedules. Thanks also go to Diane Palmason, who cofounded and codirects the camps with Maureen. Diane's wealth of knowledge on the health of women runners was invaluable to me in my research. My thanks to both Maureen and Diane for allowing me to use their camp as a forum for discussing the issues covered in this book with other women runners.

Dr Thomas Shonka deserves thanks not only for his assistance with this book but also for his attentive treatment of my own litany of injuries. Thomas is a runner's dream podiatrist: he understands our fervent need to get back on our feet quickly, and he finds time in his busy schedule to see that he makes it so. Thomas provided invaluable help with this book.

Countless other experts contributed their wisdom to this book, among them Henley Gabeau, Judy Mahle Lutter, Lynn Jaffee, Susan Kalish, Lewis Maharam, Jack Daniels, David Martin, Neal Pire, Ray Browning, Amy Roberts, Steven Ungerleider, Carol Otis, Nancy Clark, Susan Kundrat, Jerilynn Prior, Douglas Hall, Jerry Lynch, Roy Benson and Lisa Callahan.

Special thanks go to the runners and friends who shared their thoughts and tips throughout these chapters: Shelly Steely, Nadia Prasad, Jane Welzel, Libbie Hickman, Kim Jones, Ann Boyd, Lorraine Moller, Anne Audain, JoAnn Behm Scott, Shirley Van Slooten, Mya Jones, Laurie Mizener, Mary Kirsling and so many more.

Running truly is the most global of sports – understood and appreciated in just about every country and culture – so it was a thrill to hear that this book would be published in the UK.

My thanks to Alison Hamlett at *Runner's World* in London and Liz Gough at Rodale UK for their work in shepherding the book across the ocean, rewriting, editing and generally ensuring that it is fully relevant to its newest audience.

Finally, to Bianca, my daughter, an endless expression of gratitude for her grace and wisdom. She's the best inspiration a runner, a mother, a writer could have.

Foreword

THESE DAYS, IN CASE YOU HAVEN'T HEARD, women are running the world. By many measures – shoe company surveys, retail sales, new subscriptions to *Runner's World* magazine, even entries in road races – women runners have reached 50 per cent of the total running population. And their participation is growing.

Twenty-five years ago, women made up only 5 per cent of all runners. This is a revolution, make no mistake about it. And it has happened because running is the perfect sport for women.

I actually worked this out a long time ago. It was simple, really. You didn't need a crystal ball to see it. You just had to think for a moment about women and all the attributes they bring to running.

Many women are disciplined and determined and incredibly well organized. They have to be to succeed in all the roles society layers on them – job, housework, mother, wife. And more. Running comes easily to these women, because all running takes is discipline, determination and organization – exactly what women have.

And there's a bonus: running doesn't require any special athletic skills. You don't have to be able to hit a backhand. You don't have to know a three-iron from a nine-iron or a slalom from a mogul. You just have to make up your mind that you're going to do it.

Women also excel at running because they understand the importance of patience and following directions. Men? Not always so bright. My wife cooks meals according to recipes, and they always turn out delicious. I make things up as I go along, yet I can't understand why everyone refuses to eat my concoctions.

In running, it turns out, following a plan is the key to success. There's a beginning plan, an intermediate plan, an advanced plan, a first-time marathon plan and so on. Follow the plan, and you'll succeed at running. Women value plans, and they reap the benefits.

Women also understand the emotional side of running better than men. Men sometimes make the mistake of thinking that running is a never-ending race against the stopwatch. We want to go fast. All the time. As a result, we too often become injured, fatigued and burned out. Worse, we get depressed when we reach an age where we can no longer run as fast as we did in our youth.

Women like to run fast, too. I'm not saying that they don't train as hard as men, or don't try to make it to the Olympics. But more women than men accept running for what it is – a simple and immensely satisfying fitness activity. A time for solitary reflection, or for group social banter. An opportunity to drain out all of the stress of daily living and to celebrate the joy of good health.

Over the years, I have been lucky enough to run with some famous women. I ran with Joan Benoit long before she became a Boston Marathon and Olympic champ. I ran with Oprah Winfrey long after she became an international TV and movie star. And I watched Paula Radcliffe storm to victory in the New York City Marathon less than a year after giving birth to her daughter.

And here's what I've learned from Joan, Oprah and Paula and hundreds of other women runners: you can make your running into whatever you want it to be. You can go for the gold, or you can simply set out to achieve something you never dreamed possible (even if no one else notices).

It's entirely up to you. I know you can do it, because tens of millions of other women runners have done it. In the pages that follow, Dagny Scott, a wise and experienced woman runner, has laid out all the plans and recipes and wisdom you'll need. The next step is yours.

Amby Burfoot

Amby Burfoot
Executive Editor
Runner's World magazine

Introduction

As I sit down to write this, I am sweaty, grimy even, from a windy November run that has coated me with dust. Although it's the weekend, I've logged on to the computer in an attempt to capitalize on the fresh mindset that is the gift of a run – as I so often do.

Today, I saw two friends out on the run that meanders along the outskirts of town. It is a vast and hushed landscape where the mountains give way to the quieter majesty of the endless plains to the east. Beth and Jennifer were with their three dogs, a spectrum of shaggy, golden- and cream-coloured beauties. We chatted about the run, the day, yesterday's workout, the dogs. The two mentioned how they looked forward to this time each week, this Sunday ritual. Time away from husbands and boyfriends, from work and home, from tidier pursuits. This is what it's all about, they said. Yes, I said. This is what it's all about. I felt a chill and noticed that I had goose bumps, although the air was not cold yet.

So I watched Beth and Jennifer resume running with their dogs, enjoying their piece of the day. And I tried to work out why such a simple thing moved me so. Dozens of women were out running today – some in groups, some alone. In fact, there were far more women than men. And then it struck me just how far we've come. A generation ago, women had no such model for companionship. Men alone participated in athletics and reaped its ensuing benefits: the bonds of friendship, the revitalization of time away, the healthy glow from movement. Women's participation in sports – and, in particular, in the hugely popular second running boom – has given us a new paradigm. A refuge in the day that holds only good things. A place in which we develop friendships, love and trust as solid and uncomplicated as the beat of our feet and the rhythm of our breathing.

When I learned that I would have the honour of writing this book – and it is an honour – I felt a deep sense of responsibility. How could I do service to the depths of feeling that I have for this sport? How could I possibly enumerate all the gifts that running has given me: strength and health; love and friendship; a sense of self, of discipline, of capability and power and even a profession and a husband?

As I sat down over the course of a year to write this book, my goal was to impart the breadth and depth of what running can mean to women: more than just fitness or friendship or sanity but rather all those things together. I can only hope that this book offers you at least a portion of the strength and inspiration that I have drawn from other women along the way.

I hope to see you out on the roads, the trails or the track. May your feet and your heart feel light.

CHAPTER 1

Women and Running

THERE'S AN IMPORTANT STORY YOU SHOULD KNOW ABOUT. It's the story of millions of women finding their legs. Along the way, they found their voices, their hearts and their dreams. This story can be yours, too. All of running's benefits are right here for you to grab.

Why a women's running book? Are women runners different from men? After all, we both put one foot in front of the other, again and again. We both revel as we become fit and strong. We both struggle through days of plodding on leaden legs and celebrate days when our feet feel fitted with wings. In these ways women runners are no different from their male counterparts.

But wait.

Listen to those millions of women runners. Listen to their quiet breaths as they talk in pre-dawn pairs before the rest of the family wakes or with their group of friends on Saturday morning before lattes. Listen to the lessons and the laughter, the questions and the camaraderie they share to the rhythm of steady footsteps: 'I feel so much stronger . . . ', 'I'm ready to take on a new challenge . . . ', 'I never thought I could, but now . . . '.

Women develop a special sorority on the roads. The bond is based on an understanding of the empowerment that comes with running, full realization of the capabilities of mind and body, appreciation of how far they have come and a knowing wink that says how much is yet to be gained. Running, in short, is growth. Movement. Progress. To run is to feel alive. And so they talk and share – and run. Singly and in groups, swiftly and slowly, they run.

THE WOMEN'S RUNNING BOOM

Running has always had some women enthusiasts. But as millions of women have taken up the sport, they have redefined it even as it has redefined them.

At the onset of the first running boom, which hit its stride in the 1970s, female runners were the exception. The key players were men. Frank Shorter won the gold medal in the 1972 Olympic Marathon in Munich. Famed New Zealand track coach Arthur Lydiard created the idea of long, slow-distance running for professionals, and at the same time spread the gospel of jogging as exercise around the globe. In Oregon, a coach named Bowerman and a runner named Knight teamed up to create from scratch the running shoes that would eventually become the Nike brand. Sure, there were some women here and there, but they were oddities, a sideshow to the main event. Running was a man's world.

At that time, strenuous sports activities had long been considered unfeminine and even harmful for women. Most women stuck to traditional, polite activities such as golf and tennis. It was unusual to see a woman running down the street, and those who did were sometimes asked who was chasing them. But around the same time that running was becoming a phenomenon, the women's movement was challenging and changing assumptions about what women were capable of. By the 1980s, men still dominated the sport, but it was no longer uncommon to see women jogging in parks, on tracks and on trails around the world.

All the while, running was gradually evolving as it grew from a fairly obscure sport that a few hard-core athletes took part in to a fitness activity of the masses. Good for the heart and lungs, easy on the budget, and possessing only the shallowest of learning curves, running grew in popularity as more people began to recognize the value of aerobic exercise. During the 1990s, as fitness morphed from healthy pursuit to holistic health and wellness lifestyle, many countries experienced a second running boom. More than ever, running filled the bill for more and more people, providing a social circle, stress relief, personal growth, contribution to community and more.

Now into a new millennium, women are clearly driving both the resurgence and recharacterization of the sport. For one thing, women have been fuelling the sport's growth in terms of numbers. Part of this is down to what *Runner's World* Publishing Director, Steven Seaton, refers to as the two S's:

simplicity and success. 'Running is a simple sport and we all know how to do it,' says Seaton. 'That is its universal appeal but I think a lot of women are specifically drawn to it by its record of success. It works. Whether you want to use it to lose weight, relieve stress or simply feel better about yourself, running will do it more effectively than any other form of exercise. Of course you have to commit to the activity but it's an honest exercise and rewards your effort.'

An older generation of women continues to discover the sport for its own reasons. As time has become a commodity in seemingly ever-dwindling supply, women have felt increasingly pressed to balance career and family while attempting to maintain a healthy lifestyle. For growing numbers of women, running has been a saving grace. A workout for the whole body, running requires a minimum of time, instruction, equipment and planning.

Although many women have entered the sport for its easily accessible physical benefits, its surprise bonuses are what spur their enthusiasm. Running works both socially and in solitude, for relieving stress and solving problems, for relaxing and venting. Running has become a simple route to fitness that fits the complicated lifestyle of today's woman.

Women's enthusiasm for running has carried over into organized events, accentuating the sport's social and community elements. More and more races, fun runs and walk/run events cater to women. Women-only events and charity fund-raisers regularly draw tens of thousands of women. It's not unusual for women to make up a large minority in a marathon or a 10-K race, activities which were once vastly male. 'Midpackers' are recognized with special awards, as are finishers in their golden years. The cumulative result is a sport that celebrates everyone who participates, not just those who are fleet of foot. Says Seaton, 'Those changes to the racing culture and the sport are directly effected by women – they are the new "midpackers".'

They're also, he points out, redefining the front of the pack. Races now regularly offer equal prize money for women and men, something that was unheard of in the sport even a few years ago and is still not the case in many other sports. The gap between male and female world best times is closing. It's not that women will ever match men's times, but the 'softness' in women's records – the way records were easily broken and reset, caused by a lack of serious competition – is all but gone. 'More women are racing, there are more role models, so women's effect is filtering up as well as down,' Seaton says.

Women have been able to have such an impact in part because of running's egalitarian nature. Join a running club for a Sunday outing or the starting line of your local road race, and all are equals: young and old, wealthy and poor, all races, colours and creeds. And yes, male and female. It's one of the unique elements of the sport that Seaton appreciates. 'There's no gender discrimination in running,' he says. 'I regularly train with women and men and what's important is whether I can run at their pace not their gender.'

Friendships that might seem odd in another context are struck up when two strides fall into sync somewhere out on an otherwise lonely road. The speedy and the slow traditionally meet at the end, sharing their tales over a cup of tea and a piece of chocolate cake. And on race day, the tortoise shares the starting line with the hare, and the jogger can literally follow in the foot-

TRAINING LOG

So who am I and why did I write this book? After all, you haven't seen my name in the annals of Olympic-gold history. I'm not a hero or a household name, like Paula Radcliffe or Grete Waitz.

No, when it comes to running, I'm probably far more like you. I've had my dreams of athletic glory since I was a little girl. I've come tantalizingly close to some of those dreams over the years – close enough to taste them at times, mostly salty and bittersweet in my mouth. But in the end, I did not become a professional runner. I became a journalist, focusing my pen and thoughts on female athletes and on runners in particular.

Writing and running have woven together to define my life and my career. The two passions have built upon each other, becoming virtually indistinguishable. The lessons I've learned while pursuing my goals of excellence on the track and on the road are the foundation upon which I've built a career as a journalist. The women who have crossed my reporter's path have been an unending source of inspiration.

Throughout these chapters, I share some of my personal running experiences in these 'Training Log' sections. It's fair to say that these experiences range from the sublime to the ridiculous – with the ridiculous winning out most often. In running, after all, we learn as we go, bumps and bruises along with the triumphs. At most, I hope you can glean some enlightenment from my journey – at least that you can come away from it with a good laugh.

In the end, I've learned that this journey is what counts. It is a lesson that comes sooner or later to every woman who runs. More than any medals earned or weight lost or races run, the journey is always the thing. That's why we run. It's what we share. And that's why I wrote this book.

steps of her professional heroes. It's within the context of such an open social fabric that women have made their mark on all levels of the sport.

BRINGING IT ALL BACK HOME

As more women have become runners, the body of research documenting the sport's effect on women's bodies has grown. Now it seems that for every similarity between men and women runners there's a significant difference. For example, although the training principles of gaining speed and fitness remain the same for men and women, fluctuations in women's hormone levels can mean that it's more complicated for them to peak for an event. On the other hand – possibly thanks to those same hormones – women seem better cut out for endurance than men are, due to higher pain thresholds and differences in energy metabolism. And though the principles of biomechanics are the same for both sexes, women are more prone to developing knee and foot problems than men, because they have wider hips. The female metabolism even seems to react differently to exercise, resulting in different nutritional needs. The list goes on.

In addition to such biological nuts and bolts, many women find that their questions and concerns about running veer in different directions than men's. Yes, the story of women's running is a story of how to become fit, and, should you desire it, even how to get fast. But it's also a story of how to set and reach goals, make time for yourself, make peace with yourself and more. It is a story of relishing the moment and working toward the future, of appreciating the little things in life and never losing sight of the larger picture. These are the benefits women find when they become runners – benefits every bit as noticeable as trimmer thighs and faster times.

CHAPTER 2

Tools of the Trade

RUNNING IS SUCH A SIMPLE ENDEAVOUR. To get ready, you just lace up your shoes and head out the door.

It's so simple that plenty of women think that they can lace up any old shoes. They'll rummage in the wardrobe for some worn antique pair of trainers and head off happily on collapsed heels and flapping soles. Well, that won't do. Running doesn't require a great investment in gear, but it does require a special pair of running shoes. Not those shoes you used to wear in aerobics class or those cheap summer pumps but real running shoes, built for running – and ideally used only for running.

Why? Wearing only good shoes can keep a runner training year after year on uncomplaining knees, but the wrong shoes can lead to unhappy, debilitated joints, muscle soreness and even injury. Shoes can mean the difference between an enjoyable experience and one miserable enough to quit the sport. So don't even think of trying to save a few pounds on shoes. A visit to the podiatrist will cost a lot more than a pair of running shoes.

Just as you shouldn't run in any old shoe, you also shouldn't run in any old bra. For fairly obvious reasons, the right sports bra also can make the difference between misery and enjoyment out on the trail. A bit extra spent here won't be a mistake.

And that's really all the must-haves. Of course, the longer you run the more accessories you'll start to consider your must-haves. Beyond shoes and bras, you may opt for performance clothing that keeps you cool and dry in the summer and warm in the winter. Or you may notice the watches, sunglasses, hydration systems and other gadgets marketed to runners. Some are helpful, some less so. Some work wonders but cost a small fortune. Should you buy them?

Ultimately, the amount of gear you end up with is a matter of personal preference. Some runners wear enough of these gizmos to get them through an ultramarathon even when they're out for a 30-minute jaunt. Other runners are ascetics, sticking to simple shorts and a T-shirt and replacing even those items only when they wear thin. Much of the fancy clothing and gear is suited more to the competitive runner who logs many miles than to the 3-times-a-week jogger. On the other hand, many recreational runners find that purchasing a treat such as a new jacket or a pair of sunglasses can be just the thing to jump-start flagging motivation.

The bottom line is that before you start running, or if you're an old pro who hasn't paid proper attention to her body, it's time to hit the shops. Choose some shoes and a bra. Beyond that, it's your choice: knock yourself out on the extras or exit the shops with your budget intact. Read on to learn what to look for when choosing any of these items.

SHOES

Running shoes are high-tech insulation between your feet and the ground. 'When you run, your feet might strike the ground between 70 and 100 times per minute, each time with a force two to three times the weight of your body,' says Tim Hilden, an exercise physiologist and biomechanics specialist. 'Each time you contact the ground, that force is transmitted up into the body. The right pair of shoes can help to attenuate that force.'

Today's running shoes are small scientific wonders, backed by multi-million-pound research and development labs. Hundreds of different models exist to accommodate different foot and body variations. The shoes are designed to complement your natural structure of bones, ligaments and tendons – commonly referred to as the body's biomechanics – and therefore minimize damage from incessant pounding. The right shoe for you will depend on several factors, including the way your foot strikes the ground, your gait, your weight and your running programme.

Some of the most impressive advances in shoes in the past few years are in the technology that has essentially replaced the conventional foam midsole cushioning. Mark Plaatjes, one-time world champion marathon runner explains that new engineering of the midsole infrastructure that relies on air or other technology means shoe durability has been greatly extended.

For shoes with more traditional materials, the midsole is often the first element to break down, often with no visible clues. It's a good rule of thumb to replace these shoes after 300 to 400 miles. (Mark a calendar when you purchase a new pair to help you remember when to replace them.) The newer generation of shoes, Plaatjes says, might last another 200 miles.

Expect to pay a minimum of £40 for your running shoes. Anything less than that and they're not really performance-oriented shoes designed to keep you free from injury. They may look good, but chances are they won't be offering you the support and cushioning you need.

Beginning runners often ask which brand of shoe they should buy. The answer is whichever one suits your needs and feels best. This is one case when asking your friend what she runs in won't help: a model that fits one woman like a dream can be an invitation to an injury on another.

All the major running shoe manufacturers produce a variety of shoes for runners' varying needs. Since each manufacturer tends to have a 'signature' shape and feel – such as wider in the heel or narrow through the middle – you should try several brands to find the one that fits your feet best. While a few companies were pioneers in creating true women's shoes – which were more than sized-down men's shoes in a feminine colour palate – these days the major shoe manufacturers all offer a wide range of true women's shoes, built for a woman's particular needs and on a female last.

The easiest and most reliable way to choose a shoe is to shop at a specialist running shop. The salespeople at such locations typically are experienced and well trained in runners' needs. They will be likely to ask about your training schedule and injury history and may even watch you run. Then they'll be able to recommend several pairs of shoes that are best suited to your needs for you to try on. Many running stores have treadmills set up so that the salesperson can analyse your gait and your needs, and so that you can actually run in the shoes you're considering.

While you might get lucky and find such service at a large sport shop, they are less likely to have salespeople trained to this degree of specificity. In addition, their selection of running shoes isn't typically as large as that of a specialist running shop.

If you don't have a running shop near by and must choose shoes without the help of a knowledgeable salesperson, your next best bet is to seek the assistance of a good website. Many offer shoe-buying guides that can help you with the process. (See 'Why a Woman's Shoe?' on page 11.)

In any case, it's a good idea to do a little research on your own feet. The most important distinction to learn is whether you *overpronate*, *supinate* or are *neutral*. That's not as complicated as it sounds. Some pronation is a natural part of the shock-absorbing action that takes place as your foot hits the ground and proceeds to roll forward. Ideally, when you run, your foot hits first on the outside portion of your heel, and then your weight shifts toward the inside and front of your foot, until finally you push off on the ball of your foot and your toes.

If you *overpronate*, your arch doesn't offer adequate support, and your foot collapses inward too much upon landing. This lack of arch support without proper shoes to control the excessive motion can result in pain and numerous types of injuries.

On the other end of the spectrum, feet that are rigid and don't roll inward enough are also problematic because they don't provide adequate shock absorption for your legs. This condition – less common than overpronation, and even less common among women than among men – is called *supination*.

Runners whose feet pronate normally do neither of the above and are generally called *neutral*.

Knowing which category you fit into is perhaps the most important element in finding the right shoe. You'll want to start by looking at the proper shoe category based on the way your feet move when you run. Then you can look at models from several different brands in order to find your best shoe.

Here are two simple ways to help you determine which category you fit into:

Look at an old pair of shoes. The pattern of wear tells a story. The soles and midsoles of an overpronator's shoes tend to wear down and compress toward the inside of the heel and the inside of the big toe. A supinator's shoes tend to wear down and compress all along the outside. Women with neutral feet will generally have evenly worn shoes.

Observe your arches. Stand with your feet shoulder width apart, and then bend your knees so that you're in a semi-squatting position. See if your arches naturally collapse inward or stay rather high. Now twist your trunk slightly from side to side and look again: do your arches collapse and your ankles roll inward, or do they maintain their position? The more your arches flatten and your ankles roll in the greater your degree of pronation.

Now that you know which category your feet fit into, you know what kind of running shoe you need. Running shoes generally fall into 3 categories to parallel the categories outlined above.

✳ **Motion Control.** For the most excessive pronators and heavier runners. These shoes will be the most rigid in your hand, literally difficult to twist when you grab the shoe at the heel and the toe and attempt to torque in opposite directions. They will feature firm technical elements in the arch or heel area to discourage the foot from rolling in. Also, these shoes tend to be built on a fairly straight last; if you turn them upside down and look at the bottom, you can see a straight line from heel to toe.

✳ **Stability.** For moderate overpronators or those who are lighter weight and therefore do not need excessive control. These shoes offer elements of both cushioning and support, but the arch control isn't nearly as intense as those in a motion-control shoe.

✳ **Neutral.** Cushioned shoes for neutral runners or those who supinate. These shoes offer minimal support, allowing maximum flexibility for those with an already rigid arch. They are long on cushioning and are typically built with a more curved shape (turn the shoe over to see a curved line from heel to toe).

Once you've established which category of shoe you need, follow these tips to help you find the perfect pair.

Try on a number of styles from different manufacturers. Each will have a slightly different shape, and one will mould to your foot better than the others.

Run in the shoes. Walking in a pair of shoes won't tell you how they'll feel when you're running. Try a few strides down an aisle or a hallway. Better yet, if the shop allows, take them for a spin outside or on a treadmill. Pay particular attention to pinching, slippage, tight spots and rubbing. *Running shoes should fit perfectly when you try them on.* There's no such thing as breaking in a running shoe. If any part of your foot feels confined, pinched or squeezed, you can bet your feet will hurt after a few miles of running.

Wear socks of the same thickness as the ones you'll be running in. If necessary, ask to borrow a pair from the shop.

Get measured, and ask a salesperson to check the shoes for proper sizing. A whopping 85 per cent of women wear shoes that are too small, according to researchers at Homerton Hospital in London. For some women, improper sizing is a vanity issue. Others simply don't realize that their foot size increases with age, especially after pregnancy. Make sure you allow a finger's width of space between the end of your toes and the shoe; otherwise you'll suffer from jammed toes and black toenails. Also make sure the shoe

Why a Woman's Shoe?

Years ago, when manufacturers first began producing women's running shoes, the models were little more than scaled-down men's models offered in powder blue. Today women's shoes truly are built to work with women's bodies and feet. Some of the differences typical to women include:

❯ Lighter overall weight, with respect to foot length, as well as less muscle mass.

❯ Feet with a lower overall profile – not as high – than men's, therefore requiring less overall volume in a shoe.

❯ A tendency toward bunions, often exacerbated by the wearing of pointed shoes and high heels.

❯ A greater tendency to pronate, partly due to wider hips and the ensuing angle of the leg meeting the ground.

---

is wide enough. If the front of your foot feels confined against the edges of the shoe, look for a brand such as New Balance that comes in different widths.

SPORTS BRAS

Just like your old tennis shoes, your old everyday bra wasn't meant for running. Sports bras are designed to minimize the bouncing associated with impact sports. The good ones also wick sweat away from your body to reduce chafing and keep you at a comfortable temperature.

Athletics are more forgiving for small-breasted women because control is less of an issue; they can get away with simpler styles of bras. Women with larger breasts need more supportive bras, of course – these tend to be engineered to a greater degree. That might sound obvious, but it doesn't take too many trips to the local park to see that many large-breasted women either don't know about the importance of a special running bra or don't realize that styles exist that actually do offer them adequate support.

Be aware that as sports have become more of an everyday influence on fashion, athletic styles of bras are quite commonplace. But there's a distinction between a garment that simply appears sporty and one intended for exercise. As a runner, you'll want to choose a bra clearly intended for impact-sport performance. You're most likely to find these from reputable name brands of sporting goods manufacturers.

When choosing a bra, try on a few and pay attention to the following:

❋ The band around your rib cage should be snug but not stifling. You should be able to breathe freely. Try raising your arms above your head, bending them and swinging them around. The band should not move. If it does, the fabric will rub and irritate your skin.

❋ The fabric over your breasts should likewise be snug but not stifling. Jump up and down a bit. Your breasts should feel comfortable, and the bounce should be minimal. Remember that any movement you feel now will only be multiplied on a run.

❋ Look for well-crafted seams. This is where most chafing occurs. Seams should be sewn flat and free of extraneous material – or better yet, they should be on the outside of the bra.

❋ Make sure the fabric is meant to handle activity and sweat. Look on the label to see which fabrics the bra is made from. Steer clear of cotton in the liner; it will keep sweat clinging to your body. Instead, look for a label that touts the fabric's wicking properties. This is one case where seeing the word *polyester* on the label is not a bad thing. Most bras intended for sports performance will have hang tags indicating properties such as wicking.

❋ Expect to pay between £25 and £35 for a quality sports bra, and more for styles intended for large-breasted women.

❋ If you wear a C cup or larger, you might find greater comfort and support with a bra that encapsulates each breast separately instead of compressing the entire chest. Many manufacturers now produce special offerings for women with larger breasts. It really shouldn't be necessary for women to layer two bras on top of each other – once a poor but common solution for well-endowed women.

To maintain the life of your sports bras, wash them on a gentle cycle and let them air-dry. This will maintain the elastic for a longer period of time. And clean out your drawer annually. Replace your bras when they no longer provide adequate support.

SHORTS AND TOPS

Today's fabrics can help wick away sweat so that it evaporates, keeping you dry and free from chafing. This feature can be especially helpful in shorts. Look for a liner made of CoolMax or a similar synthetic fabric. Shorts are available in a variety of cuts and lengths to accommodate different tastes. Be aware that what you gain in modesty with longer shorts, you'll give up in range of motion. That's not a problem unless you're running at fast speeds and need full leg lift. Expect to pay around £20 for running shorts. Although that might seem steep, you'll appreciate the comfort from the first step.

Traditionally runners have worn cotton T-shirts, but if you live in an especially humid climate or run for more than 30 minutes at a stretch, you might want to invest in a tank top or singlet made from one of those great synthetic wicking fabrics. Cotton, which tends to hold moisture, can get pretty heavy and cause some nasty chafing when it's hanging on to an hour's worth of your sweat.

APPAREL FOR RAIN AND COLD

The elements just aren't what they used to be. Today, a runner can be out in the rain or cold for hours and remain comfortable. High-tech fabrics have been developed specifically for exertion in the cold and rain. These materials repel water from the outside while allowing perspiration to evaporate from the inside.

When buying running jackets and tights, read the label to ensure that they're constructed of a material designed for this one-way moisture transport. A heavy lining will provide more warmth, but if you're going to purchase only one running outfit, a more versatile option is to choose items with very light linings (or no lining at all) that can be worn year-round. On rainy days, wear the jacket over a light underlayer of shorts and a wicking top. In colder weather, start with a base layer of tights and a wicking top. If necessary, add a middle layer of insulating fleece. (Cotton should never be used as a layer in cold and damp conditions. It absorbs water and quickly grows heavy and cold.) When choosing a running outfit, look for these features.

❋ The jacket's zip and/or collar should not scratch your chin when fully zipped.

❋ The collar should fit fairly snugly around your neck to keep cold air out.

❋ Sleeves with Velcro or elastic allow easy access to your watch.

❋ Vents in the jacket's sides, back or underarms provide breathability.

✱ A jacket panel can cover your rear end during very cold weather.

✱ Zips at the ankles of tights should enable easy ins and outs with your shoes still on.

SOCKS

Running socks are available in every weight, length and material. The main ones to avoid are those made of 100 per cent cotton. Cotton tends to keep your feet clammy and cold in the winter and cause blisters and chafing in the summer. Instead, look for synthetic blends made from polyester, acrylic, CoolMax and even Teflon. Wool blends such as SmartWool are good for winter. Wool or synthetic-blend socks will provide superior wicking and lessen the chance of blisters. Double-layer socks are also effective at reducing the risk of blisters.

The thicker the sock the more cushioning it will provide. Many women prefer thicker socks for easy runs because of their superior comfort and cushioning. For faster runs or races, look for a thinner sock. The reduction in cushioning allows for greater 'road feel' and responsiveness.

It's important to try on socks with the shoes in which you will be running. Some thicker socks can require a shoe up to a half-size larger.

ELECTRONIC DEVICES

Watches

Sports watches today are really miniature computers. They can do everything from sounding an alarm at regular intervals to storing your workouts so you can download them onto your home computer. Of course, if you're running only 30 minutes a day, you can do without the bells and whistles – and the added expense.

No matter how simple or complex a model you decide upon, look for large, easy-to-press buttons and large, easy-to-see digits. These models are easier to use while running. An easily audible beep accompanying each press of the buttons is helpful, too.

Many experienced women runners prefer to avoid so-called women's models. Their petite size means smaller, harder-to-press buttons, not to mention fewer memory features. For most women, the men's models fit just fine and are superior products. Stick to plastic or fabric straps, which are durable and comfortable. When it's time to change the battery, take the watch to a jeweller to have a new one installed. If you try to do it yourself, your watch might become disposable before its time.

Heart-rate Monitors

Until the 1990s, the heart-rate monitor was an obscure gadget used mostly by professional athletes. Today it has gained widespread acceptance as a useful tool for runners of all levels. Heart-rate monitors can be used to target specific zones of effort on harder runs and to ensure that a run doesn't get too difficult on easy days. Most monitors consist of two parts: the pulse-reading monitor band, which straps around your rib cage just under your bust, and the display unit, which looks and works much like a watch.

Monitors come with a wide range of functions and settings. As with any electronic device, that can sometimes be more overwhelming than helpful. When buying a heart-rate monitor, look for one that's simple enough that you will actually use it. Most runners prefer a stopwatch feature and an alarm that sounds when you exceed or fall short of your target pace. Expect to pay at least £40 for a monitor with these functions.

Should You Use a Heart-rate Monitor?

Plenty of runners and coaches love to use heart-rate monitors, but are they right for you? Heart-rate monitors provide an easy, high-tech method of taking your pulse. By displaying your heart rate, they give you instant feedback on a run, essentially telling you how hard you're working. You can then adjust your effort by running faster or slower to reach the rate you desire.

Proponents appreciate this objective measure of a workout. After all, numbers never lie. So why doesn't everybody take advantage of the feedback that a monitor can offer?

Some runners love the sport because it puts them closely in tune with their bodies. For these athletes, it's a challenge – and a joy – to learn to read their physical responses during training. Mechanical input can be seen as an intrusion on what should be a natural and flowing effort.

Others argue that numbers can in fact lie, and that if you do nothing but follow the beep on a machine, you lose the benefit of *feeling* that you might possibly be able to push harder, regardless of what the monitor is telling you.

There is no right or wrong when it comes to heart-rate monitors. Runners of all levels benefit from their feedback; likewise, runners of all levels succeed in training without them. Should you try one? It all boils down to your personality.

GPS Devices

If you thrill at the idea of knowing precisely how fast your last mile was, exactly how far you went on each run, and even mapping out your route on your computer when you get home, then GPS (global position) devices were made for you. If the thought of wearing a computer on your arm that tells you all this and more sounds a little, well, beside the point, then you can

When Just a Shoe Isn't Enough

Athletic shoe inserts are designed to take the place of your shoe's removable insole or to work in conjunction with it. Made in a variety of materials, inserts range from arch supports to heel cups, from half-length to full-length and more.

For many women, the insoles that come with their running shoes perform perfectly fine. But if your arches deviate from 'normal' – meaning they're either very high or very flat – you may benefit from special insoles, says internationally renowned podiatrist Dr Thomas Shonka. The more you deviate from a perfect arch, the more likely you'll benefit from an orthotic device added to the shoe. Another tip-off is the onset of running-related injuries after increasing mileage. 'If you develop an injury every time you go over a certain number of miles per week, that can be an indication of an overuse injury that is biomechanically related. Shoe inserts can alleviate that kind of injury,' Dr Shonka says.

First try running in shoes that are well suited for you without additional accessories. If pain develops in your feet, knees, hips or back, inserts might be a simple solution. (You can try them without the expense of consulting a physician – a specialist at a running shoe shop should be able to help you choose an appropriate model.) If you don't get relief from an over-the-counter model within a few weeks, more aggressive customized orthotics can be crafted from a personalized mould. See a sports physician; podiatrists who specialize in running or sports medicine are best qualified to make running shoe inserts. Expect to pay between £150 and £200.

Here's a rundown of the most common inserts and their functions.

Arch supports. Designed for different arch types, these insoles are moulded for varying degrees of support. Primarily for overpronators, whose

save the money you would have spent on one of these to help with race-entry fees.

One nice thing is that you needn't be a technophile in order to figure out how to use the latest models. 'These devices have become so much better,' says running-shop owner Mark Plaatjes. 'They're simple now – to the point where you can simply hit "start" and "stop" and get your distance and pace.' Indeed,

feet collapse inward too much upon landing, they stabilize the foot and ankle. To find a pair that feels comfortable, try them with your running shoes in the store before you buy them. If these don't provide relief, custom-made orthotics might be in order.

Cushioned insoles. Although these inserts are used mainly for additional cushioning and comfort, some runners also place them over custom-made orthotics when the orthotics don't provide their own cushioning. Each insert is a flat, thin layer of foam that is either full-length or half-length. When used only in the back of your shoe, the insert can raise your heel to alleviate stress on tight calf muscles. The inserts are also easily trimmed into any shape: you can glue trimmed pieces to specific areas of your shoe's insole to build up cushioning where you need it. Play around to find a formula that works for you, or go to a podiatrist for guidance.

Heel cups. These look like what the name implies, with the cup cradling and cushioning the heel. Heel cups are typically used to provide relief from the pain of plantar fasciitis (inflammation of the band of tissue on the bottom of the foot), which is felt just under the heel. Heel cups may alleviate the pain but they don't solve the problem, which is usually related to overpronation. Sturdier shoes or arch supports might be more appropriate.

Metatarsal cushions. You insert a metatarsal cushion in the front of your shoe under the ball of your foot. It can help alleviate the pounding on the bones that are just behind your toes – and the ensuing pain – by providing both support and cushioning.

Replacement insoles. These are beefed-up versions of the insoles that come in shoes. Replacement insoles can provide better, more durable cushioning than regular shoe insoles. They essentially upgrade your shoe without changing its characteristics.

that's how most runners use them. You can easily programme in your desired pace, and an alert will tell you if you're falling behind or running too hard. But there's more, Plaatjes points out. 'Then if you want, if you're really techy, you can go to the website and map the route you just ran, it will give you your elevation change, you can store all your workouts, everything.'

A drawback is that the technology is dependent on a clear satellite line. Running in areas with lots of trees or tall buildings or even running on a cloudy day can throw off the results. Still, most GPS devices promise roughly 95 per cent accuracy.

An entry-level GPS will likely run about £100 (the Garmin Forerunner is a popular model). Spending upwards of £200 should get you a heart-rate monitor in the mix, as well as superior satellite technology.

There's no doubt that these devices are addictive – start wearing one and you'll wonder how you ever functioned without it. And yet . . . must we really know our distance each day to the tenth of the mile? Isn't learning your pacing part of the natural progression of learning your body? OK, call me a Luddite. And a hypocrite. Let's put it this way: I haven't bought one. I don't like the idea of tracking my runs to this degree. Running is just about the only thing in my life that's possible without any thought, quantification or technology. But I admit it: I really enjoy it when one of my training partners has one of these gadgets.

Tracking Devices

The newest technology allows you to track your runs based not on GPS but rather on your stride and cadence. Nike coupled with Apple to pioneer a version of the technology that works through an iPod to create a computerized record of your run. A chip embedded in the running shoe measures stride length based on the frequency of stride and the amount of time the runner's foot remains on the ground. Tests have proven the technology to be highly accurate, especially after you've personally calibrated your device. When the run is finished, information from the workout can be downloaded into your computer and tracked online. Nike's website allows runners to have plenty of fun beyond this, encouraging community and camaraderie by comparing yourself to others, training virtually with others, and offering support along the way. The chip itself costs around £20, but you'll also need the correct iPod version. Nike sells shoes enabled for the devices, but it's not essential that you purchase these to use the chip.

Adidas has coupled with Polar to create a computerized tracking device

Smart Tips

A running shop is your best bet for finding the right gear, especially proper shoes and a sports bra. If you don't have a running shop near by, try one of these speciality online or catalogue retailers.

→ www.alexandrasports.com

www.wiggle.co.uk

www.sweatshop.co.uk

www.sportshoes.com

→ Women's-specific retailers include She Active and Sweaty Betty

www.sheactive.co.uk

www.sweatybetty.com

→ If you're looking for a sports bra, the ladies at Less Bounce are happy to answer questions and offer advice on the best sports bra for you. To find out more, visit www.lessbounce.com

---

that works in conjunction with a heart-rate monitor. It offers feedback on pace, distance, stride efficiency, heart rate and even elevation. It doesn't come cheap – you'll need to purchase the device for about £300 (online price), as well as special shoes and apparel to house the required sensors – but for the runner who wants to track virtually every aspect of her training, it's the ultimate in information.

SUNGLASSES

Sunglasses for running are designed to provide protection from sun, wind, glare and flying objects such as insects. Some runners won't leave home without them; others never wear them. If you do purchase a pair, look for shatterproof lenses that offer broad-spectrum protection, filtering out both UVA and UVB rays. Although prices on name brands with superior styling easily top £100, you actually can find models for £20 that have polarized lenses and good UV protection. (They might not be as durable or protected by as good a warranty as the fancier models.)

The glasses should fit snugly, so that they don't bounce when you're running, but they shouldn't fit so tightly that they give you a headache. When trying them on, prop them up to see if they'll stay on top of your head: since weather can change while you're out running, it's an added convenience if they stay put in that position.

TRAINING LOG

At the risk of sounding like everybody's grandmother, here's an 'I remember when' story. I was 8 years old when I started running. That was back around 1970 – the Stone Age of the sport. No women's running shoes existed; no children's running shoes existed. Men's running shoes were a relatively new concept, and even those were hard to find. (In those days, tennis shoes and high-tops pretty much covered the sporting gamut.) My parents bought shoes for me from a guy named Dick Pond, who travelled around to cross-country meets selling running shoes from the back of his van. We'd get the smallest size he had, and I would stuff them with paper towels to fill out the toes.

And so it's with great fondness that I remember my first pair of true women's running shoes. They fit. They were fast. They looked cool. (For about a week, that is. A rainy day turned their cheery blue into a mildewed green that never quite cleaned up.) Having them made me feel like a certified member of this sweaty, gruelling sport, despite the fact that I was 'just a girl'.

Of course, I didn't know it then, but many early versions of women's shoes were just downsized men's models in pastel shades. Plenty of them were cheaper quality as well, because, the thinking went, a woman didn't need 'serious' shoes.

Well, women's shoes have come a long way. Virtually all of today's women's shoes made by reputable manufacturers are truly built for women's feet and are offered in the same range of quality as men's models. Indeed, manufacturers consider the female market a hot segment: they realize that all those women runners mean pound signs. Their economic opportunism is good news for you: now when women go to the running shop, they have the luxury of choosing from a large number of shoes that truly offer an excellent range of options. Shoes come in every price, shape, style and size imaginable. May your choice bring you as much joy and inspiration as my first pair brought me.

HYDRATION SYSTEMS

In most climates and locations, you needn't worry about carrying water unless you're running for more than an hour. In especially humid and hot weather and on remote trail runs, carrying your own liquid is always a good precaution, even on shorter runs.

Even the simple concept of a portable water container has evolved over the past several years. New belt models feature several holsters and disperse the weight of the fluid over several smaller bottles. These are far more comfortable than a belt that holds a single bottle in the middle of your back. The drawback is that they typically can't carry as much liquid. For many runners, they're sufficient on all but the longest runs.

Other hydration systems come in backpack or bumbag form, with a bladder connected to a tube for sipping. These are best suited to runners who plan to be out for several hours. For shorter workouts, their extra weight isn't worthwhile.

In all cases, look for a model with a small pocket in which you can carry a key, some money and an energy gel. And yes, these do come in sizes, so be sure to choose the model that suits your running needs and body size.

CHAPTER 3

A Beginner's Guide to Frequently Asked Questions

You walk out the door, you start to jog, and you feel . . . awkward. Silly. Clumsy. Fat. Slow. Any number of things. Any number of things except like a runner.

Stop right there. Before you take another step, remember: everybody started somewhere. The best of runners began with the same slow steps that you are about to take. Your first run can feel anything but normal. You're full of uncertainties: can I really do this? What if it hurts?

To start you off, here are answers to novice runners' most commonly asked questions. This quick primer will alleviate your fears and speed you on your way out the door with confidence.

Q: Can't I just walk?

A: Well, sure. Walking is better than the alternative, if the alternative is watching a season's worth of sitcoms on the sofa or spending your lunch hour surfing the Internet aimlessly – walking is healthy compared to those and plenty of other options. And for some women, walking is as much exercise as they can imagine and muster – and that's just fine. But as long as you're not suffering from any debility that eliminates the possibility of adding some 'oomph' to your fitness routine, running does make sense from a health-benefit perspective.

Running burns more calories than walking, utilizes your muscles to a more intense degree and gives your heart and lungs a better workout than walking. The more researchers learn, the more it's believed that all these things are connected with our long-term mental and emotional health, too, so the intensity of your workout just might matter. This doesn't mean you have to run fast; even jogging at a very slow pace will up the ante from walking.

Q: Do I really need to get a health check from my doctor?

A: It's the first admonishment you hear when you begin any exercise programme: get a health check-up. So what exactly is everybody getting checked for?

The primary concern for anyone starting a workout programme – particularly an aerobic one, such as running – is heart disease. Every adult woman has some buildup of plaque in her arteries, explains Dr Amy Roberts, sports nutritionist and director of sports science for leading lifestyle website, www.asimba.com. That's dangerous only if you have advanced buildup – whether from diet, lack of exercise or genetics – and suddenly begin exercising heavily. Women under the age of 50 aren't at particularly high risk, Dr Roberts says, unless they are overweight or have a family history of high blood pressure, high cholesterol or heart disease. If any of these are the case, no matter what your age, you absolutely must have that health check-up.

Ultimately, it's not a bad idea to be examined even if you don't have any of the red flags for heart disease. Depending on your age, your GP may check for other conditions as well. Minor health conditions can sometimes grow worse with the additional physical requirements of a workout programme. Your doctor may investigate your overall nutrition and check for anaemia and osteoporosis. If nothing else, finding out your cholesterol level, blood pressure, resting heart rate and body fat percentage at the beginning of your programme can inspire you down the road when those numbers improve. So go ahead and make an appointment for a check-up.

Q: Should I eat something before running?

A: You should be neither famished nor stuffed when you head out for a run. A good rule of thumb for beginners is to drink a glass of water and eat a light high-carbohydrate meal or snack half an hour to an hour before running. Rich and high-fibre foods often cause stomach distress, especially for beginners, so stay away from any significant intake of fats, protein, salad and fruit. (Bananas are an exception – they're easy on the stomach for most people.)

Mornings are less problematic, since you'll wake with an empty stomach. Have some toast, cereal or a banana – and coffee if you like – and give yourself a little bit of time before running. If you're fitting a run into a busy day, be sure to wait two to three hours after you've eaten a large lunch or one that contains rich or fibrous items, or you might suffer from uncomfortable bloating. By the way, many runners will attest to the fact that as you progress and get used to running, your stomach will most likely become less sensitive to what and when you eat. That's yet another reason to stay motivated and keep running!

Q: How should I dress?

A: Check the weather outside. The exertion of running will keep you warmer than if you were standing around, so choose clothes that leave you on the cool side when you start out. If you haven't purchased specific running clothes, any pair of athletic shorts or tights will do to start. You will be more comfortable in items meant for running, though – they're designed not to bunch up in the crotch area or chafe anywhere, and they tend to be best at keeping sweat away from your body.

If it's hot outside, a sports bra with a T-shirt or vest top will suffice on top. If it's cooler, wear a long-sleeved top made from synthetic fibre to wick moisture away from your skin and keep you comfortable. Layer a windproof jacket on top for cold or windy weather.

A nylon vest will stand in for a jacket in a wide range of temperatures. Check for clouds on the horizon; a baseball cap will save your vision in a sudden downpour. (Actually, many runners like baseball caps all summer long, as they protect the face from unnecessary sun exposure.) And if it's at all chilly, wear a hat and gloves. Much of your body's heat can escape through your scalp. Also, many women find that their hands stay cold while they're running, even if they're working up a sweat.

Q: Do I have to wear something over my sports bra?

A: Most sports bras today can be worn without T-shirts. (The exceptions are some of the bras for large-breasted women that are designed like more traditional undergarments.) Plenty of women are comfortable running without T-shirts, but others wouldn't be caught dead with their stomachs showing. It's a matter of personal preference. Just beware of white bras, which can lose their opacity when drenched with sweat, especially if the fabric is thin.

Q: What if I feel self-conscious?

A: If you do, you're in good company. A bunch of elite women runners I know were chatting when one confided that, during runs, she regularly looked down at her thighs 'to see if they looked fat'. Expecting ridicule at such a confession, she was instead met with a chorus of 'Me, too!' from the group. Some might scoff at such insecurity, but women can be hard on themselves, and taking up a new physical activity can exacerbate such concerns.

Remember that one of the wonderful benefits of running is improved self-confidence. The sooner you start, the more quickly you will become comfortable with your body, your speed and your stride.

Also, remind yourself that everyone *isn't* watching you. Running today is everywoman's sport. Consider checking out the local park before your first run. You'll see women and men of every age, every weight and every speed. They're all enjoying themselves too much to be judging the colour of your shorts or the girth of your thighs.

Q: Where should I go?

A: If you're lucky, right out of the front door. For convenience, many women run from home. Try to find a nearby park, bike path or trail. Getting off the street is always safer than dealing with cars, and the fewer junctions you deal with the happier you'll be and the more you'll be able to relax and enjoy your run. Soft surfaces are easier on your joints than pavement or concrete surfaces, and they'll reduce your next-day soreness. If a soft surface isn't available, a road is fine, but look for the following for safety and enjoyment:

- Minimal traffic
- Minimal traffic lights
- A wide shoulder
- A soft running surface (gravel is softest, followed by asphalt and then concrete)
- Low speed limits

If local roads are not conducive to a safe and pleasant run, it might be worth a short drive to a park or trail with a runner-friendly surface such as dirt, grass, pine needles or bark mulch. Another option is a track. Municipal tracks are open to the public, as are some school tracks. Tracks can be fun for beginners who want to know how far they go each day. Most tracks are 400 metres (roughly ¼ mile) around. If you run regularly at a track, be sure to alternate directions (clockwise and anticlockwise) to ensure your legs are working equally. And stay in the outside lane – the inner lanes should be reserved for runners who are engaging in challenging efforts.

Q: How fast should I run?

A: Speed shouldn't be a concern. It's impossible to go too slow, and it's risky to go too fast. Start by walking for 5 to 10 minutes to warm up, and then break into a shuffle. If you wish, increase your pace slightly until you find a stride that feels comfortable and natural. Don't compare your speed with other runners around you. The sooner this lesson is learned the better. Even professional runners have easy training days when they barely break above a shuffling speed, no matter what the competition is doing near by. On your first runs, maintain a pace at which breathing remains comfortable. If you find yourself growing tired or breathing heavily, slow down or walk.

Q: How should I breathe?

A: Breathe through your mouth. Your nose can't deliver enough oxygen for your body when you're running. Long, deep breaths will help you take in more air and prevent side stitches, which are caused by a buildup of lactic acid. For now, run at a pace at which you can breathe easily. (A good test is whether you can carry on a conversation.) If you're gasping for breath, slow down or walk if necessary. 'Most people will be short of breath when they start an exercise programme,' says Dr Roberts. Shortness of breath that's caused by running isn't particularly troublesome, but tightness in the chest and pains that shoot from the chest are symptoms that should be checked by a GP.

Q: How should I run? I don't think I look like everybody else!

A: Runners refer to the way they move as their 'form'. Each woman has her own unique form, rather like her running fingerprint. Generally speaking, your body finds the gait that feels right for a reason: your natural running form is a product of the alignment of all your limbs and joints, as well as the balance – or imbalance – of your musculature. While you don't want to change your form radically, there are elements you can be aware of that will help you run more efficiently:

✷ Don't bend forward at the waist or neck. Retain good posture: upright but not rigidly erect.

✷ Swing your arms at roughly a 90-degree angle at the elbow, careful not to let them cross too far over the midline of your chest.

✷ Let your feet fall naturally – for most people that's a gentle landing on the heel or midfoot, which then rolls forward and pushes off at the toes.

✷ Don't bounce up off the ground, but as you gain strength, do try to lengthen your stride naturally past a shuffle.

In general, think of your energy and motion moving forward rather than side to side or up and down.

Q: What if it hurts?
A: If you're wearing the right running shoes for your foot type and starting off slowly, nothing should hurt at first. But beginning runners can soon expect to experience minor discomfort, usually in the knees, shins, feet or chest. Faint soreness is caused by your body's adaptation to a new source of stress, and the irritation will dissipate over the next few weeks. On the other hand, a sharp pain is always a sign to stop. Walk for a bit and see if the pain diminishes. If it resumes upon running, cut the run short and walk home. Ice and rest will take care of most minor sore spots; more serious injuries call for a trip to the doctor.

Q: What if I have to go to the toilet?
A: Welcome to one of the realities of running. There's something about the activity that makes some women have to go. A little precaution goes a long way toward ensuring a pleasant run. If you want to drink anything before your run, do it at least half an hour before you set out. This will give you time to go to the toilet before your run and reduce the chances of needing to stop. (And you don't need to down a huge water bottle of water – just a few sips will do when you're starting out.)

Leave half an hour to an hour between eating and going for your run, and stay away from high-fibre foods, such as fruit or muesli. If you do need to go while you're running, by all means stop and find a place to do so. There's no rule that says you must finish your run without a break, and you'll be far more comfortable afterwards.

Q: How far should I go?

A: As a beginner, don't be concerned with the distance you cover. For now, just listen to your body and think in terms of total time rather than miles. This eliminates pressure to perform at a certain pace. Your first run should be a comfortable combination of walking and jogging to introduce your body to the activity. For most women, a total of 30 minutes of activity is a good start. Warm up by walking for 5 to 10 minutes, then alternate jogging and walking so that your breathing and your legs remain comfortable. Cool down with another 10 minutes of walking. For a full beginner's running programme, see chapter 5.

Okay. You have your clean bill of health in hand and new shoes on your feet. You're ready and raring to go. So relax. Remember to breathe. Start off at a brisk walk. When you're ready, let yourself break into a jog. Now you're a runner.

Q: Should I run with an iPod?

A: These days, portable music players practically seem like a required piece of equipment for running. But safety experts still warn against wearing headphones, especially for women. They greatly reduce your ability to hear your surroundings, and they also contribute to a generally removed sensibility, meaning we're less alert. That said, running with music is indeed a great pleasure, one that can help women find the motivation to run at all. If you want to wear headphones, keep the volume low enough that you can monitor your surroundings, and try to run in a park or other area where cars and traffic are not a danger. And don't rule out running without a soundtrack: you might be pleasantly surprised by the sound of silence.

DEBUNKING THE MYTH OF PAIN

For such a healthy sport, running has a bad reputation. 'All that pounding!' 'Doesn't it give you arthritis?' 'I've heard it makes your breasts hurt.'

But the fact is, almost anybody can run – comfortably.

Most running horror stories surface from misguided first outings. Any activity you jump into too quickly will leave you with achy muscles and sore spots. (Think of how sore your legs were the last time you played football with your kids.) Because running is so simple, people have a tendency to overdo it on the first try. 'The reason that people think they can't run is that when they've started in the past, they've gone kamikaze,' says Maureen

Roben, a five-time Olympic Trials Marathon qualifier. By starting a running programme smartly – and slowly – you can avoid painful pitfalls.

Sore knees are almost always due to two factors: the wrong shoes and previous inactivity. If you start out slowly with a walk/run programme, you should never experience anything more than a mild ache. After 2 to 3 weeks of consistent activity, most soreness will be gone.

Other concerns: 'Some women think their breasts are going to sag,' Roben says. 'I still hear people who think running is going to loosen the uterus!' Other rumoured side effects include loose skin, chunky muscles and exacerbated incontinence. None is true. All stem from the Dark Ages when women were discouraged from participating in the sport altogether.

Far from causing all these deteriorations, running conveys many benefits that can boost health as women advance in age. Women who are regular runners retain greater range of motion as they age. Their bone health actu-

TRAINING LOG

Growing up, my older brother and I would race around our garden as if it were a cross-country course. I raced my little heart out, each time thinking this might be the day I would beat him – but I never did. I didn't know it then, but those sprints were my introduction to a lifetime of running. They also ensured that I would never know the self-consciousness that comes with taking up the sport as an adult.

As it turns out, that's a good thing. When it comes to trying new sports, I've developed the track record of a chicken. I shied away from golf for years, thinking that it was a requirement to whack the ball onto the green in one shot. I avoided mountain bikes, too, not realizing that it was acceptable, when faced with a slope of loose rock, to simply get off and walk.

Even an uncomplicated sport such as running holds mysteries and challenges. Over the years, I've been awed by the women I've met who were taking up the sport: some battling cancer, some struggling with obesity or the pains of advancing age, still others seeking strength to start new passages in their lives. All have stood at a crossroads and taken those pivotal first steps, becoming more fearless with every day. Those women are a constant reminder to me that it's never too late to make running part of your life, and if I had to do it now, I could only hope that I would exhibit the same courage and grace.

ally tends to be superior to that of their sedentary counterparts because weight-bearing activity improves bone strength. Roben tells of a study in which she and coaching colleague Diane Palmason were asked to take part. Both women, who had competed at world-class levels for decades, showed bone density in their legs comparable to that of 20-year-olds. At the time of the test, Roben was in her 40s and Palmason in her 60s.

CHAPTER 4

The Principles of Training

WHY DO YOU RUN? Simple question. A thousand possible answers. The reasons run the gamut: time alone, time with others, fitness, sanity, freedom, health, to eat more without gaining weight, to worry less, to stay young, to push limits, to eliminate limits.

Although there's really only one way to run, there are many ways of being a runner. When you pinpoint why you run, you focus your goals, which will determine how you train. Each day you head out the door, you are faced with choices: how far, how fast and how hard. Your decisions will depend on your goals.

If you've had a hard day at work, for instance, and you're looking for some stress release, you might amble along while you contemplate the beauty of nature. On the other hand, if you're feeling competitive and want to beat your partner in an upcoming 5-K, you might decide to hammer out some speed repeats on the track.

Setting goals is the first step on your path to fulfilment as a runner. Learning the basic principles of training is the second step. Combine the two, and you can determine the level at which you wish to run and the type of training schedule that's most appropriate for you.

WHAT DO YOU WANT FROM RUNNING?

Having goals enriches any endeavour. By having goals, you become more keenly aware of what you have accomplished and what you still wish to achieve. But goals can be frightening, dangerous things, too. Some people avoid them at all costs. Why? Because by acknowledging a goal, you face the possibility of that awful 'f' word: failure. You can make setting goals less frightening if you keep the following two points in mind.

Goals are not immutable. They can and will change over time. Your life is a complex tapestry of work, love, family, hobbies and obligations. One year may bring freedom and lightheartedness and a zest for adventure, while another brings tough challenges and a longing for security. Your goals – for work, running or anything else – are likely to shift at these times, even if you have not attained your original hopes. This brings up the next point:

Not meeting a goal is not failure. In fact, if success were a certainty, you wouldn't have much of a challenge to begin with. There is little point in setting an easily attainable goal. Goals are meant to stimulate you and inspire greatness. A goal that is obviously attainable is without value. That means that any worthy goal comes with the implication that you might not meet it. Learning and growth come only in the struggle to attain your goal.

YOUR PERSONAL RUNNING PROGRAMME

There is one fundamental truth about running that can spare you much frustration when it comes to setting goals: your potential speed, aerobic capacity and body shape are greatly determined by genetics. Some women can run for years and never turn into the sleek, petite whippets they envisioned they would become. Others take up the sport at 60 and find themselves, to their own astonishment, walking away with age-group trophies.

That's genetics. And no, it's not fair. But here's the good part. No matter who you are or what your starting point is, you can and will improve. Your heart and lungs will become better conditioned. Your legs will grow stronger. Running can help you achieve the greatest possible health for your body type. Also, hard work and determination can go a long way toward expanding your possibilities. One elite women's distance coach I know has turned away talented runners, saying, 'Give me a runner with heart over one with talent any day.'

So don't despair or bemoan your genetics. Rather, recognize that your physical makeup is the luck of the draw. Instead of wasting time trying to change it, learn to work with it. You can learn to take advantage of your strengths and work on your weaknesses. Don't compare your running with that of others or become self-critical if you aren't progressing as quickly as you thought you would. Such comparisons can lead to frustration and demoralization – as well as to inappropriate training that will only compound physical problems.

Just as every runner progresses at a different rate, every runner responds differently to training, nutrition and all other aspects of the sport. The workout that one runner swears by as her secret training weapon will leave another runner broken down. The vegetarian diet that gives one runner energy will seem Spartan to another, leaving her weak.

Books and coaches often promote a single 'winning formula' that they say will yield guaranteed results. That sounds great, but there's no such thing. It's not that such programmes are always completely wrong, but they simply can't be applied universally. While garnering advice from any source – including this book – remember your individuality, and weigh the advice as it relates to your own situation. To apply advice successfully, you need to know yourself, body and mind.

Listening to your body is the foundation for a successful and enjoyable running programme. It's also surprisingly hard to do. Self-knowledge becomes more evident over time and miles. It is an accumulation of learning that never stops, since your body continues to change. Self-knowledge can be as literal as learning that you need water every half-hour on your runs or that you're the kind of runner who can run indefinitely without feeling dehydrated. It can also be evident in less tangible factors: time might teach you, for example, that you push yourself too hard when you run with a group, so you need to run alone on days when you want to take it easy.

As you get to know your body's capabilities, you develop a valuable sense of confidence. You learn when to push and when to back off. You can predict how you will feel if you notch up the intensity of a run and just how long you can last at a given pace. You learn what builds confidence and what is destructive. In short, knowing yourself results in the ability to create a personalized training formula. And in the end, no book or coach can provide such information. It's a matter of logging the miles and paying attention while you do so.

THE RULES OF RUNNING

Putting one foot in front of the other isn't exactly rocket science. But just as you can make your runs as hard or as easy as you wish, you can make your training as complex or simple as you wish. Ultimately, your reasons for running will determine how much of the science of training you need to know.

If your goal as a runner is to relax, have fun and maintain your health, you may never want or need to run more than 30 to 40 minutes at a time. Many women find running at this recreational level to be a great stress reliever and fitness booster. They don't need to test their endurance, and indeed, they would rather not undertake anything so strenuous that it becomes another energy drain. These women are perfectly content never to know what it feels like to enter a state of oxygen debt.

For other women, fitness is just the beginning. They derive pleasure from pushing themselves and their limits. They are driven by wanting to know how fast or how far they can possibly go. To investigate the boundaries of potential, these runners will need to push beyond levels of comfort.

Regardless of the level at which you wish to run, some principles of training and improvement remain the same. If you sidestep or shortcut these rules, you'll experience burnout, discomfort and injury. But if you understand them, you'll be able to do more than simply follow the workout schedules in this book; you will actually be able to customize a schedule to fit your specific needs and goals. You'll know 'how far, how fast' each time you head out for a run.

1 Do the minimal training needed for optimal results. 'If I'm improving this much by running 30 miles a week, think how much better I could be by running 50 miles a week!' What could be wrong with that logic? Plenty. Finding your optimal training schedule – for fitness or for racing – is not a matter of cramming in as many miles as your legs can possibly handle. Instead, it's about finding the optimal number of miles and training days per week to help you reach maximum fitness while still feeling energized and strong. Just because a friend is running 6 days a week doesn't mean that you should too. Perhaps she has a more advanced fitness background, or maybe she has a desk job and you work on your feet. For a myriad reasons, different runners thrive on different workloads.

Anyone can fall victim to the 'more is better' disease. Although it's something that advanced runners need to worry about more than beginners, anyone can overtrain. Overtraining happens when you exert yourself past the point of positive returns. The price you pay might be exhaustion, burnout, or injury. For runners who wish to improve, training wisely is just as important as training hard.

2 Balance your hard efforts with rest. You don't get faster or fitter on the days that you push yourself. Improvement comes during your rest *after* the days when you run hard. 'The benefits of stressing the body come during recovery,' explains Dr Jack Daniels, coach and author of the bestselling book *Daniels' Running Formula*. He illustrates the principle with this extreme example: imagine yourself running as hard as you can one day, then again the next day, and the next. Sooner or later, you'd barely be able to run at all.

In this scenario, 'you'd never be giving your body a chance to recover, to strengthen itself, to ward off injury, or to just feel good again,' Dr Daniels says.

During recovery time, he explains, your body is busy: repairing muscle fibres, building new blood vessels into your muscles, increasing your muscle fibres' ability to process nutrients and oxygen, and eliminating waste products from them. On off days, your body can repair muscle damage, fortify your immune system and prepare for the next onslaught. If you don't give your body a chance to recover, over time, you will tear yourself down.

This rule of rest holds true for runners of all types; only the level of effort and rest change. Recreational runners will balance their running days with days of complete rest, meaning no running. More serious runners will rest from their hard workouts by running a short distance slowly or by cross-training on off days. For competitive distance runners, a 10-mile day may serve as a 'rest' day. Even these runners, however, benefit from the occasional day *completely* off to rest their muscles and tendons.

❸ Expect peaks and plateaus in your running. Just because you lopped 5 minutes off your 10-K last summer doesn't mean it will happen again this summer. This is quite simply the law of diminishing returns. If you stress your body by running 20 miles a week, for example, you will improve until you eventually reach a fitness level that this amount of work allows. Your 10-K time might drop by 5 minutes over the course of one summer spent this way, but when you increase your training to 40 miles a week, you won't double your fitness or necessarily cut your time by 5 minutes again. In general, your greatest improvements come as you begin your running career. Although improvement can continue for years thereafter, the pace of improvement is likely to slow down.

Not only will the pace of improvement slow, but you'll also hit peaks and plateaus along the way. Your body adapts to the demands you place upon it, and it will be at varying levels of stress and recovery depending on where you are in your training. Dr Daniels cites studies in which researchers measured adrenaline secretions in runners and non-runners to gauge their stress levels. When study subjects who ran 10 miles a day had trained for a certain length of time, they had the same adrenaline levels as non-runners.

Although a plateau is probably a good indication that it's time to increase your training intensity, more advanced runners must read plateaus with caution. Ironically, they can also be signs of overtraining. 'The people who are training really hard and don't notice improvement might

Smart Tips

You usually won't reach your running goals within days or weeks. Instead, it typically takes months or years. Although a beginning runner might improve virtually overnight, both progress and setbacks can continue for a lifetime. Because of that, it's a good idea to set short-term goals that help motivate you along the way to reaching your long-term goals.

Set short-term goals so that you can easily attain them within a certain time period, and then set some more once you achieve them. Reaching these intermediate objectives can keep you inspired and on target to meet long-term goals. Here are some tips for making and reaching both short-term and long-term goals:

> Choose short-term goals that seem attainable within one season – such as being able to run for 30 minutes without stopping by the end of the summer or taking 30 seconds off your best 5-K time.

> Choose long-term goals that span the course of a year or more – perhaps running your first marathon or breaking 40 minutes for a 10-K.

> Set goals that will help you develop the strengths you value. If you're not concerned about going fast, don't set a goal based on your 10-K time. Instead, set a goal of running with friends at least once a week for the duration of the summer. Other examples are learning 10 new routes by the end of the year or losing a modest amount of weight in 2 months.

> If you do set goals for a personal best (PB), set both short-term and long-term marks.

> Write it down. Note your goals in a diary, training log or calendar. Having concrete evidence of your goals is a wonderful motivator. In the future, it will also serve as a fun reminder of how far you've come.

> Re-evaluate your goals once a year. Choose whatever date you wish: New Year's Day, your birthday, the beginning of spring, the anniversary of the day you started running. Look at how far you've come in the past year, and use this time to set new goals or recommit to old ones.

have an opposite scenario,' Dr Daniels explains. 'These people are probably training too hard and need more recovery.'

It's a good idea to pay attention to your peaks and plateaus, especially if you train hard. But you shouldn't obsess over them. They're a normal part of the running experience.

❹ Be consistent. Sorry, last summer's workouts won't keep you trim and fit this spring. If you stopped running over the winter, you'll have to start almost from scratch, slowly building up to the level at which you left off. Don't make the mistake of trying to jump in where you were 6 months ago – you'll find yourself out of breath, frustrated and sore as can be. The good news is that fitness tends to come back more quickly the 2nd, 3rd or 10th time around. On some level, your body remembers those 'miles in the bank'.

That's why persistence is crucial to your success as a runner. Ask coaches what the one most important factor is in training, and most will answer, 'consistency'. That applies to runners of all levels. Recreational runners won't see improvement if they run once a week, because that's not often enough for the body to make physiological changes. Likewise, more serious runners won't improve if they regularly run hard for a week but then take the next week off.

Consistency *doesn't* mean never missing a day out of foolish stubbornness, no matter the cost. If you feel a cold coming on, for example, it's better to miss a day or two and allow yourself to get healthy than it is to keep running until you're really ill and forced to take several weeks off.

❺ Practise patience. Your body is an amazing machine. It adapts to the stresses of working out by becoming fitter and stronger. Even at an advanced age or after years of neglect and abuse, your body can regain strength and endurance. Getting in shape is a gradual process, however. No matter how much of a hurry you might be in to lose weight or run faster, you can't shortcut the process of fitness. Piling on the intensity in your running programme at the start of your training, after a winter layoff, or to break through a plateau won't get you in shape faster. It might get you injured, though. Increase any training gradually. Get comfortable before increasing quantity or quality. A good rule of thumb is the 10 per cent rule: don't increase your workload in time or distance by more than 10 per cent a week.

❻ Train your entire body. It takes a whole body to make a running stride. Although hamstring muscles might seem like the workhorses of running, you ignore the rest of your body at your own peril. Tendons and

TRAINING LOG

Why do I run? Over time, the answer to that question has evolved, as have my goals.

When I was a child, I ran because it felt good. By the time I reached senior school and was competing on athletic teams, I ran not out of joy but because of pressure for results from adults. Because of that, my enjoyment was limited to rare glimpses of triumph when others felt I had done well. I stopped running at university because I no longer felt any connection to the thing that had once given me such pleasure.

When I turned 30, I began running to keep my bottom from drooping onto my thighs. I was a journalist married to a desk, and running was a way to defy gravity. But something happened along the way: my legs and trunk became stronger, my heart and lungs grew powerful and I rediscovered my child's delight in the sport.

By my mid-30s, it seemed as if I had learned to fly. I ran to feel my feet skim over the ground, to feel my heart swell in my chest, to feel invincible. I ran to be free; I ran to avoid pain; I ran to feel pain; I ran out of love and hate and anger and joy. Somewhere along the path, running became the canvas upon which I documented my life.

For a brief year during that time, I ran to see how fast I could be. The more I believed that I was approaching my limits, the less I understood what those limits were – and the less I knew whether they had to do with legs and lungs at all but rather with heart and head. That's when I realized that I was no longer running to see how fast I could be, but instead to learn what other stuff I was made of.

I now work more than I run, which means I no longer wish for my running to be work. I run to feel the slap of cold air on my face or the heat melting into my bones. I run for the sunsets, for the way the shadows play over the hills, to keep pace with my beloved in a silent contest that only running partners know.

The way I see it, I've had at least four different running careers over the last 25 years – and I'm nowhere near finished. During each stage, the training most appropriate for the time has been different, and I've adapted accordingly: different workouts, different training partners, different sources of joy and accomplishment. Over time, my running has faithfully and graciously transformed to suit my circumstances. Through it all, each morning has patiently asked me, 'Why do you run today?' And over the course of the years, one simple answer has quietly become more clearly heard than all the others: because I must.

ligaments, for example, are integral to the running process, yet they adapt and strengthen very slowly. That's why many running injuries involve these connective tissues. The small muscle groups of your feet and legs come into play with each stride, as do your arms, shoulders, trunk and back. Respect these parts of your body. Strengthen and stretch them. Gradually you'll see the difference in your running. (For more on total-body stretching and strengthening, see chapter 18.)

Over time, you'll come to understand these training principles as you see them in action. You will feel the bounce in your step after you take your rest day; you will become aware of the microcycles of improvement in your running from month to month; you will recognize when you push too hard or when you're being inconsistent and your training suffers accordingly. Pay attention to these principles and to the messages your body sends. Eventually you'll find that you can tailor a training programme to your own needs, no matter what type of runner you are.

CHAPTER 5

From Walking to Jogging: Training for the Beginner

THE BEGINNING OF YOUR RUNNING PROGRAMME is a time of immense excitement, progress and growth. You'll see your legs in a new light, as powerful and capable. You'll take pride in one day's accomplishment and use it to motivate yourself the next day, when temptation is tugging you to slow down. You'll feel triumphant at the end of your first steady runs.

But the beginning is also a time of challenge and discomfort. You'll discover sore spots and worry about them. You may tire quickly and feel discouraged. You may have days when the kids are ill and the phone won't stop ringing, and before you know it, you'll have missed your workout and feel like all progress is lost.

When you start running, you'll experience both extremes. That much is guaranteed. For some women, this stage will be relatively easy and pass rapidly. For others, it will require more patience. These ups and downs are part of the process of conditioning your body and mind in a new way. The tough days might not be fun, but they are the days when you make real progress – physical and mental. The easy days when the pavement skips lightly underfoot, well, those are the days that make all the work worthwhile!

RUNNING STYLE

Beginners often worry about how to run. How should I carry my arms, they ask. How high should I lift my feet? Should I look down or ahead?

The first answer is that it's best not to worry too much. Every runner has a unique style that she'll fall into naturally. Most coaches agree that it's not a good idea to stray too far from the form toward which your body innately gravitates.

On the other hand, vastly improper form can be taxing and can make you tire early. Sometimes inefficiencies are so pronounced that they can lead to soreness or injury.

Generally speaking, the best running style is the one that is most efficient. You should strive to avoid wasted motion. Think about it this way: since running is primarily a forward-driving action, no part of a runner's body should display excessive side-to-side or up-and-down motion.

The following guidelines will help you develop an efficient running style. These are generalizations that work best for most runners, but if something feels uncomfortable, don't force it. Also, don't concentrate relentlessly on your form, or you'll wind up tripping over your own feet. (And you certainly won't enjoy your run.) Instead, consciously practise these points for a minute or so during your runs. Eventually they'll become second nature.

Maintain erect, but not stiff, posture. Don't bend forward or lean backward at the waist. Hold your neck and head erect as well. Most runners prefer to look at a spot on the road several strides ahead. One helpful trick is to imagine a helicopter drifting above you and just slightly ahead (a nice, quiet, relaxing helicopter). Now envision a hook dropped from the helicopter and attached to the shirt at the back of your neck. How does this help? Imagine that hook pulling you both upwards and forwards: you're running tall, not slouched or 'sitting'. The fact that the hook is pulling you just the tiniest bit forwards helps you maintain an efficient forward momentum. This little bit of visualization can even help you when you're tiring on your run and feel as if you could use a little outside help.

Relax your shoulders. Don't hunch them forwards or up near your ears.

Swing your arms loosely at your sides. Your elbows should be bent at approximately a 90-degree angle. Let your arms come slightly across your waist in a natural motion. Your hands, held in loose, relaxed fists, should swing no higher than your chest and should not cross the centre of your body.

Raise your legs a few inches off the ground. There's no benefit to lifting your knees and feet in an exaggerated motion. Start with something slightly more animated than a shuffle. As you develop more power, you'll naturally take longer strides.

Land lightly on your heels. Your foot placement is highly individual and depends greatly on the structure of your feet. Beginning runners, however, shouldn't run on their toes, as so many ill-advised sports teachers insist. Generally, your foot should strike somewhere on the outside portion of your heel and roll forward until your toes push off.

Relax. From time to time as you run, take stock of your body. Is your jaw set? Is your face screwed up tight? Are your fists clenched? Relax, relax, relax. One of life's little paradoxes is that sometimes when we strain hard, we accomplish less. This is certainly true in running.

SET YOUR OWN PACE

I'll assign your very first running goal right now: you want to be able to run for half an hour without stopping. The aim of the schedule offered here is gradually to integrate running with walking so that in 8 weeks' time, you'll meet this goal.

You've probably heard of people who start running programmes only to quit within the first couple of months. Why? Typically, they try to accomplish too much too soon. Instead of working up to half an hour of running, they try to do it all on day one. This leads to an array of problems: side stitches, shin pain, breathing discomfort, lethargy and so on. Ideally, running should never hurt when you're a beginner. If it does, you're trying too hard.

Smart Tip

Here's a great tip that doesn't so much change your form as it helps you move your body in an efficient manner.

Think about the way you run now: How many moving parts do you count? Probably four: two legs, two arms.

Now think of a marionette, with arms and legs *attached*, so that each set – left leg and right arm, right leg and left arm – moves in synchronization.

Next time you run, try to imagine you only have *two* moving parts. Let your opposing arms and legs flow as a pair. Don't exaggerate or change the motion – you don't want to move like a marionette. Just think of those two sets of limbs doing the work instead of four separate parts. The result should feel as if you're creating an X of motion. It's a subtle change, but in making it, you might be eliminating excess motion and jerkiness. It may feel awkward at first, but eventually you should find yourself moving more smoothly than ever.

The walk-to-jog transition programme in this chapter assumes that you can already comfortably walk for 30 minutes three or four times a week. This base of walking activity ensures that your heart, lungs and legs are ready for the additional stresses of running. If you've been especially sedentary or if you aren't sure of your fitness level, first work up to half an hour a day of walking several times a week.

As you make the transition from walking to running, you'll continue to exercise in 30-minute sessions, but you'll incorporate jogging into your walks. Each week, extend the length of time spent running and reduce the amount of time spent walking. Plan to exercise in this manner for 3 to 5 days a week. Fewer than 3 days will not be enough to condition your cardiovascular system. More than 5 days might not give your muscles the rest they need.

Knowing when to run and when to walk is the tricky part for beginners. Pushing too hard and not pushing at all are both potential pitfalls. The first will leave you hurting; the second will mean you won't see much progress. Maureen Roben, a five-time Olympic Trials Marathon qualifier who has coached hundreds of women, tells beginners to run until they are slightly uncomfortable, then try to keep running for another 30 seconds or so. 'I tell them, "When you think you can't go any further, go a bit further." You get more benefit that way, and it gets you out of the habit of stopping the second that running becomes uncomfortable,' Roben says. 'And when you walk, don't stroll. Pump your arms, and really work to keep that heart rate up.'

The sample schedule in this chapter is meant to offer a comfortable, conservative transition to running, but each woman's body will react differently. The 8-week plan is just a guideline. You might want to go more slowly, taking twice the time, or you might want to advance more quickly. You should never feel pressed beyond your limits based on how much somebody else is running or what somebody else tells you to do. Books, coaches and friends can offer suggestions and advice, but in the end your body will tell you how hard to push.

When listening to your body, it's important to understand that you can't separate your running from the rest of your life. If you're tired from other activities, it can and will affect your running. You might find your energy drained from a family problem, a bad night's sleep or office stress. You can't fight the impact of those things; nor should you ignore them. Factor them in when gauging how hard to push in your workouts. Running at this stage should remain a positive, enjoyable complement to the rest of your activities.

If any day proves too challenging – your legs hurt or your breathing is uncomfortably laboured – back off. Walk as much as you need in order to finish. Take the next day off, and repeat the previous workout until you can complete it comfortably. Do this as many times as necessary.

But be honest. Don't create excuses to curl up on the sofa as soon as you're the least bit weary. If you haven't exercised before, you'll soon find that running gives you more energy than ever. To get to that point, however, you must go through a phase of several weeks or even months when your body will protest while adapting to the increased activity.

If, on the other hand, the workouts feel unchallenging, increase the jogging portion more rapidly, by a minute or two more than the schedule shows. Don't overdo it, though: your body's aerobic capacity usually adapts more quickly than your muscles and tendons do. You might feel fine while you're jogging, but your muscles will pay the price the next day in increased

Now Is a Good Time to . . .

❯ Begin a cooldown programme of regular light stretching after your runs to avoid muscle tightness. Gently stretch your legs, arms and torso without bouncing. Hold each stretch for about 20 seconds.

❯ Strengthen your back and abdomen by exercising these muscle groups two or three times a week, after a run. A common pitfall for beginning runners is to hunch over when their core tires. A strong core will help you retain proper form and keep you running longer.

❯ Take stock of your nutrition. The sandwich-and-salad diet that many women stick to lacks protein and fat. These nutrients are more important now that you're revving up your muscles regularly. Try to include at least a small amount of protein in every meal. You should be getting 20 to 30 per cent of your calories from fat.

❯ Participate in a fun-run event. Races are no longer just for hard-core runners. Sign up with friends to jog in a low-key 5-K a month from now. The party atmosphere, the food and drink, and the women of all abilities and backgrounds are sure to inspire your workouts for weeks to follow.

By the Numbers

If you decide to run with a heart-rate monitor, you can use it to determine when to walk and run during your 30-minute sessions. A beginner should stay at around 60 per cent of her maximum heart rate (MHR), according to Nick Anderson, who coaches the British cross-country team. (Your heart-rate monitor's instruction manual should tell you how to work out your maximum heart rate. To calculate 60 per cent of your MHR, multiply the maximum rate by 0.60. Then programme the number into your monitor.) 'Once you can exercise at 60 per cent of your MHR for 30 minutes, you can start to include short periods of running at around 75 per cent of your MHR,' says Anderson.

---

soreness if you do too much too soon. The idea is to increase slowly enough that you never experience significant soreness the next day. Remember that speed is not important. The point is to get your body used to the activity of jogging.

8-WEEK SCHEDULE

Use the following schedule as a guideline for your transition from walking to running. You'll notice that no distances are listed. For now, don't worry about miles. They can be a pain for beginners to measure, and knowing how far you've gone each day can create unnecessary pressure to improve each time you run. Remember, if any day feels too hard, take a break, and then repeat that workout until it feels comfortable.

Week 1. Walk 10 minutes to begin and end each 30-minute session. Alternate between walking and running for the middle 10 minutes, starting the week with running segments of a minute or less and working up to 2-minute segments.

Goal by week's end: 2-minute running segments.

Week 2. Walk 8 minutes to begin and end each 30-minute session. Alternate walking and running during the middle 14 minutes, starting the week with 2-minute running segments and working up to 4-minute running segments.

Goal by week's end: 4-minute running segments.

Week 3. Walk 5 minutes to begin and end each 30-minute session. Alternate walking and running during the middle 20 minutes, starting the week with 4-minute running segments and working up to 6-minute running segments.

Goal by week's end: 6-minute running segments.

Week 4. Walk a few minutes to begin. Run 7 minutes. Walk until rested. Run 7 minutes. Walk the rest of the half-hour. As the week progresses, extend the running portions by 1 minute at a time, aiming for 10-minute runs by the end of the week.

Goal by week's end: two 10-minute running segments.

Week 5. Walk 3 minutes, then run 12 minutes, then repeat. By the end of the week, walk 3 minutes, run 15 minutes, walk until rested, then run the rest of the session.

Goal by week's end: a 15-minute running segment.

TRAINING LOG

I remember the day I learned to jog. It all came about rather backwards for me, since I had grown up competing at school and at university. Workouts were a matter of grave intensity, hardly the stuff of stress relief and sunsets. In fact, *jogging* was the 'j' word, and whenever somebody used it, teammates and I were quick to point out that we didn't jog, we ran.

Then I got busy with a career, and running became something that I used to do as a girl. Until, after several sedentary years, quite out of the blue, the urge struck. It must have been the first hint of spring in the air. I trotted off along the trail into the bright morning, feeling like I hadn't skipped a day. Momentarily. The first few minutes of exhilaration quickly turned into oxygen debt as my out-of-shape body struggled for breath. I slowed. I walked. I stopped.

That's when I noticed my surroundings. Going out for a run had given me the opportunity to take time to marvel at the brilliant golds and greens of the new leaves.

As I marvelled at such hopeful beauty, I realized that I never would have noticed the spectacular day had I been running as I used to. When I took off again, I was *jogging*. I did so deliberately, joyously, at a pace that my out-of-shape body could comfortably maintain while taking in the wonder of it all. But most importantly, I knew that this day on the trail would be the first of many.

Week 6. Walk 5 minutes to begin and end the workout. Run the 20 minutes in the middle.

Goal by week's end: 20 minutes of continuous running.

Week 7. Walk 3 minutes to begin and end the workout. Run the 24 minutes in the middle.

Goal by week's end: 24 minutes of continuous running.

Week 8. Walk only a block or so to limber up your body, then proceed to run slowly for the full 30 minutes, walking only if and when you need to.

Goal by week's end: 30 minutes of continuous running.

THE NEXT STEP

Many beginners find it motivational to sign up for an organized run when they start out. A 5-kilometre walk/run a month or two down the road, for example, can be a fun event to participate in with friends and a good celebration of your 30-minute run accomplishment. It doesn't matter if you don't finish the 5-K in half an hour – simply walk the rest. You might, however, surprise yourself with the adrenaline of the event pumping through your veins and run the entire way. If a race sounds intimidating, choose one of the many women-only or charity events; these are designed specifically to be fun for beginners.

Once you've accomplished your first 30-minute jog, a next logical step is to build up to running 30 minutes regularly and comfortably. For at least a few weeks, alternate your 30-minute runs with 30-minute walk/run sessions. When that feels comfortable, try running 3 days a week, but still do 1 walk/run day during the week. When you can comfortably run for 30 minutes 3 to 5 times a week, you'll be ready to take on more rigorous workouts if you want to.

CHAPTER 6

From Jogging to Running: Training for the Intermediate Runner

WHEN DOES A JOGGER BECOME A RUNNER? Here's a hint: it has little to do with going faster. There is no cut-off speed per mile, no magic number of miles per week, no firm starting point at which the moniker is bestowed.

The difference between the two exists primarily as a mindset. While some women are content with jogging as a fitness activity, others find that running gets under their skin and becomes a part of their fibre. Much like playing an instrument or keeping a journal, what you get out of running isn't determined by how good you are at it. The joy of participation is not an exclusive commodity reserved for the elite runner any more than it is for the concert pianist.

Women turn from joggers into runners for different reasons and at different stages. For one woman, the transformation might occur when she realizes that she no longer runs to keep her weight down but rather to keep her sanity. For another, it might be the night before a trip, when, as she's packing, she realizes that she must take her running shoes because she can't bear to miss a week of workouts. For still another woman, it might be that her schedule barely allows her a morning jog, yet she surprises herself when she finds that she describes herself as a runner.

Once a woman becomes a runner, she finds that the sport is woven into the fabric of her life. Whereas running might have been only a vehicle before – to fitness or to weight loss, for example – it now becomes that rarest of things: a means *and* an end. To a runner, running is still a means of strength and health, of exploration and socialization. But unlike the jogger, who might take up the sport primarily out of a sense of duty or for the extrinsic benefits, such as weight loss, the runner finds that the very act itself is enough. Running is the thing she craves. Within it is a new sense of wonder at the power of movement – whether laboured or light – over ground, the rise and fall of breath in her chest. When a woman knows *this* feeling, she knows that she cannot do without running. And thus is born a runner.

LONGER, STRONGER, FASTER

Many women feel the urge to improve their running, and that can mean many different things. Some simply want to get faster. Some want to be able to run for longer periods of time so they can enjoy new routes or challenging trails. Others want to increase their fitness levels in order to join new groups of running friends. Some wish to go faster just for the feeling it gives them.

'I've been plodding while I run, and that's fine, but in another way, it's frustrating to run 9.5-minute miles, because I know that my body is capable of running faster,' says Jean, 37, an accomplished climber and outdoor enthusiast who runs for fitness. Jean has been running since she was a teenager, but in the last 2 years, she has developed a yearning to reach a new level in the sport. For Jean, speeding up has nothing to do with competition. It has to do with recognizing her potential. 'I want to use my body in that way because it's a beautiful feeling, like you're free and flying and using the machine you have in an efficient way. I've felt that way a few times when running – and it's when I'm running a little bit faster.'

Running more often, running for longer periods of time, becoming more comfortable with running, becoming fitter, running faster, finding more running friends, expanding your running routes, training more intensely and beginning to race: if you have any of these goals, it's clear that you're becoming more serious about running. Yet many women get stuck in beginner mode because they don't know how to proceed to the next step.

'I feel as though I don't know how to take my running to the next level. There's so much information about what to do and what not to do that I become overstimulated and do nothing,' jokes Katherine, 31, who has been running since she was 20. 'I end up sticking to my tired, less-than-challenging routine and not experiencing the growth and progression of which I believe I'm capable. It really compromises the motivation factor.'

She's not alone. Some runners get stuck in a rut when they find that they are comfortable at a certain level of training. Each day's workout is easy, familiar and safe. Even if they want to improve, they don't know how, or they're intimidated by the idea of taking on more. The reaction is to overdo it or to not change anything. But taking your running to the next level needn't be complicated or painful. It can and should be a gradual transition.

You'll probably be pleased to find that the workout schedule offered in this chapter is, above all, simple. The new workouts you'll be doing are playful and non-restrictive. There is no need for regimented track workouts at this stage or for marathon long runs. Will you have to work harder? Of course – that's how you improve. But you needn't fear or dread it.

As you become more serious about your training, you should follow a simple and logical progression of steps to improvement, just as when you first started running. In making this transition, the principles that got you to this point still apply. But this is precisely where many runners become impatient to improve. Raring to go, they throw caution to the wind. ('Well, my friends were doing that 10-mile trail run, so I thought I'd just join in . . .') The result is typically extreme discomfort, discouragement or injury.

Don't rush. Mastery of any endurance sport is an exercise in patience. Change happens gradually at every level. Improvement in running is a slow process of adaptation, and it can't be rushed. Never bump up your training to a new level overnight. In your quest for a new level of expertise, you are essentially a beginner again, with challenged legs, lungs and mind.

NEW LIMITS

Until now, you have stayed in your comfort zone, which was good. If you had pushed too hard or too fast as a novice, you could have ended up injured and discouraged. But now you have a strong foundation. The muscles in your legs are used to running. So are your heart and lungs. You're ready for more.

In order to take on more, you'll need to train your brain as well as your body. Pushing yourself to new limits is as much mental as it is physical. If you didn't grow up playing sports or exercising, pushing yourself may feel frightening and strange. Simply put, it hurts. As you increase your pace, you'll breathe harder and pick your legs up higher. You'll get acquainted with oxygen debt – the feeling that you can't breathe fast enough to supply your body with the oxygen it needs. You'll sweat. And at first you may even feel some post-workout soreness in your ribs, thighs and even abdomen.

It sounds dreadful. But the right mindset can turn negatives into positives.

It helps to understand that discomfort is a given. Discomfort is your body telling you that it's working hard to achieve the challenge you've set for it. This is progress. Although the old saying 'no pain, no gain' is exaggerated and misguided, it is true that you must stress your limits in order to expand them. If you're following the rules about gradually increasing your training distances and speed, then the discomfort you feel will be a normal part of the improvement process.

As you progress to new levels of training, your mind takes on a more important role. As a beginner it's fine to let your mind wander on runs, to chat with friends, to construct shopping lists in your head – in short, to make each run as painless and as pleasurable as possible. This type of mental distraction is called dissociation, and it can be extremely helpful at times. Your internal dialogue while running up a tough hill might go something like this: *Look at those pretty flowers over there. I didn't realize spring was coming along so quickly. I'd better start watering my garden. . . .*

When you're dissociating, you're doing your best to focus on anything but the task at hand, specifically *that* hill.

Dissociation will still work on your easy runs. When your goal is to pick up the pace or to improve your form, however, it won't do you any favours. It's far more helpful to train your mind to enter into a partnership with your body. How so? You can use your mind to monitor your every step and to dispense feedback. You can pay attention to your breathing and your form, staying relaxed and positive. Your internal dialogue on that same killer hill might go something like this: *Okay, hold together here. This hill isn't all that tough. Just another few hundred yards. How's my posture? Oops, I'm hunched over at the waist. Stay upright; that's it. Now my legs are lifting more easily. Nice and steady. Even breathing. Here's the top – great! Now relax and recover on the downhill.*

That's a big difference in approach. It takes concentration to run a notch harder than what you're used to; your body would love nothing more than to slip into its old, comfortable pace. Stop paying attention for a moment and it will do just that. Several studies have shown that when runners let their minds wander, their bodies actually slow down. The mental concentration required to maintain a tough effort doesn't come naturally or easily. On your early attempts, you may be surprised to find your mind working against you: *I'm so tired, I'll never make it up that hill. I want to stop. Why am I doing this anyway?*

With a mind like that, who *wouldn't* rather daydream about the landscape? It's crucial that your feedback remains positive; otherwise, you'll use your brain's powerful impact to talk you right out of a workout.

Concentration is most important during your more challenging workouts, but it's a good idea to develop it by practising on other runs. After all, it's easier to work on maintaining a positive attitude during a comfortable run when everything is going well. Try doing regular 'check-ins' to monitor your form, breathing, stride and mental attitude. Use these periods to correct yourself gently: drop your hunched shoulders, take a few deep breaths and exhale slowly, lengthen a stride that has turned short and choppy, stop any negative thoughts midstream. If you get used to this process on easier runs, you'll be more prepared when all the challenges come lumped together at the end of a long run or other tough stretch.

Like anything else, training the brain takes time. Become aware of your dialogue, and when it turns negative, consciously correct yourself, but be kind, and reaffirm that you are up to the task at hand. Over time, you'll naturally develop a more positive association between body and brain.

TRAINING CONSIDERATIONS

You're now ready to explore workouts that are longer and more involved than the short, steady jogs you're used to. 'It's good for women to start on something other than slow jogging as soon as they have the necessary base,' says Maureen Roben, who coaches many beginners making the leap to a higher level. 'When you do the same thing every day, you use the same muscles and develop the same systems. Adding some variety to the programme is healthy.'

As you add more intense workouts to your schedule, you'll need to keep the emphasis on smart training. Here's how.

Add distance first. When increasing your workload, never boost distance and intensity at the same time. The combination can overload your body, leading to injury or fatigue. In this training schedule, your distance will increase first, in order to improve your general fitness. Only then will you add workouts of a greater intensity. As always, take the necessary time to get comfortable with the training programme. If you find that a certain week is particularly difficult, keep training at that week's level until it becomes comfortable.

Run for time, not miles. At this stage of your training, it's still most practical and useful to run 'by the clock' – for set amounts of time as opposed to distance. So that's how the workouts in this chapter are structured.

Some runners will be curious to see how far they are going, though, or to see how fast they are covering a route of a certain distance. Look for signs: many bike paths and park trails are already measured and marked. Or you might want to buy a GPS device that will measure your distance and pace. (For more information, see chapter 2.) Even if you decide to spend the money and have the ability to monitor your every step, I recommend you avoid the temptation to monitor every route you run. As you become more serious about running, you may find yourself feeling tempted to time every mile on every outing and to compare them from day to day. That's one sure way to press too hard in your training, since some runs should be done at an easy recovery pace. You'll also be setting yourself up for disappointment, as there's simply no way you can improve on a micro, day-to-day level. So leave some runs unmeasured and untimed. You can even leave your watch at home sometimes.

Keep easy days in the mix. To increase your training level effectively, this schedule requires that you apply the 'hard–easy' approach. Since you'll be running harder or longer on some days, it goes hand in hand that you'll also need recovery days. If you need to depart from the suggested schedule, be sure to keep the hard–easy approach intact.

Never schedule your more challenging workouts on consecutive days. (For now, a challenging workout is anything longer, faster or harder than your typical 30-minute run.) In general, your week should alternate one longer or harder run with days of easy 30-minute jogs or a day off.

Also, run no more than 4 days in a row. After running this many days at a stretch, take a day off completely. If you crave some form of exercise, try swimming, cycling or another activity that's less demanding of your joints.

VARIETY AND INTENSITY

These workouts are designed to increase your strength, endurance, speed and overall fitness. They are essentially simpler, scaled-back versions of workouts that advanced runners do.

The long run. The long run can sound intimidating, and indeed, some advanced runners will eventually hit the pavement for upwards of 3 hours during one of these workouts. But fear not. Your long run won't start out that long. Pick a day that works best for you, and gradually increase your running time each week until you build up to an hour. (Typically, runners do this workout at the weekend since that is when they have the most time.) Don't bump up the length of this run too quickly. Follow a progression like the one in the sample training schedule outlined in the 16-week plan, which starts on page 55, increasing your long run by 5 minutes maximum each week.

Your long run will build your endurance, enhance your fitness, and get your body comfortable working for a longer period of time. Speed is not important on your long-run day. Run at a comfortable pace, walking every now and then if you need to. Once you can run for an hour, keep your long runs at that duration for several weeks or months until you are comfortable with it.

Fartlek. This strange-sounding word is a Swedish term that means, roughly, speed play. And indeed, these workouts can seem like child's play, interspersing fast bursts with slower recovery jogging. More advanced runners will do a fartlek workout in a regimented style, sometimes including a set number of timed intervals so that it resembles a traditional speed workout. But for the intermediate runner, fartlek can be simply a fun, unintimidating introduction to faster running.

To do fartlek, vary the speed and intensity of your pace, creating work and allowing recovery without stopping. Warm up by starting your run as you ordinarily would, jogging at a comfortable pace for about 10 minutes. Then, for a set period of time, 'play' by alternating slow, medium and faster paces for short periods of time. (See 'Intermediate Training Schedule' on page 60.) These timed intervals can last anywhere from 30 seconds to 3 minutes. You don't even have to look at your watch. Try running each segment by picking out a different landmark: run harder to the fifth lamppost, for example; then recover by jogging to the tree at the end of the street; then pick up the pace again. Follow faster bursts with slower ones for recovery.

Never go so fast that you're sprinting. Alternate tempos so that the overall effect is one of breathing more heavily than you're used to but so that you can still recover within a minute or so and have enough energy left for your next 'burst'. Think of it in terms of changing gear in a car: you want to shift from first to second gear, and sometimes from second to third. But leave fourth and fifth gear out of it – you won't be able to complete the workout if you're pushing that hard. Fartlek will begin to train your mind and your body to feel the difference in paces and to recover efficiently. That's valuable information, especially if you're going to be racing. So although these workouts can indeed feel like playtime, pay attention to what you're feeling: you can learn a lot.

Hills. Ask any runner about her least favourite terrain and she's likely to talk about hills. Hills slow you down, and worse, they hurt. So mythic is their reputation that particular hills in races and on training courses have even acquired names: Heartbreak Hill, the Beast and so on.

In order to overcome such monsters, runners tend to attack them head-on, intentionally training on hills for a tough workout. Typically, this has meant finding a hill and sprinting up it as fast as possible, then trickling down slowly, then hammering up, and doing it over and over again. And yes, it is better to train on hills than to avoid them. There's really no getting around it – if you ignore hills in your training and you race on an undulating course, you'll be sure to pay the price. Plus, running on hills has all sorts of benefits. You rely on your power muscles, which can be underutilized on long, flat runs, so it's a fast, efficient way to build strength. And hills will build your confidence along with your strength, so you won't need to fear any course or terrain.

Still, there's a less regimented, more whimsical way to train on hills, especially at this stage of the game. Coach Maureen Roben explains her kinder, gentler approach to hills this way: 'I tell women to find a hilly course or park to run and then, every time they hit an incline, to pick up the pace. If it's a short hill, run a little harder. If it's a long, extended hill, don't go quite so fast. This workout is much more fun and less intimidating than doing hill repeats. Plus, it tends to put less stress on the joints during the downhills.' You'll reap all the benefits of running hills, and you may even have some fun along the way.

So instead of going up and down the nearest big hill, look for a route that includes rolling hills. As you run each hill, concentrate on maintaining good form. In particular, avoid slumping forward at the waist, which makes it more difficult to lift your legs. It also helps to shorten your stride by a small amount. And slightly exaggerate the pumping motion of your arms to help drive your body up the hill. Pick up the pace until you reach the top of the hill, then relax and ease back to your regular pace until the next hill.

16-WEEK PLAN

The Intermediate Training Schedule will help you reach the next level safely and comfortably. Although the schedule covers 16 weeks of training, remember that this is only a guide and that every woman responds differently to training. Move along more slowly if your body dictates. If a certain week proves particularly difficult, repeat that week's training before progressing to the next week. In fact, every 4 weeks, it's a good idea to repeat the last week's workouts until you feel comfortable at that level. If you feel very sore or are ill, be sure to take a few days off. Resume training where you left off; don't ever jump ahead without taking the incremental steps. Don't worry if you take several extra weeks or months to get through the entire programme.

In Weeks 1 to 8, this schedule concentrates on building distance, particularly during your long run and on one other day of the week. Week 9 adds a day of training, bringing you up to 5 days a week. Finally, Weeks 13 to 16 increase the intensity of 1 workout per week.

You can alter this schedule to meet your own personal needs. If you want to run only 4 days a week, for example, that's fine. You can still work your way through the rest of the schedule. Just repeat the Week 8 workout for several weeks, until you feel comfortable at that level. Then head into Week 9 and subsequent workouts, deleting the fifth day's 20-minute run so that you remain at 4 runs per week.

THE NEXT STEP

When you reach the end of this programme, the first thing you might want to do is take a break. That can mean taking a week off entirely to rest your legs. After increasing the intensity of their training, runners are particularly prone to injury. So if you've made it this far already, a short break is good, cheap insurance for maintaining your health. Have some fun with other workouts while you're resting: you can swim, cycle or join some classes at the gym.

When you start up again, rebuild with a few weeks of distance runs only. No hard workouts just yet. Get back to your baseline of comfort, running 4, 5 or 6 days a week before you resume hills, fartlek and long runs.

After that, it's a good idea to stick with a variation of the schedule in this chapter for a while before attempting anything more strenuous. If you did your 16-week buildup during the spring or summer, for example, continue this level of training – 5 days a week, with a long run of an hour and 1 other difficult workout – during the winter. Get to the point where hills and fartlek workouts feel truly comfortable. Don't think about increasing your workload again until the following summer.

Now Is a Good Time to . . .

➔ Try a new running route, preferably one that takes you to a place of beauty. Once a week, drive to a local park or trail for your run. The scenery will be good for your soul, and the change of location will help keep your running fresh. Also, running on dirt or grass at least once a week is good for your feet and legs. Running on a softer surface reduces the impact on your joints, and the uneven terrain helps to develop tiny muscles and tendons to strengthen your feet and ankles.

➔ Check out your local running club. These clubs attract runners of all abilities, ages and levels of experience. You're sure to find someone at your level to run with as well as someone to inspire you to new levels.

➔ Incorporate flexibility and strengthening exercises into your fitness routine. Stretch lightly for 10 to 15 minutes after running. It feels great, wakes up your body and will keep your muscles from tightening as you physically challenge yourself.

➔ Start a tradition. Race with friends for a festive day of fitness. Many towns and villages in the UK, especially in areas like the Lake District and Derbyshire Dales, hold races as part of a summer fete or festival. These can be a great opportunity to try a fell race or take part in a fun run with your children. Some runners like to choose one local race and make it an annual family event. It's a great motivator and helps to encourage others to have a go.

➔ Cross-train once a week. By swimming, cycling or walking 1 day out of the week, you can keep your muscles and mind fresh and engaged.

➔ Consider attending a running camp or clinic. Women of all ages, experience levels and abilities attend these. Participation in a camp or clinic virtually guarantees that you'll be inspired, motivated and challenged. Plus, devoting a day or a week to nothing but your health and fitness is a worthwhile indulgence. To find a camp, consult your local university or running shop, or check out *Runner's World* magazine's website, www.runnersworld.co.uk, which posts a listing of camps.

TRAINING LOG

The runner's path isn't necessarily a straight one. Sometimes it's a bell curve: a new runner becomes more serious and steps up her training for years until she's maximized her improvement; then she tapers off her mileage and intensity with the eventual demands of age. Others have paths that look like EKGs: bursts of inspired training interspersed with periods of little activity.

My own curve hasn't been very predictable. It continues to develop peaks and troughs that make no particular sense, except within the ragged rhythm of my own life. I trained hard as a child and then stopped completely at university. After that there's a flat line on the graph showing when I took some years off. Then the line on the chart skyrockets, showing when I attacked my running flat out to see how good I could get before getting too old.

Now, despite more than 20 years of running, I find myself at the intermediate level once more. This time around, work and family dictate that level of activity.

When I first withdrew from hard training, my body and mind rebelled. But now, after several years, I've settled into my stride at this new and perhaps more sane level of training. I run as time allows, usually 4 times a week. Once a week, I try to fit in one long run of more than an hour, usually heading off into the hills on Sunday. During the week, I also try to fit in one harder effort, with fartlek or a sustained faster tempo. Other than that, I run when I can.

I've learned to appreciate the beauty of running according to how I feel each day, rather than sticking to a regimented schedule. On days when I'm truly worn out from stress, I allow myself to take my time, taking notice of the clouds, the newborn lambs in the field, the neighbours' latest lawn ornaments. And at those serendipitous times when it all still comes together, I allow myself to fly, the lovely strain of effort leaving no room in my mind for anything but the sensation that is running.

When I first cut back on my training, I thought that I would slip backwards, but I've found that there is no such thing when you're a runner. Between the growing pains of the beginner and the growing pressure of the advanced runner, I've rediscovered a beautiful stage of running freedom. To know that you have the strength to run however long and hard you wish, to know that you have the choice of when you will do so – therein lies the sweet spot of running.

If you don't want to engage in advanced training for racing but you do want to maximize the fitness benefits of running, the end point of this schedule is a good base from which to work. You might eventually want to bump your long run up – by only a few minutes each week – until you reach 90 minutes. You can also increase your easy midweek runs from 20 or 30 minutes to 45 minutes or an hour.

INTERMEDIATE TRAINING SCHEDULE

	MON	TUES	WED	THURS	FRI	SAT	SUN
WEEK 1	Off	30 min	Off	30 min	Off	30 min	35 min
WEEK 2	Off	30 min	Off	30 min	Off	30 min	40 min
WEEK 3	Off	30 min	Off	35 min	Off	30 min	45 min
WEEK 4	Off	30 min	Off	35 min	Off	30 min	50 min
WEEK 5	Off	30 min	Off	35 min	Off	30 min	55 min
WEEK 6	Off	30 min	Off	35 min	Off	30 min	60 min
WEEK 7	Off	30 min	Off	40 min	Off	30 min	60 min
WEEK 8	Off	30 min	Off	45 min	Off	30 min	60 min

	MON	TUES	WED	THURS	FRI	SAT	SUN
WEEK 9	Off	30 min	20 min	30 min	Off	30 min	60 min
WEEK 10	Off	30 min	20 min	35 min	Off	30 min	60 min
WEEK 11	Off	30 min	20 min	40 min	Off	30 min	60 min
WEEK 12	Off	30 min	20 min	45 min	Off	30 min	60 min
WEEK 13	Off	30 min	20 min	45 min (middle 20 fartlek)	Off	30 min	60 min
WEEK 14	Off	30 min	20 min	45 min with hills	Off	30 min	60 min
WEEK 15	Off	30 min	20 min	45 min (middle 20 fartlek)	Off	30 min	60 min
WEEK 16	Off	30 min	20 min	45 min with hills	Off	30 min	60 min

CHAPTER 7

From Running to Racing: Training for the Advanced Runner

IF YOU WANT TO EXPLORE YOUR FULL RUNNING POTENTIAL, this is the chapter for you. Let's be clear: this doesn't just mean the speedster who breaks 40 minutes in a 10-K or the woman who's always the fastest in her group. In running, we can only truly measure ourselves against ourselves. Every woman can work toward becoming her best running self within her own realm of capability. If that's what you wish to do, this chapter is for you, whether your goal is to break a certain time in a 5-K or 10-K or just to see how fast you can go.

That said, this chapter concentrates mainly on runners who wish to race competitively. Beginning and recreational runners can and certainly do race, too, and I strongly recommend racing for runners of all levels, for its social and goal-setting benefits. This chapter will focus on runners who wish to race up to their potential. By that I mean that it's important to you to see how fast you can get, how well you can do, to explore the boundaries of what's possible for you as a runner.

Before you attempt the level of training outlined here, you need a strong base of training to prepare yourself physically for the more intense programme.

That means you should have at least a year of running experience behind you. You should also be at a plateau. In other words, you should have maximized your improvement within the intermediate running programme in this book before moving up to this level. 'As long as you are improving your racing with aerobic training – and when you're starting out, you can continue to do so for several years – you should continue with that programme,' says Lorraine Moller, a four-time Olympic marathon runner and winner of the bronze medal in the 1992 Olympic Games. 'It's when you start to plateau that you should start to incorporate changes.' Bear in mind that even with an advanced workout programme that includes track sessions and sustained hard runs, you won't see your best results until you've been doing this training for several years.

Why race? Why take on the extra work and dedication that an advanced training programme entails? After all, most of the sport's general health benefits peak at the intermediate level of training – in which you work out about 5 times a week, between 30 minutes and an hour each day. Running more than that is not about health. It's not even about superior fitness, which could be achieved with supplementary cross-training. No, the bottom line is that anyone who's training at an advanced level is pursuing something more than health and fitness. She may be pursuing excellence. She may be testing herself. She may be investigating limits. She may be doing all of the above. Runners race to see what they are made of. Some runners feel that the training and racing process contains a microcosm of life's challenges and that through the one they learn about the other.

Taking on the commitment to become the best you can be is a bold move. It entails hard work, time, dedication, triumphs and setbacks. It almost certainly entails frustration and, just as certainly, delivers spectacular fulfilment. But specific results are never guaranteed. Most runners eventually find that it's the journey, not the destination, that provides the greatest value. In the end, the ultimate reward does not reside in the number of minutes and seconds on a watch, but rather within that process of work, learning and discipline.

BE YOUR BEST

The process of becoming the best runner – or the best at any other pursuit, for that matter – involves discipline, dedication and mental fortitude. One of the benefits of pursuing serious training is that it helps develop these attributes, which can in turn come in handy in other areas of life.

In advanced training, you will need to run more miles, more intense workouts and more days per week. You must push yourself constantly. That takes increased time and an increased energy expenditure from your body. In order to accomplish your goals, you'll need to be smart, listen to your body and make wise choices.

The more miles you put in, and the more intense your workouts, the more stress you place on your body. Runners who do large amounts of training are more susceptible to colds and flu, due to their strained immune systems. They are also more susceptible to injury. Obviously the goal is to minimize those troubles, which are counterproductive not only for running but in the rest of your life as well.

You can minimize negative effects by training smart. For advanced runners, that may be even more important than training hard. Most injuries can be avoided by following the rules of wise training. That means never increasing either quantity or quality too quickly and adjusting your schedule at early signs of overtraining or extreme fatigue. It also means giving proper attention to your body's biomechanics. Because any misalignment will be exacerbated by greater training loads, it's doubly important that you wear the proper shoes and replace them often when training at this level.

You'll also have to make choices about how you commit your time and energy. 'At a high fitness level, you're going to have to work a whole lot more just to get a little more benefit,' says Dr Jack Daniels, coach and author of best-selling running book *Daniels' Running Formula*. It comes down to the law of diminishing returns. Basically, you see your greatest improvement when you start running. At each subsequent level, you have to work harder for what will almost undoubtedly be a smaller increment of improvement. In order to reach your potential, you will train extraordinarily hard to shave what might amount to seconds or a minute off your time in a race. The question then arises whether the amount of work needed to get to the next level is worth it.

Because of all there is to gain in the pursuit of excellence, for plenty of women the answer is yes. But that answer is likely to require some rearrangements in your personal life. The rest of the world isn't set up to work around your tough training schedule. It might mean using up some of the free time you currently spend on other pursuits. It might necessitate shifting a work schedule around in order to meet with a training group.

When intrusions become tempting, remind yourself of your goals and the benefits you get from pushing yourself. View your commitment not as a sacrifice, but as an investment in yourself. Finally, allow yourself to break form every once in a while – to miss an easy run to go on a country hike with friends, for example. The change of pace will help keep you from going stale. As always, balance is key.

MASTERS OF BALANCE

Ask most coaches and elite runners what the single key to success in the sport is and they'll answer, 'consistency'. Do the work day after day, month after month, year after year, and improvement is virtually guaranteed. Consistency has many enemies, however: injury, boredom and lack of discipline among them. Consistency can even be a cannibal. Some of the most focused runners – those who will never, ever, under any circumstances miss a workout – are the ones who discipline themselves right into a debilitating injury, one that could have been avoided by taking a few days off early on.

Former world-class runner and coach Benji Durden believes that the truly great runners are masters of balance. 'Ultimately, the best runners are the ones who are willing to work very hard but who have a little bit of a lazy streak in them,' he says. What he means is that these runners will be prone to take a day off when they feel worn out rather than pushing through fatigue even when their bodies cry out for them to back off.

Only you can determine your optimal balance between pushing and backing off, between consistency in training and necessary breaks. Master that formula and you've mastered running at the expert level.

So how on earth do you master the balance? Above all, it's a function of time. The longer you've been running, the more information you'll have gathered to make those decisions. You will have learned the difference between laziness and true exhaustion, between minor tweaks and serious pain in need of attention.

But it's also a function of mindfulness. Some women can run for years and never learn to listen to their bodies. Others have an uncanny sense of how hard to push. You can develop this mindfulness just as you would build your muscles – by exercising it. That means paying attention when your body talks to you.

CLIMB TO YOUR PEAK

To race well, you need to understand peaking. You can maintain peak fitness only for a few weeks, so that's when you want to race. Then you want to rest before building up again. Professional runners might plan to peak several times in a year – for example, for track season, for an autumn road race, and then for indoor track over the winter. For most other runners, this science is a little too precise, so it's more realistic to peak just once a year. Because most races are held in the period from spring to autumn, and because the weather can create a challenge to training in the winter, the seasons can help guide your programme.

Start by choosing one major event in which you hope to run an optimal performance. This is the race you should peak for. You can and certainly should run other races along the way, but bear in mind that you might not be in your best shape, and therefore you might not run up to your capacity. You'll probably want to 'train through' these interim races, which means you won't taper your training before them. Otherwise you won't be able to train consistently enough to reach your peak. Interim races are useful to learn about your fitness at the time and to experiment with pacing and racing tactics.

If you've never raced before, choose a shorter race that you can easily tackle. A 5-K is a typical starting point, not only because you can go the distance but also because the shorter the race, the fewer mistakes can happen. If you go out too fast and find your pace woefully slowed, for example, you won't have that far to run to finish the race. But if you attempt a half-marathon before you can correctly gauge your pacing, you could be in for a very long final 5 or 6 miles. Plan to run a few 5-Ks and 10-Ks before attempting the half-marathon.

Next, break your training into 4 segments: base building, strengthening, sharpening and tapering.

Base building. Traditionally done during the winter, base building consists of easy distance running. You can certainly add some hilly runs and fartlek, but overall you should concentrate on logging miles. 'This phase gives you a good opportunity for development of all the things that happen as a function of time spent running, as opposed to intensity,' says Dr Daniels. Muscle cell adaptation, an increased capacity for your blood cells to deliver oxygen to your body and other physiological improvements occur during this phase of long, slow distance.

Since building a base is the least exciting, least 'glamorous' part of training, it often receives short shrift. Runners will run track sessions all winter, for example, or they won't log enough miles because of cold weather. But the importance of this phase of training can't be understated. Think of your base as the foundation on which you build the rest of your training programme – the broader and stronger it is, the higher a peak you will ultimately be able to climb.

Strengthening. During this phase you build up your strength with longer intervals, tempo runs and harder long runs. This stage typically takes place during the spring and can last several months. 'At this point, you're working on your running economy, improving lactate threshold and aerobic capacity,' Dr Daniels says. These scientific terms may sound scary, but they're crucial to understanding running performance.

Lactate threshold is the point at which lactic acid, a waste product created during exertion, builds up in your system faster than your muscles can flush it out. This happens when your cardiovascular system can't process enough oxygen to get rid of it, a condition called anaerobic ('without air') threshold. If you've ever run too fast too early in a workout and felt as if your legs had become jelly-like, you've felt the effects of surpassing your lactate threshold. By training near the threshold, you can extend it. These workouts are often referred to as tempo runs or as lactate or anaerobic threshold runs.

Aerobic capacity refers to your body's ability to process oxygen. Not all the oxygen we inhale is used when we exercise. The amount used depends on your max VO_2, or maximum oxygen uptake, the amount of oxygen your body is able to deliver to your muscles during exercise. Though this figure is partly determined by genetics, training can help you maximize your potential aerobic capacity. Such training is typically done in track workouts in which you run close to or slightly faster than your usual 5-K pace.

Sharpening. As you approach your goal race and want to build speed, it's time to start sharpening. Interval workouts focus on shorter distances, and workouts in general should develop your speed without leaving you overly fatigued. Your mileage might drop off slightly at this stage to speed leg recovery. Your body will be able to store reserves, and you'll feel bouncy and ready for the race efforts to come.

Tapering. Depending on your race distance, 1 to 2 weeks before your race you should reduce your mileage drastically. This final reduction will allow any sore spots to heal and help your body to store an optimal amount of fuel to use during the race. (For more on tapering before a race, see chapter 8.)

These phases are not entirely exclusive of one another. You'll still do easy distance runs during your strengthening phase, and you might still run a few strength workouts while you are sharpening. The point is that the overall focus of the training shifts over time.

After your big race, it's not a bad idea to take a few weeks off to let your body recover and to give your mental concentration a break. Some runners swim or cross-train during this break, while others prefer to be completely sedentary. Once you start back, you'll want to begin again at the base-building phase. (The sample training schedules on pages 80 to 83 start at the strengthening phase.)

OPTIMIZE YOUR TRAINING

Here's a look at some of the most important considerations that should go into your running programme at the race preparation level. These are things that you might not have worried about before, but when training this hard, they magnify in importance.

Flexibility

The harder you train, the more important it is to listen to your body and make the necessary changes. Our bodies talk to us all the time, but we don't always pay attention. Try to recognize the difference between niggling soreness and pain. Do the same with the general tiredness from a busy schedule versus the exhaustion that signals overtraining.

When you find clues that you're heading down a destructive path, take action. Take a few days off, have a massage and get a good night's sleep. Don't be so obsessive that you won't miss a workout. If you begin a hard workout, such as a track session or tempo run, and find that you're 'dead' – you can't stay focused, or you're just physically exhausted – take the day off or go for an easy jog instead. It's far better to be proactive than to miss weeks or months down the line once you've driven yourself too hard. Bear in mind that you can't make up for lost time. Don't try to cram in missed workouts or put hard workouts back-to-back after taking time off. If you skip a hard workout, try to do it the next day if you have several easy days scheduled after that; otherwise, skip it altogether.

When to Push

Some coaches ask runners to 'give their all' every day in training. They are liable to end up with runners who have nothing left to give on race day.

'There is racing energy and there is training energy,' says Lorraine Moller, 'and you don't want to use racing energy up in training. There's only one time when you should use that kind of energy, and that's in a race.' Though it's important to run hard in track sessions and tempo runs, you shouldn't run to exhaustion. 'Your energy levels will plummet if you give your all every time you train,' agrees British coach Nick Anderson. A good rule of thumb is that you should be able to run your last repeat in track sessions as fast as your first one. If you're getting slower with each repeat, you're running too hard. Likewise, in tempo runs, when you finish, you should feel able to continue running at the same pace if you had to. If you complete the workout and collapse at the finish line, you're using up your race energy.

A Mental Edge

It's important to ensure that your programme builds your confidence, and not the opposite. Some women thrive on hard training; others wind up feeling demoralized and insecure about their abilities. To reach your potential, you must begin every workout and race with utter faith in your coaching and training.

If your programme isn't inspiring this kind of confidence, think of ways to change it. That might mean finding a new coach, new training partners or a different location. Details count, too. Run your quality workouts – the interval sessions, tempo runs, fartlek and long runs – at a pace that is reasonable for you (as outlined in chapter 6). Don't overextend yourself to train with a group that competes beyond your current ability. Don't ruin your workout by either slowing down or speeding up based on how somebody else is running. Make sure you're getting enough rest between hard workouts. All these little things add up, either building into a ladder of successes that will give you confidence for your race or slowly eroding your belief in your abilities. Ultimately, you are responsible for this process, so don't be afraid to take control of it and make changes in your training if necessary.

Days Off

You'll benefit from days of complete rest. Typically, that means taking 1 day off each 7 to 10 days. A rest will allow your legs to recover more fully for upcoming hard efforts. It can also fend off injuries that might be creeping up. If you're the obsessive type, you can use your day off as a cross-training day, but choose an exercise such as swimming that doesn't tax the legs with impact.

Two-a-Days

The purpose of running twice a day is to add miles with a minimum amount of stress on your legs. For example, let's say that you're already running 6 afternoons a week, up to an hour each day, with a long run on weekends, and you want gradually to increase your miles. Instead of going even longer than an hour, add a short run in the morning on 1 day. Start at 20 minutes and build up to 30 minutes. You'll find that doing so is a lot easier – physically and mentally – than a long, 90-minute run in the middle of the week. When you are comfortable with your additional run on 1 day, you can increase to 2 or 3 days of 'doubling'.

While there is an argument for running twice a day, most women will find that the added time required (changing clothes, showering, not to mention child-care and work concerns) mean it's just not worthwhile. And certainly only professional runners should run twice a day more than a few times a week.

If you've been training at an advanced level for several years and feel you really want to try two-a-days, limit them to your hard workout days during the week. (If you double on other days, you'll be making your recovery days too difficult.) Add 20 to 40 minutes of easy distance for your second run. Make sure that you have at least 6 hours between runs, preferably more. Finally, take care to eat enough on these days; otherwise, you stand a chance of running out of energy on your second outing. After your morning run, eat a substantial meal right away. That will leave enough time to digest your food before your second run.

Effort and Recovery

The harder you run, the more recovery you need. Hard workouts are the bread and butter of an expert runner. These are the days when the real training is accomplished. But without recovery days, hard workouts are worthless: there must be easy runs in order for the training effect to be felt.

Most serious runners will do either 2 or 3 hard workouts per week. Newer runners will want to start at 2 hard efforts and perhaps eventually build up to 3. Older runners typically come upon a time when they have to drop from the 3 workouts they're used to down to 2. What really determines this number is the number of recovery days your body requires between hard efforts. If you do a track session on Tuesday and an easy run on Wednesday, for example, you'll need to be fairly well recovered to do a tempo run on Thursday. If you haven't recovered enough, you might need 2 or even 3 easy days between these efforts. The sample schedules on pages 80 to 83 show what a training programme may look like at the beginning and advanced competitive levels.

The principle of effort and recovery applies not only on a daily basis but also over the long haul. Just as you need recovery days, you should have recovery weeks as well. For every 3 to 5 weeks of hard training, you should cut your mileage and your quality back for 1 week. This proactive approach can keep you from overtraining, injury and burnout.

Quality versus Quantity

Although I've alluded to this in many places throughout this book, it bears spelling out especially for runners who are training at an advanced level. Doing the *right* training (or 'smart' training) is more important than doing the *most* training. Increasing your weekly mileage is not a certain recipe for success. Some runners do successfully run 80, 90 or 100 miles a week over long periods of time, but they are rarities who seem to be genetically blessed with the ability to avoid injury or illness. And there's no guarantee that they're running any faster; they might even be hurting their performance with chronically tired legs.

For runners who are not competing professionally, most performance gains can be maximized at a level of 40 to 60 miles a week. Even some elite runners succeed on far fewer miles than their peers who boast of large numbers in their running logs. So don't feel pressured to run more miles because your friends or training partners are doing so. If you are able to improve on less work, consider yourself lucky.

THE WORKOUTS

The quality workouts you'll be running in this training programme are meant to prepare you for the effort of racing. You'll concentrate on both strength and speed.

The other runs during the week should be considered recovery workouts and run at an easy pace. This means that you shouldn't worry at all about time on these runs. Go with whatever effort feels comfortable to your body.

Long Runs

Before starting on this programme, you should already have built your long run up to about an hour in duration. Now you'll work on increasing that time and distance. For the 5-K, the 10-K, and even the half-marathon, 90 minutes is the maximum time necessary for this workout. (For marathon training, see chapter 9.) Incrementally extend your long run by 5 to 10 minutes each week until you reach 90 minutes.

When you're comfortable with this amount of time on your feet, mix some intensity into your long run. Whenever you pick up the pace in your long run, do it gradually – anywhere from 30 to 60 seconds per mile faster than your easy pace. You don't want to be sprinting when you still have 45 minutes to go. Here are some long run variations you can try:

✳ **Surges.** Pick up the pace slightly for short periods of time in the middle of your run. Warm up by going easy for at least the first 20 minutes. Then surge for a total of 15 to 25 minutes of harder running. The surges can be loosely structured ('I'll pick it up until the next big tree') or timed segments of planned duration. Between surges, return to your standard pace. Start with shorter surges the first time you attempt this, and build up to several minutes. Play with variety, for example, running up and down a ladder of surges of different duration – say, 2 minutes, 4 minutes, 6 minutes, 4 minutes and 2 minutes.

✳ **Segments.** Divide your long run into longer segments, running the middle or latter portion at a faster pace. For example, run 30 minutes at your usual pace, 30 minutes slightly faster, then 30 minutes back at your usual pace. Or divide the run into 20-minute chunks, gradually picking up the pace with each one. With these segments, the shift in pace should be very slight, or you'll find yourself unable to complete the workout. As you'll discover for yourself, you'll not only be training yourself to run at a faster pace, but you'll also be getting an invaluable lesson in pacing and in your body's tolerance of different speeds.

✳ **The fast long run.** Of course, one way to increase the intensity of the long run is to run the entire workout faster. This can be a very demanding workout and generally should not be done more than a few times in a training season. Start conservatively to ensure that you can complete the workout strongly, picking up the pace rather than slowing down over the course of the run.

Tempo Runs

Also called lactate threshold or anaerobic threshold runs, these workouts are as close as you'll come to simulating competitive conditions. You'll be running at a certain tempo – namely, close to your racing pace – for a prolonged period of time. Ideally, these runs are conducted a little bit slower than your anaerobic threshold, in which lactic acid accumulates in your muscles faster than your body can flush it away.

If you've ever suffered the dreaded 'leaden legs' or 'jelly legs' feeling after starting out too fast on a run, you know what it means to surpass your anaerobic threshold. By running just under that threshold, your body develops its ability to process lactic acid more efficiently, which essentially raises your threshold and allows you to run harder. In addition to these physiological benefits, tempo runs also help you to develop a sense of pacing as well as a confidence in your ability to maintain a strenuous pace for longer duration.

Tempo runs can last for a predetermined amount of time or distance. It's best to start with a short time or distance and move up from there. For 5-K and 10-K races, you'll eventually want to build up to a 3- or 4-mile tempo run. For half-marathons, these runs might reach 6 miles. Always plan to warm up before and cool down after your tempo run with an easy 2-mile or 15-minute jog. Look for a relatively flat place to do this workout; changes in terrain defeat the purpose of your attempt to keep a consistent pace. Gently rolling hills are acceptable, especially if you know you'll be racing on hills. Run the same course each week in order to track your times.

Your pace should be somewhat slower than your 10-K race pace. It should feel brisk but not exhausting. My former coach used to describe it as 'fresh' pace: a point at which you could talk if you absolutely had to, but you really don't want to. Ideally, your pace should remain the same throughout the duration of each tempo run. When you bump up the distance of the tempo run, don't be surprised to see your pace drop accordingly. As you grow fitter, however, you should be able to increase the distance you can run while maintaining your goal pace.

Track Sessions

Track workouts are similar in form to fartlek workouts, in that they alternate hard efforts with a recovery pace. But track workouts add the dimension of regimentation: you'll be on a perfectly flat, measured surface. That's why these workouts are invaluable for learning a sense of pacing. They also make it easier to compare times from one repeat to the next, in order to gauge consistency, and from one session to another, in order to gauge your fitness and performance levels.

Track sessions are typically called interval workouts. They consist of repeated hard efforts of a specific distance (commonly called repeats) alternated with periods of rest (known as intervals). The lengths of the repeats and intervals vary depending on the purpose of the workout and where the workout falls within the overall training schedule. The track sessions in this chapter's training schedules consist of distances ranging from 200 metres to 1,000 metres (2½ laps around a typical 400-metre track).

Run your track repeats around or slightly faster than your goal 5-K race pace. You'll want to become comfortable running at this pace, and become familiar with the effort so that you can duplicate this pace in a race. Either jog very slowly or walk during your rest interval, but don't sit or lie down; that will leave you stiff for your next repeat and won't allow your system to flush out lactic acid efficiently. A 400-metre jog should be sufficient rest for repeats of 400 metres and up. A 200-metre jog should suffice when you are doing repeats of only 200 metres.

The point of these sessions is not to replicate a race effort. 'People

Too Much Running

Here's one of the most perplexing contradictions about running: more isn't always better. Yes, you must put in more miles and run more intensely to get faster. But there is such a thing as running too much. Insiders call it over-training.

When you overtrain, you feel sluggish. Your times slow down, no matter how consistent your workouts are. Training partners with whom you ordinarily keep up pass you by easily. When this happens, most women's logical response is to train harder. Wrong answer.

Overtraining can create a nasty little cycle that leads to frustration and debilitation. The last thing that serious runners want to admit is that they might have limits, so overtraining often goes unrecognized. Coaches and training partners can be helpful in spotting the signs.

Pay attention to the following symptoms of overtraining:

→ Chronic fatigue

→ Trouble sleeping

→ Elevated heart rate

→ Slowing times

→ Loss of appetite

→ Irritability

→ Lack of motivation

→ Frequent illnesses (typically cold and flu)

Overtraining should not be taken lightly. Some runners who overdo it become chronically tired and ill. It can take months for your body to recover when it's been pushed past the point of healthy training.

think that the minute you put your feet on the track you have to go as hard as you possibly can, preferably until you're sick,' jokes five-time Olympic Trials Marathon qualifier Maureen Roben. She cautions that most runners could stand to run these workouts more conservatively, especially the ones who are always struggling to complete a given session. You should aim to complete your final repeat as fast or faster than your

Although formal evidence is lacking, many runners and coaches believe that there is even a point of no return, from which runners who have pushed too hard for too long can no longer return to their former strength. 'You see a lot of people who should have made it but didn't because they pushed themselves too hard and weren't patient enough to progress,' says Ann Boyd, an elite runner turned coach. 'They have success for a short while, but then they disappear from the racing scene and never come back to that level.' Shelly Steely, a four-time World Championship cross-country team member who coaches women, agrees. She says that overtraining is the number-one pitfall of serious runners of all levels. 'Everyone who starts training consistently sees some improvement, so then they think that more work must be even better,' Steely says. 'Then, when faced with a little injury or exhaustion, they're already hooked, so they can't imagine taking a day off.'

Steely urges her runners to realize that with such behaviour, they have the opposite effect of their intentions. 'They are, in fact, not investing in long-term consistency at all,' she cautions.

If you suspect that you have been overdoing it recently, take a week or two off to allow for a full recovery. Get extra sleep, eat well, and do something other than running if you feel the need to exercise. If you've been pushing too hard for a long period of time – say, for a few months or more – you might want to take several weeks to a month off and run only easy distances until you recover. The payoff will be worthwhile: a stronger, healthier, more resilient you.

first. If you find yourself fading throughout the session, you're starting out too fast.

Start your track workouts with a warmup of about 2 miles of easy jogging. Stretch thoroughly, and then do some strides to get your body prepared to move at a faster pace. A good method is to choose a straight on the track and do 'pickups', starting out slowly and gradually picking up the pace until you are striding at around your 5-K pace by the end of the 100-metre stretch. At that point, slow down, stop, rest and repeat. Do 6 to 8 of these before the track session. Finally, always finish with a sufficient cooldown.

Now Is a Good Time to . . .

❯ Get together with a team or a group of friends for hard workouts. For most people, intense training sessions seem easier and more enjoyable when they're run with others. Some friendly competition can also push you to work harder.

❯ Begin keeping a training log if you're not already doing so. A record of your workouts will help you determine what works and what doesn't work for you. Besides your workouts, you might want to record what you eat, how you sleep, any stressful events, when you buy new running shoes and anything else that might affect your training.

❯ Run a race for time. Set a realistic goal based on your past performances. Choose a race at least 2 months away, and then follow an appropriate training schedule for your training level. For an optimal performance based on a full peaking schedule, you'll want to have 4 to 6 months. If you already have a sufficient base of easy miles, you can begin at the strengthening phase outlined in this chapter's workouts. Regardless of whether you hit your goal, remain positive and choose another target race. Analyse what went right and wrong in the race and how you can improve your training for the next time around.

❯ Consider consulting with a coach. He or she can help determine your individual strengths and weaknesses and can tailor a training programme just for you. At this level, it can be very beneficial to have someone who can serve as a sounding board.

Jog slowly for about 2 miles after your repeats. This will help reduce any muscle soreness that might set in the next day.

Race Preparations

The first 2 workout schedules presented here will prepare you for either a 5-K or a 10-K race.

Use the Beginning Competitor Training Schedule if you want to race more seriously but have been running at an intermediate level for only a year or so. This will allow you gradually to increase the intensity of your workouts. Try

---

→ Invest in racing shoes. If you're training this hard, you deserve to have every advantage when you compete.

→ Evaluate your diet – again. It's crucial to get enough calories and the right kind. As women grow more serious about their running, they often start to cut corners on their diets to keep their weight as low as possible. Consider seeing a nutritionist at your local gym to see whether you are eating adequately for your training level.

→ Be sure that you're getting enough sleep. Now is not the time to stress yourself in other areas of your life. If you're in the midst of a busy work schedule or have particularly tough family demands, you may want to reschedule your heavy training for another time.

→ Get sports massages. Tired, sore muscles can benefit from therapeutic massage. Consider scheduling a regular session, anywhere from once a month to once a week.

→ Have your form analysed. Many podiatrists and sports physiotherapists offer form analysis, which can help ensure that you run as efficiently as possible. If you don't know where to get one in your area, your local running club or running shop can help.
Or you can simply ask a friend to video you while you run and then watch the recording at home. While you watch, look at your feet to make sure they're not rolling in or toeing out. See if your arms are crossing too far over your chest. Are your shoulders hunched? Is your head poked forward?

this schedule in the spring, after a winter of building your base at an intermediate level, as you train for your first serious 5-K or 10-K.

Use the Advanced Competitor Training Schedule once you have spent a racing season completing the Beginning Competitor Schedule. Rebuild your base over the winter, and implement the advanced schedule in the spring.

The last workout schedule is for training for a half-marathon. Plan to race some 5-Ks and 10-Ks before you attempt this distance.

THE NEXT STEP

As you progress, you may want to continue to notch up your training. If you do, always be aware of the issues raised at the beginning of the chapter. Improvement at this level will require a great amount of effort. Your risk of overtraining and injury increases. Be careful to monitor your body at all times and back off when warning signs hit.

BEGINNING COMPETITOR TRAINING SCHEDULE

	MON	TUES	WED	THURS	FRI	SAT	SUN
WEEK 1	Off	30 min easy	40 min (middle 20 fartlek)	40 min easy	Off	40 min easy	75 min with 2 8-min faster segments
WEEK 2	Off	30 min easy	Track: 4 × 400 m with 400-m jog	40 min easy	Off	40 min easy	75 min (middle 15 faster)
WEEK 3	Off	30 min easy	40 min (middle 20 fartlek)	40 min easy	Off	40 min easy	75 min (20-min or 2.5-mile faster segment in middle)

The rules of training won't change much over the course of time. You can use the same workout programme presented here whether you've been running hard for a few years or for 10; the only difference is that your speed will change with your level of fitness. The level of effort should remain the same.

If you wish to continue to compete in races of up to a half-marathon, your overall mileage needn't increase greatly. You may wish to do some doubles, adding some easy miles in a second run on your tempo-run days and track days. You can add a few more repeats to your track workouts, but in general the quality portion of each of these workouts should never amount to more than 10 per cent of your total weekly mileage. Concentrate on quality rather than quantity, aiming to become faster in the same workouts than you were the year before. Remember, more isn't always better. Many world-class runners do the same workout programmes year in and year out with good results.

	MON	TUES	WED	THURS	FRI	SAT	SUN
WEEK 4	Off	30 min easy	Track: 4 × 400 m, 400-m jog; 4 × 200 m, 200-m jog	40 min easy	Off	40 min easy	75 min (25-min or 3-mile faster segment in middle)
WEEK 5	Off	30 min easy	Track: 10 × 200 m with 200-m jog	40 min easy	Off	40 min easy	75 min (middle 20 fartlek)
WEEK 6	Off	30 min easy	40 min easy	30 min easy	Off	20 min easy with strides	Race (5-K or 10-K)

ADVANCED COMPETITOR TRAINING SCHEDULE

	MON	TUES	WED	THURS	FRI	SAT	SUN
WEEK 1	Off	60 min (10 × 2 min fartlek)	45 min easy	Tempo run: 2 miles warmup, 2 miles tempo, 2 miles cool-down	45 min easy	30 to 60 min easy	Long run: 75 min (15 easy, 45 faster, 15 easy)
WEEK 2	Off	Track: 6 × 800 m with 400m jog	45 min easy	Tempo run: 2 miles warmup, 2 miles tempo, 2 miles cool-down	45 min easy	30 to 60 min easy	Long run: 90 min easy with surges
WEEK 3	Off	Track: 6 × 800 m with 400-m jog	45 min easy	Tempo run: 2 miles warmup, 3 miles tempo, 2 miles cool-down	45 min easy	30 to 60 min easy	Long run: 75 min at slightly faster than easy pace
WEEK 4 (RECOVERY WEEK)	Off	60 min: 15 easy, 30 easy fartlek, 15 easy	45 min easy	Off	45 min easy	45 min easy	60 min easy (or interim race)

	MON	TUES	WED	THURS	FRI	SAT	SUN
WEEK 5	Off	Track: 2 × 800 m, 2 × 400 m, 2 × 800 m, all with 400-m jog in between	45 min easy	Tempo run: 2 miles warmup, 3 miles tempo, 2 miles cool-down	45 min easy	30 to 60 min easy	Long run: 90 min easy with 10 surges in middle
WEEK 6	Off	Track: 4 × 400 m, 400-m jog; 8 × 200 m, 200-m jog; 2 × 400 m, 400-m jog	45 min easy	Tempo run: 2 miles warmup, 3 miles tempo, 2 miles cool-down	45 min easy	30 to 60 min easy	Long run: 75 min at slightly faster than easy pace
WEEK 7	Off	Track: 4 × 400 m, 400-m jog; 8 × 200 m, 200-m jog	45 min easy	60 min (15 × 1 min fartlek)	45 min easy	30 to 60 min easy	Long run: 80 min easy
WEEK 8	Off	Track: 4 × 400 m at goal race pace, with 400-m jog	30 min easy	30 min easy with 10 × 100-m strides	Off	15 to 20 min easy with easy strides	Race (5-K or 10-K)

HALF-MARATHON TRAINING SCHEDULE

	MON	TUES	WED	THURS	FRI	SAT	SUN
WEEK 1	Off	60 min (6 × 4 min fartlek)	45 min easy	Tempo run: 2 miles warmup, 3 miles tempo, 2 miles cool-down	45 min easy	30 to 60 min easy	Long run: 75 min (15 easy, 45 faster, 15 easy)
WEEK 2	Off	Track: 3 × 1000 m with 400-m jog	45 min easy	Tempo run: 1.5 miles warmup, 4 miles tempo, 1.5 miles cool-down	45 min easy	30 to 60 min easy	Long run: 90 min easy with surges
WEEK 3	Off	60 min (8 × 3 min fartlek)	45 min easy	Tempo run: 1 mile warmup, 5 miles tempo, 1 mile cool-down	45 min easy	30 to 60 min easy	Long run: 90 min easy
WEEK 4 (RECOV-ERY WEEK)	Off	60 min: 15 easy, 30 easy fartlek, 15 easy	45 min easy	Off	45 min easy	45 min easy	60 min easy (or interim 10-K race)

	MON	TUES	WED	THURS	FRI	SAT	SUN
WEEK 5	Off	Track: 6 × 800 m with 400-m jog	45 min easy	Tempo run: 1.5 miles warmup, 4 miles tempo, 1.5 miles cool-down	45 min easy	30 to 60 min easy	Long run: 90 min easy with 10 surges in middle
WEEK 6	Off	Track: 2 × 800 m, 2 × 400 m, 2 × 800 m, all with 400-m jog	45 min easy	Tempo run: 2 miles warmup, 3 miles tempo, 2 miles cool-down	45 min easy	30 to 60 min easy	Long run: 75 min, slightly faster than easy pace
WEEK 7	Off	Track: 8 × 400 m with 400-m jog	30 min easy	60 min (15 × 1 min fartlek)	30 min easy	30 min easy	Long run: 60 min easy
WEEK 8	Off	Track: 6 × 400 m at goal race pace, with 400-m jog	30 min easy	30 min easy with 10 × 100-m strides	Off	15 to 20 min easy with easy strides	Race (half-mara-thon)

TRAINING LOG

I once found myself engaged in office chitchat with a woman who was curious about my running. She was asking me to explain my – at that time – slavish devotion to my workout schedule and my obsession with racing.

After I spoke for a minute or so about what I perceived as the benefit of those things, she replied, 'Well, I run for the love of the sport.' Within that sideways retort was a smug commentary: hers, it was implied, was a purer version of running, having nothing to do with the unyielding world of times, miles and goals. Competition, it was implied, was a dirty word.

How odd, I thought. Because I, too, ran for the love of the sport. So I tried to explain. I tried to explain what I found so beautiful about a simple footrace, the oldest game in the world. I tried to explain that for me, the love of the sport at that point in time included the test to see how far I could push myself. That it was in fact the very thing I sought from the sport: to know that I had gone as far as I could possibly go. That I sought refuge in the one corner of my life that was cut-and-dried: a time on a watch, a number on a page. So simple, so unquestionable, compared with the editorial mumbo jumbo of the rest of my life.

Now that I'm no longer training at that level, I do miss the feeling of being at my absolute physical peak. I miss feeling that I could run through a mountain if I had to, because that's how tough I felt I was. (Wow, that *was* a long time ago!) I love my running today, but in a vastly different way, as a mother loves each child utterly for his or her own unique gifts. That's a beautiful aspect of this sport: it is what you make it. The recreational runner is no greater or less than the competitive woman and vice versa. And there should be no apology required for either pursuit.

CHAPTER 8

On Racing Well

SOME RUNNERS ARE GREAT RACERS. They perform consistently, delivering solid results even when the stakes are high and the pressure is on. Other runners – equally talented ones – never seem to perform up to their potential. All the promise of their workouts fades in disappointment when, time and again, they fail to run up to expectation during a race.

The difference between these two scenarios is sometimes the result of fairly obvious factors. Training too hard, though it's likely to result in some impressive workouts, can leave you depleted when race day dawns. A lack of tapering can likewise leave you with inadequate reserves.

But the difference between a great race and a below-par performance can also be the result of less tangible factors. The best training in the world will not produce results if you're not mentally ready for a race.

To truly succeed at racing, you'll require a formula of equal parts cockiness and calm. You must master the seemingly antithetical arts of concentration and relaxation. You'll learn to both pace and push. You'll also need pre-race planning, physical preparation, a positive attitude, self-control, wise choices and, yes, a bit of dumb luck.

While some great racers certainly seem to have been born with an uncanny confidence in the art, most runners can improve in all the required elements – except for luck. 'Racing is a learned skill,' says Lorraine Moller, a four-time Olympic marathon runner and winner of the bronze medal in the 1992 Olympic Games. 'It's like anything else in running: you can practise it.'

MENTAL READINESS

The only thing you can control in a race is your performance. It sounds obvious, but plenty of women toss that concept out the car window when they pull into the race car park.

'Some women will look around at the competition at the start of a race and predict where they will finish,' says Ant Smith, a personal trainer from London. 'They'll say to themselves, "So-and-so's here and she can beat me, and so can she, but I can beat her and her. Looks like I'll finish . . . third in my age group." And they do themselves a huge disservice by doing this.'

Instead of tallying up your limitations before the starting gun, adjust your mindset. Put yourself in the right frame of mind before your next race:

Worry only about yourself. Since you can't control who shows up or who will race well, stop wasting energy worrying about how other people will perform. A woman I know named Sarah recalls a race she entered with hopes of winning. During her warmup, she saw a tall, lean woman preparing for the race. The woman was dressed in the latest flashy running apparel. She looked fit. She looked fast. 'I was even intimidated because of her tan, figuring that she'd been working out a lot!' Sarah jokes. As it turned out, the 'threat' finished well back in the pack. But Sarah did finish second – to another woman wearing a plain old T-shirt.

The more relaxed and confident you are, the more likely you'll be to perform up to your potential, to learn from your mistakes and to have a more positive racing experience in general. Even if you're the type of person who comes down with insomnia, dry mouth, gastrointestinal distress and just plain jitters during everything from job interviews to speeches, you can still learn to race well. Just as your training determines your level of physical preparedness heading into a race, it also moulds your emotional state and your mental capabilities. During training, practise mental concentration. It will help you in a race.

Face your fears in practice. Moller looks for mental stumbling blocks in her runners and then specifically tailors workouts that play to those weaknesses. 'An athlete should practise the situations of which she might be fearful,' she says. 'For example, some runners go to pieces when somebody passes them. That's something you can easily stage in a workout situation with your running partners.' Other stumbling blocks might be fear of leading, or of not running in front of the pack, or of having a long distance to make up on a competitor. All of these situations can be recreated in workouts. One runner can start in front and then be passed, for example. Or runners can trade sharing the lead and following. Or they can stagger their starts to practise catching up with a runner who has a hefty lead.

Listen to your body objectively. The best racers learn to view 'negative' sensations – heavy breathing, a slight burn in the legs – as information from their bodies and brains rather than as signs of impending doom. Fatigue, for example, is a given in racing. Of course you're going to feel tired. But quite often, if you can hang on through a rough segment of a run or race, you'll eventually feel fresher – in fact, chances are that you'll go through several such ups and downs in the course of a race.

If you're busy destroying your momentum with negative thinking *(That's it; I blew it. My race is over. Here they come, passing me . . .)* you'll never feel that second wind. By becoming used to the sensation of fatigue and responding with assurance *(Okay, I knew this feeling would hit; just hang in there and it will pass. It's not so bad . . .)* you can train yourself to run through it.

To do this, choose some track sessions or tempo runs and execute them mindfully, with the specific goal of developing a confident outlook. Aim to complete the workout with self-assurance and self-control. Focus at the start as if it were a race. If nervousness or doubt about the upcoming effort creeps into your mind, replace such thoughts by reminding yourself that running your best is all you can do. Tell yourself that you're calm and confident. Remember that nerves are often a function of worrying about external factors over which you have no control.

Visualize yourself relaxed. Visualization is a powerful tool that can help change your behaviour. As you test yourself during hard workouts, picture yourself on the starting line with a positive attitude, knowing that you belong there with your worthy competitors. As the workout progresses and you grow tired, concentrate on gently pushing despite your fatigue. Become accustomed to the feeling of weary legs. Towards the end of a workout, visualize yourself coming on strong and successful, as if the workout were the finishing stretch of a race.

Pay attention to the emotional and physical responses that arise as you run the workout. Work with your training partners, trading off during hard efforts to practise running in the lead or from behind the pack. Practise responding calmly and positively in your training situation, and you'll be prepared to do the same in your race.

CHOOSING YOUR RACE

If you're running in the hope of achieving a personal best (PB), choose a race that will optimize your chances. Flat courses are generally faster than hilly ones. Running at low altitude is always faster than a race at high altitude. Other factors can come into play too. Find out about the average temperature and humidity level on race day, and choose a race that plays to your strengths in those areas. Some runners perform well in heat, for example, while others wilt. If you live at high altitude, you might do better running in the mountains than in the humidity customarily found at sea level.

Consider the size of the field as well. Most runners find it easier to run a

Race Travel

Racing away from home is fun and exciting. It's a great way to see new places, challenge yourself against different competitors and discover new courses. But when your race is in a different town, a whole host of complications can crop up to threaten your performance. While attempting to concentrate on your running, you are in new and unfamiliar territory that can present distractions ranging from the merely tempting to the thoroughly aggravating. The key is to keep your routine as similar as possible to the one you follow at home. Here are some specific tips to keep you on track.

➲ Save the sightseeing and socializing for after the race. More than one Sunday race has been ruined by a Saturday of exploring a new city on foot. Beware of large pre-race expos for the same reason. It's fine to look around for an hour or so, but spending the day walking around on cement floors can sap the energy from your legs.

➲ Review the race course before the event. By familiarizing yourself with the course, you can prepare for hills, get a rough idea of mile markers and make a mental note of markers near the finish so you can decide ahead of time where to make your final push. The best review is done by foot; running allows you to notice the subtlest changes in terrain. If you arrive too late for this, however, or if it's too long a race to jog, at least drive the course in a car.

➲ Drink, drink, drink. Air travel can be dehydrating, and any type of travel can throw you off your normal, healthy patterns, including that of drinking

fast time in a race of at least several hundred people, where they know they'll have cheering crowds and company and competition, than in a smaller race, where they might find themselves alone out on the course. On the other hand, there's a point of diminishing returns, when a race's size makes the course too crowded for unimpeded racing.

THE TAPER

A week or two before your race, start cutting back on your training. A 1-week taper is sufficient for shorter, less crucial races. For longer or more significant events, you might want to gradually back off hard training for up to 2 weeks. Some runners don't taper at all for small local races that they run

enough. Carry a water bottle, preferably filled with a diluted sports drink, and drink regularly while you travel and in the days prior to the race.

➤ Don't be tempted by exotic restaurants until after the race. Search out a pre-race meal like the ones you're used to eating at home – the simpler the better, to avoid any possibility of stomach upset. Play it safe with menu choices: pasta is always a good, conservative bet.

➤ Bring a selection of familiar pre-race foods for the day before and the morning of the race. Otherwise, you'll be sorry if bagels, bananas and energy bars are in short supply at the local shops.

➤ Enquire in advance about things you'll need on the day of the race so you won't have to rush that morning. Ask the hotel's receptionist where you can get a cup of coffee at 5:00 a.m. Find the shuttle-bus stop for transportation to the start of the race. Know where to go to pick up your race number.

➤ Get plenty of rest in the days before the race. Try to go to bed at the usual time. If you're in a different time zone and have trouble falling asleep early enough the night before the race, don't despair. Being well-rested in general is more important than the last night's sleep just before the race.

➤ Don't just ask for a wake-up call; set a backup alarm as well. You'll sleep better trusting that you'll be up in time for the race.

as workouts rather than as serious races. That's fine – just remember to adjust your expectations for the race accordingly.

Some runners have a tough time tapering. When they cut back on their training, they can't help but think that their fitness is slowly slipping away. It's not. In fact, during this rest, the body is getting stronger. It's repairing muscle damage, topping off the fuel stored on a cellular level and restocking energy. Tapering actually helps maximize fitness for race day.

This means, however, that cramming last-minute workouts into the week before the race won't help. Missing previous workouts due to injury or illness leaves runners especially susceptible to this temptation. Remember that there are no shortcuts to fitness, and you can't make up for lost time. Training hard too close to the race can only hurt by tiring the body without adequate recovery time.

If you're in doubt about your time frame, you may find yourself wondering, 'Can I squeeze in one more hard workout?' Bear in mind that most runners are best served by erring on the side of recovery before their race efforts. The running world is full of anecdotal accounts of runners crushed with disappointment having caught a bad cold a few weeks before their race, then running PB's and realizing that the enforced rest was probably the best thing that could have happened to them.

Although there are general rules for tapering training, every runner responds differently. You will have to experiment over the course of several races to find the formula that works best for you. Generally speaking, however, you'll want to follow this advice:

Cut back on your mileage. During the week leading up to a 5-K or 10-K race, you should cut your mileage in half. For a half-marathon, start halving your mileage about 10 days out. A marathon taper should last about 3 weeks, each week cutting the mileage by about a quarter. For example, if you were averaging 40 miles a week, 3 weeks before the race you would run 30 miles, 2 weeks before you would run 20 miles, and the week before you would run 10 miles.

But keep running. Several studies have shown that a complete lack of physical activity in the days preceding a race leaves runners not energized but sluggish on race day. Assuming that the race is on a weekend, do a short, modified fartlek or track session on Tuesday to keep your speed and sense of pacing honed. A set of 4 400-metre repeats at race pace or up to 10 200-metre repeats will do. Trade your Thursday tempo run for an easier run with several pickup strides thrown in. On Friday and Saturday, 20 to 30 minutes of easy running should suffice, with plenty of stretching and a few strides tossed in to keep you sharp. If you want to take a day off, research shows that 2 days before your race is actually a better time for it than the day before.

Resist temptation. Some runners feel edgy from the excess energy that comes with cutting back their routines, while others feel sluggish from the change in pattern. Avoid the temptation to modify your taper based on these feelings. Your body is storing energy for the race, and it's expected that you will feel different. A hard run might make you feel better temporarily, but you'll be burning off the very energy you're trying to store.

Women in particular also report feeling 'fat' during their tapers, and many panic that they'll gain weight before the race. Such feelings are typically more psychological than physical. (A minor weight gain can result from a return to proper hydration, which typically comes with a decrease in exercise.) Since your calorie expenditure has dropped, it's not a bad idea to cut back slightly on your food intake. But don't fast or miss meals or take any other drastic measures. It's crucial to eat enough to maintain your energy and health. You'll hurt your performance far more by sabotaging your energy than by gaining a little weight before the race.

COUNTDOWN TO THE START

A good warmup will prepare your body for an optimal performance. By the conclusion of the warmup, your mind and muscles should feel loose and relaxed. You should not feel overly tired. Over time, you'll probably develop a personal warmup strategy that will bring out your best.

Your warmup will depend on the length of the race, the weather and your own personal preferences. You can, however, use the following countdown as a general guide.

45 minutes to race time: Jog easily for 2 miles or about 15 minutes.

30 minutes to race time: Stretch all your muscle groups. See if any areas feel particularly tight, and do some self-massage if necessary. Find toilet facilities now if you need them; don't wait until the last minute, when queues can be very long.

15 minutes to race time: Change into your racing shoes.

10 minutes to race time: Jog a bit more, and do some strides of 100 metres or so at race pace or slightly faster. Stretch any areas that still feel tight.

5 minutes to race time: Head to the starting line and listen to any last-minute race instructions. Continue to move and stay loose, jogging very slowly or stretching lightly until the starter tells you to line up for the start.

For longer races – a half-marathon or more – the emphasis should be on

Your First Race

Your first race can be intimidating – all those fast runners, all those women with more experience. But don't be scared away: today's events are designed to welcome runners of all abilities. You'll find plenty of participants just like you, new to the sport or new to an organized event. Think positively and plan on having fun, and your race will be a good one. Here's a 5-step plan to the perfect race:

1 The night before: Prepare everything you'll need for the next day, including your running outfit, bad-weather gear, shoes, race number, sunglasses and water bottle. Now is not the time to test new attire. To ensure that they won't chafe or cause blisters, be sure to wear shoes, shorts and a bra that you've already run in a few times. Stuff some toilet paper into a pocket of your warmup clothing.

2 Race morning: Wake up at least 2 hours before the race; that will give your body plenty of time to shake off any sleepiness. Eat a simple, light meal straight away; that will allow enough time for the food to settle. Stick to foods you know your stomach is comfortable with: a banana and half a bagel are a favourite for many runners. Drink plenty of water or diluted sports drink now. If you wait until just before the race, you might need to visit the toilet at the last minute.

3 Travel to the race: Plan to arrive at the race 45 minutes to an hour before the start. That way you'll still have plenty of time to warm up if there are traffic delays or if you need to park far away from the start.

4 Warmup: Tailor your warmup to the race and your own particular comfort level.

5 The start: Line up at the start of the race in a position appropriate for your pace. Generally, the fastest runners will start in the first few rows, with the rows behind them getting successively slower. Joggers and walkers should line up at the back of the pack. Resist the temptation to line up too close to the front. Although you may lose a few seconds or minutes waiting for the pack ahead of you to cross the starting line, you will ensure that you'll start out at a conservative pace – and that you won't get trampled by faster runners behind you.

conserving energy. These distances require less of a warmup, since the pace will be slower at the start. You probably don't need to do any fast strides, since you won't be running that rapidly during the race. For the marathon, you can jog lightly and stretch for a few minutes before the race, and then essentially warm up during your first mile by easing into the pace. Not only will you have saved precious energy, but this abbreviated warmup can also work in your favour by discouraging you from going out too fast.

Shorter races, such as the 5-K, require a much more concentrated burst of energy. For these races, you must be primed and ready to go at the sound of the gun. Allow 30 to 50 minutes to warm up for this type of race. Be sure to stretch thoroughly, and do several strides at race pace or slightly faster. Leave enough time after these pickups so you're not winded from the start.

If the weather is exceptionally hot, consider cutting back on your warmup. This will help you conserve energy and avoid premature dehydration. In very hot, humid weather, you're far more likely to feel sluggish, so your primary concern should be staying cool until the race begins. In cold weather, on the other hand, be sure to allow for a full warmup, beginning with very easy jogging to ease your muscles into their working mode. Leave plenty of time to stretch, and to avoid tightening up again, keep moving until the race starts. Keep warm clothing layers on until the last possible minute.

Use your warmup to the best mental as well as physical advantage. Does the sight of other competitors before the race make you edgy? Then do your jogging and stretching on a quiet road away from the race site. Do you need to psych yourself up beforehand? Use the time to quietly compose yourself and review your race strategy. Does focusing on the event make you more nervous? Some runners actually do better by socializing and joking around with friends until the gun goes off, saving their mental energy for the race itself. There is no right or wrong; different styles work for different runners.

Although it's good to have a set warmup routine, try not to reach the point of superstition or phobia. Many runners have set patterns that they follow before a race for good luck. They might have raced well one day after warming up in a certain pair of shoes or after eating a particular brand of bagel or cereal, so now they feel that they must always prepare the same way. But what happens if your shoes get lost on the way to the race or if you don't arrive in time for your regular warmup? What if the shop has run out of Cornflakes? Does that mean your race is ruined? Beware of any rigidity in thinking. It can set you up for failure.

Mara Yamauchi prepared for the horrendously humid conditions she'd face in the marathon at the 2007 World Championships in Osaka, Japan, by training in similar conditions for 2 weeks before the race. Her race-day strategy benefited. 'I practised drinking a lot in training, and tried to estimate my sweat rate by weighing myself before and after sessions. This helped me to decide how much I needed to drink on race day,' she says. Her flexibility paid off: Yamauchi was the first British woman to finish and finished ninth overall.

If something doesn't go as planned before the race, don't worry. Great races have been run by competitors who have had all kinds of crazy mishaps and distractions beforehand or even during the race. Perhaps the most important element of your warmup is a continual reminder to yourself that nothing will

Smart Tips

Women's races have become increasingly popular over the last decade, as more women have discovered the joy of running. These female-friendly events make a point of welcoming runners of all abilities, and they often feature a charity element. Cancer Research's Race for Life series has grown hugely since it started in 1994. Millions of women have run a 5-K to raise more than £200 million in sponsorship for the charity. The nationwide series of runs now attracts more than 750,000 runners every year.

Some other popular women's events include:

▶ The Bupa Great Women's Run 10-K in Sunderland draws 3,000 women. Visit www.greatrun.org to find out more.

▶ The Adidas Women's Challenge is a series of three 5-K races in London, Liverpool and Birmingham on the same day. This event regularly attracts 20,000 women. Visit www.womenschallenge.co.uk to find out more.

▶ The Liverpool Women's 10-K – now in its 22nd year – is one of the oldest women-only events in the UK. It attracts more than 2,000 women each year who complete a lap of the city's Sefton Park. Find out more at www.runliverpool.org.uk

▶ The Glasgow Women's 10-K, which boasted almost 14,000 finishers in 2007, is the largest single-sex race in the UK. The course takes in Bellahouston, Maxwell and Pollock Parks – some of the most scenic parts of Glasgow. For more details visit www.runglasgow.org

get in the way of your having a good race: not heat, not wind, not bad petrol-station coffee, not even lost racing shoes. It's far better to believe that you're the kind of woman who runs well no matter what the circumstances than to believe that you run well only under certain conditions.

BE A TORTOISE

Hands down, the most common way for a runner to ruin a race is to start off too fast. When the gun goes off and other runners shoot out quickly, it takes great confidence to maintain your race plan and your pace. You need to exercise ferocious self-control, or you run the risk of derailing the rest of your race because of a rash decision made in the first few minutes of excitement.

Keep in mind that because you feel fresh and eager, your pace will feel deceptively slow. You may feel so good that you're sure you can go faster. Use caution: chances are that you're running faster than your body clock is telling you.

Remind yourself to run your own race. Some competitors get carried away by staying with (or passing!) faster runners because it suddenly seems like the 'right' pace to run. Most of these hares end up paying the price and slowing after a mile or two, when they find out that they've run beyond their ability. There's no way you can win by following somebody else's race strategy. It's far better to lose 10 to 15 seconds at the start of the race than it is to lose a minute or two – or 5 – at the end when you find yourself in severe oxygen debt.

The habit of starting out too fast can be hard to break. Here are a few tips to help you overcome the urge to run too fast at the start of your next race:

✻ **Put on mental blinders.** Focus only on yourself, and don't be distracted by what other runners are doing. Tell yourself that the only mistake you can make is going out too fast, and then force yourself to hold back, especially for the first 400 metres. After that, the initial adrenaline rush will be out of your system, and you can more accurately gauge how fast you're running and whether you should pick up the pace.

✻ **Line up with a similar runner.** Look for a friend or training partner who runs at your pace but knows how to pace herself. If she's a seasoned racer, that's even better.

✻ **Have a plan and check your times.** First of all, know what pace is reasonable for you to start at. Measure the first quarter- or half-mile marks on the course by bicycle or by car before the race. Calculate what time you should hit these marks based on your optimal race pace. Then check your times against this plan during the race. (Of course, if you have a GPS or a running chip that connects to your iPod, you can check your pace easily with these.) It's worth it to make the effort to check in on your pace this early. Most races will have the first mile marked, but at that point it's probably too late if you've gone out too fast.

MAINTAIN A STEADY PACE

Over the years, a number of studies have shown that the fastest races are generally those run at an even pace. This means that you stand the greatest

Smart Tips

Professional runners need to be experts at racing well. Their careers depend on their abilities to deliver consistent results. Here the elites share their secrets.

➔ 'When I enter a race, the only thing I can control is the shape I'm in, so I make sure I'm in the best shape possible to get the best from myself. Even when I know I'm going to win a race, I run as hard as I can to get the most out of the training I've done.'
– PAULA RADCLIFFE marathon world record holder

➔ 'Don't be afraid to rest. Many runners are obsessed with their weekly mileage and continue to train when they're too fatigued, ill or have a minor injury. A day off now is better than 10 weeks off in the future.'
– LIZ YELLING bronze medal winner in the marathon at the 2006 Melbourne Commonwealth Games

➔ 'I tell myself that I can't compare myself with others. The competition does help me to go beyond my own limits, but I remind myself that I am competing ultimately to go beyond my own self, not others. In racing, it's important to respect others and not to underestimate the competition – but you should respect yourself the same way!'
–NADIA PRASAD 1995 French national 10,000-metre champion

chance of running your best race when you can complete the second half of the race at the same (or faster) pace that you ran the first half. Runners who start off fast in the hopes of 'putting time in the bank' typically slow down, losing more time than they gained in the first place.

The goal, then, is to shoot for the pace that will allow you to run evenly throughout the race. Tempo runs and track workouts can help you predict this pace. But times – seemingly so objective – can be misleading guidelines, since hills, weather and running surfaces will all affect the speed of a particular race course. Ultimately, it can be more useful to rely on the way your body feels.

Your workouts are the best gauge for giving you a sense of pacing and an understanding of the effort that you can maintain over a given distance.

➡ 'When I'm tackling a hard training session, I visualize myself doing well in an upcoming race. Imagining winning a medal or beating a personal best keeps me going when the session becomes tough.'
– MARA YAMAUCHI first British woman at the 2007 London Marathon

➡ 'By knowing my strengths and weaknesses, I come up with tactics for a race. I allocate training time to address my weaker areas and make sure I ease down and taper fully to reap the rewards of my training.'
– JO PAVEY Olympic 5,000-metre finalist in 2004

➡ 'It's easy to get through a training session when I feel good, but it's on the rough days that I really challenge myself. I listen to my body and run accordingly – I finish a bad day stronger than when I started it.'
– DEENA KASTOR bronze medal winner in the marathon at the 2004 Athens Olympic Games

➡ 'Determination and hard work got me to where I wanted to be. I wasn't the best runner when I was growing up, but I did work the hardest.'
– LIZ McCOLGAN world 10,000-metre champion in 1991

Although you can certainly look at your watch for guidance during the race, always pay attention to your body signals first and foremost. If the ideal pace that you predicted feels far too hard early on, back off. If you're halfway through the race and you feel like it's your day for a breakthrough, don't let the time on your watch scare you into slowing down.

Although your *pace* should remain consistent over the course of a race, your *effort* will not. The same pace will feel like a walk in the park at the start of a race compared with how it will feel at the end. Remember this as the miles tick by. 'As you grow more tired, the same pace will feel harder and harder,' says Olympic miler Willie Rios, who specializes in coaching women distance runners. 'That means that if you feel too comfortable toward the end of a race, chances are that you've lost concentration and slowed down.'

TRAINING LOG

The races I'm most proud of are not necessarily my fastest or the ones I won. Triumph in racing can take many forms, as can disappointment. Indeed, it is a seventh-place finish in a small, local event that stands out as one of my favourite races. It was the first running of a mile race that attracted many national and world-class runners. Some were past their fastest times but others were coming into their prime.

My coach had encouraged me to enter the elite field instead of the all-comers' category. I had come off a yearlong break and had been training hard for all of 2 months in my new town with my new coach. Although I was excited to test myself, I expected the usual nervousness to afflict me at the start. Much to my surprise, it didn't.

While warming up, I saw all manner of tough competition, including a whole team of Japanese runners. When I started to feel intimidated, I shifted my focus to one of excitement: it was *energizing* to be a part of such a field. I thought back on the workouts I had done over the past 8 weeks in preparation for the event. I felt confident. Most important, when I stepped on the starting line, I felt that I belonged among these athletes.

When the race started, I stuck to my plan. I felt in my bones that I had perfectly targeted my pace, drilled into my very fibre from track workouts. For the entire race, I truly believed that I could win, no matter the calibre of the women I was running against. Noting the competition in this manner was different from anything else I

One way to ensure that you stay at your target pace is to choose regular intervals at which to check in with your body. Crank up your effort a notch if you've lost concentration and let your pace slip.

HOW TO STAY STRONG

Coaches and spectators often admonish runners to stay strong in a race. Easy for them to say. But just how do you do that? What goes on in the mind during a race is a highly individual thing. Every runner tends to develop her own secrets of success when the race grows difficult. Here are a few examples of how to practise race toughness.

Concentrate on what's in front of you. When you feel yourself struggling, it can be devastating to try to envision yourself maintaining your pace

had felt in a race before: it was less a matter of worrying about them than of feeling absolutely confident and certain that I was running my best race.

I didn't win, but I never gave up. After the turnaround at the halfway point came the tough part, as the course became slightly uphill. I ticked off the yards on the home stretch, making every step count as I never had before. Because I had followed my own game plan at the start, I was able to give everything I had and maintain my pace. Passing several runners in the last half mile, I finished in 5:17, good for seventh place and a personal best.

Now, that time won't go down in the annals of running history, but for me it felt glorious. The feeling of accomplishment I had after that race resonated far more than other efforts, even victorious ones. I felt as if I finally knew what it meant to execute every step of a race properly, to have truly done my best, not to wonder, *What if . . . ?* or to think, *I could have . . .* or *I should have. . . .*

I haven't been able to replicate that feeling in every race since then, and I eventually realized that it was foolish to believe that I could. Instead, I think of that race as my benchmark, my touchstone of what I am capable of. Why did it all come together then? It comes down to that ineffable mystery dance of mind and body. My brief training log entry from the day before that race does, however, present a strong clue: 'Feeling confident heading into race.'

for several more miles. Instead, concentrate on maintaining your pace just for the next mile. Towards the end of the race, you may need to think even shorter-term: make your goal to hold your pace to the next junction, or even to the next lamppost. When you reach your target, pick another one and repeat the process as needed.

This strategy works because, though you might not believe that you can hold on for the rest of the race, you do know that you can hold on until the next lamppost. String those segments together, and you'll have finished the race.

Count to 10. This is similar to breaking the course into short segments, as it helps you maintain your pace for a less intimidating chunk of time. Count your footsteps up to 10 over and over again in order to concentrate on the task at hand. Your goal should go no further than getting you to the next count of 10; by narrowing the task at hand it feels more manageable.

Check in with your body. Conduct an inventory of your body, monitoring how you feel from head to toe. Consciously relax your eyes, jaws, neck, shoulders, arms and feet. Correct your posture. Check your footfall. Instead of focusing on fatigue, make sure you're running as efficiently as possible. If you need to, when you reach your toes, go back and check yourself again.

Talk to yourself. If you always seem to manage to convince yourself that you *won't* be able to hold on, here's a radical idea: try to convince yourself that you *will*. Remind yourself of the hard training you've done. Tell yourself you love (fill in the blank): heat, hills, wind, whatever it is that's plaguing you. You can even tell yourself that you love the feeling of being tired because you thrive on a challenge and know you can rise above it. Do whatever it takes, even if it seems silly. Some runners tell themselves that they are warriors who feel no pain; others pretend that they are soaring birds. Some just tell themselves that they're the best damn runner out on the course that day.

For longer races, consider planning out this self-talk in stages. You might conduct an inner dialogue for the first part of the race that focuses on calm, conservation and staying cool. Then towards the end of the race, this self-talk might switch to a more aggressive stance, encouraging toughness, urgency and giving your all.

Become the meaning of tough. The bottom line is that to race well, you must be 'capable of enduring strain, hardship, or severe labour'. That, by the way, is a dictionary definition of the word *tough*. There is no fancy way around it. Some runners do best to dispense with the mental gymnastics and attack the beast head-on. When you're running at the limits of your potential, it will hurt. When you feel that discomfort, it's a reminder of the task that you have set for yourself. Don't give in, and you will reap the rewards of knowing that you've done your best.

WHY YOU CAN'T LOSE

What if, despite your best efforts, you didn't reach your goal? Maybe you didn't hit the PB you felt certain you'd reach, or perhaps you started off too fast and died, or maybe you didn't finish in the top three as you'd hoped. Not meeting a goal can be disappointing. Depending on the amount of training you've done, it can even feel devastating. But it's not a failure.

Races are simply a measurement of where you stand on a given day. They are best treated as information. Granted, you might like the information better when you run well, but you learn more when your run doesn't go exactly as planned. Did you fade on the hills? You might need to work on strength. Did you get so nervous beforehand that your legs felt like jelly? Some mental training is in order. Did you misgauge your speed? Track sessions can help develop your sense of pace.

Avoid the misguided temptation to increase your training blindly in response to a poor race. 'It's very typical for people to set standards too high, then to get disappointed after they race,' says longtime competitor Shelly Steely. 'They might not have rested enough, or their goal was unrealistic. So then they try to do more in training, when in reality what they need is to do even less, or to approach their training differently.'

The world's greatest female marathon runner would agree. In early 2007, after the birth of her daughter, Paula Radcliffe was keen to recommence her training regime but was frustrated by a stress fracture in her back. At the time she acknowledged her training had to change: 'I'm not taking silly risks or rushing anything. I can't jump straight back into 100-mile training weeks. I'm building up gradually.' Her sensible approach paid off and just 10 months after her daughter's birth, Radcliffe stormed to victory in the 2007 New York City Marathon.

Every race can teach you something if you're willing to pay attention. This attitude not only makes the last race feel a little better, but it also makes the next one a little less frightening. By keeping a positive outlook, you can walk away from every race having won something.

CHAPTER 9

Conquering the Marathon

THE STORY GOES THIS WAY: IN 490 B.C., a Greek soldier named Pheidippides ran 26 miles from Marathon to Athens to deliver word of a Greek victory over the invading Persians. After uttering the words, 'Rejoice, we conquer,' he collapsed and died.

There's some doubt as to the truth of this story, but from it a legend, and the marathon, were born. Since the modern Olympic Games were revived in 1896, the 26.2-mile odyssey has been considered the ultimate test of machismo, a rite of passage for relatively few diehards. Until recently, those diehards have virtually all been male. It wasn't until 1984 that the women's marathon became an official Olympic event.

But leave it to women to reinvent the event. By the 1990s, women succeeded in creating a wonderful oxymoron: the kinder, gentler marathon. No longer a testosterone-fest of thin, driven men, the marathon has been cheerfully overrun by women of all ages and abilities – and reshaped in their image. Groups of friends join together to train and then run one of the hundreds of marathons that are on offer both at home and abroad, with the result that races like the Dublin Marathon now attract around 40 per cent female entrants, and rising.

Who are these new women marathon runners swelling the ranks of the pack? Many are beginners who want to experience marathon magic; for many of them, a fast time is not important. Participants now combine running and walking in whatever combination it takes to get to the finish in one piece. Some women run to raise money for charity. Some decide to enter races with groups of friends for a social outing. Some women choose a race based on a travel destination and build a holiday around the event. Some just want to test themselves in 'the big one'. All have one thing in common: a focus on having an enjoyable marathon experience. In the process, these women have proved that a marathon can be completed in relative comfort.

This is not to say that all the women are at the back of the pack. Indeed, women have created a renaissance at the other end as well. The historic Boston Marathon in the US, with its mandatory qualifying standards, draws the very best marathon runners in the world. The growing number of women who qualify for the run serves as a barometer of women's serious participation in the sport. In 1993, 1,854 women entered the race, accounting for 21 per cent of all its runners. By 1998 – just 5 years later – the number of women entrants had almost doubled, with 3,549 females accounting for 31 per cent of the marathon's runners. By 2007, the number of women finishers had more than doubled, and the 7,975 women who crossed the finish line accounted for fully 39 per cent of the entrants.

That's phenomenal progress, considering that just a generation ago, the Amateur Athletic Union prohibited women from running the distance. The first woman to run the Boston Marathon, Roberta Gibb, did so unofficially in 1966, after officials refused to give her an entry form. She ran much of the way disguised in a hooded sweatshirt, finishing in a phenomenal 3 hours, 20 minutes.

The next year, women were still banned, but Kathrine Switzer made history as the first woman to run officially, registering only as K. V. Switzer. Things got physical when a race organizer attempted to remove Switzer's race number after 4 miles, but she still finished the race. The famous incident, captured in photographs and run on the front pages of newspapers around the world the next day, helped to open the door for female runners. 'Running gave me a sense of achievement and confidence,' Switzer says. 'I always felt like I was a hero in my own life. It makes sense that so many other women have discovered the endless fascination of pushing beyond their limits.'

In a way, the marathon has become two events. For those who simply want to finish, it has become the sporting world's biggest street party. For those who wish to race a certain time, it remains running's greatest challenge. Both approaches, however, require meticulous and disciplined preparation. Here you'll find training schedules and tips for finishing a marathon comfortably and for finishing one fast. The workout programmes were developed in conjunction with Maureen Roben, who has coached hundreds of women.

WHEN YOUR GOAL IS TO FINISH

'I'm going to do a marathon.' More recreational women runners are uttering those words every year, surprising family, friends, colleagues and even themselves. Heather, 27, is typical. After years of inactivity, she joined a running group, completing 1 mile in her first workout. Two months later, she'd worked up to 13 miles and was well on her way to her first marathon. 'I'd always toyed with the idea of running a marathon, but that was all,' Heather says. 'It sounded – and still does – like such an insurmountable challenge. I thought that people who ran marathons were athletes, nimble racehorses with a different genetic code.'

'I still don't consider myself an athlete per se. When I joined the running group, it rekindled thoughts that maybe I could do this. I was hooked by the progression. I like how supportive the group is and the challenge. Each week, in the deep recesses of my brain, I fear that this is the week I will figure out I'm not a marathon runner. It hasn't happened yet.'

For women like Heather, the marathon is not a cut-and-dried, 1-day effort of 26.2 miles. It's a challenge that illuminates the depths of your fortitude. As with so many things, what you get out of a marathon depends on what you put into it. In this case, the more careful and complete your preparation, the more enjoyable your experience will be. Here are some tips to keep in mind while you train.

Focus on your long runs. The most important part of any marathon training programme is the long run. The purpose of long runs is to develop endurance – particularly in the leg muscles and the connective tissue – and to develop the fitness of your cardiovascular system so that your body can withstand the rigours of the marathon distance.

It's imperative that you do the majority of these long runs; they're the bread and butter of your training programme. If you have to miss a day of running, then forego one of the shorter runs during the week or swap training days around so that you can do your long run on a different day.

You'll notice that the long runs in this programme increase steadily until you top 2 hours in length; then you have 'shorter' long runs interspersed. This is because runs of this duration can be very stressful on your joints, connective tissue, muscles and even your immune system. This programme increases your workload while giving you a break every now and then to avoid burnout and injury.

Keep these additional points in mind for successful long runs.

✳ Walk early and often in order to go the distance. Maureen Roben refers to the length of these workouts not by the amount of running but by 'total time on your feet'. It's assumed that you'll spend some time walking. Walk for 1 minute after every mile or after every 10 minutes of running.

✳ Find a safe, pleasant route. Look for a soft surface away from traffic. A dirt road or a grassy area in a large park is ideal. If you're not sure where to find such a location, ask at your local running shop or contact the local running club.

✳ Stash a sports drink. You'll be exerting yourself for several hours in these workouts, so be sure to stay hydrated. A sports drink, rather than plain water, can replenish much-needed carbohydrates and electrolytes along the way. Stash a bottle or two along your route before you run or wear a belt designed to hold your bottles.

Pay attention to time, not miles. As in the beginning and intermediate programmes, this training programme will have you running by length of time as opposed to distance. Running by the clock is simple and more convenient for most women because they don't necessarily have measured routes near by. It's also less intimidating for first-time marathon runners, who may find that a 20-mile training run sounds impossible. Obviously, different women will run these workouts at different paces, which means that some will cover more miles than others. Don't worry about your mileage in this programme.

Don't worry about going the distance ahead of time. There's a tendency in first-time marathon runners to feel that they must cover a full 26.2 miles on a training day before the race so that they know they can go the distance. Trust me, this can do more harm than good. The longest run in this programme is 3½ hours, enough for a woman running 10-minute miles to cover 21 miles. That's the most any runner need cover before tackling a marathon. But most important, even if you are going slower than 10 minutes per mile, *you needn't run any further*. Three-and-a-half hours should be considered the upper limit for any training run, no matter what mileage you cover. Anything longer and you risk becoming injured or ill before the race. Trust that if you've come through a several-hour-long training run, the cumulative effects of your training, the excitement of race day and the benefit of being rested will propel you the rest of the way when it counts. You don't want to use up the incredible amount of energy it does take to complete 26.2 miles before that.

Be flexible. Rigidity is a good way to get injured or sick. Adapt the schedule to your own needs and commitments. If the weather's bad or if you have to work late on a Wednesday, run on Thursday. If you need to swap days, space your runs so that you're not working out 3 or 4 days in a row, then missing 3. The schedule puts long runs on the weekends because that's when most people have the time. Note that days off surround the long run; try to maintain that pattern if you swap days around. If you must miss a day, try to miss one of the shorter runs during the week instead of the long run.

Build in some rest. Note that Weeks 8, 11 and 14 in the schedule are rest weeks. You won't stop running, but you will decrease your training time considerably by reducing your long runs. This gives your body a chance to recover from your training, and it builds in a 'safety valve' to avoid injury and exhaustion. Again, feel free to adapt this to your own schedule. If you

Now Is a Good Time to . . .

→ **Buy a second pair of training shoes.** Running additional miles means more stress on your shoes and your legs. Alternating runs between two pairs of shoes – preferably different models – can extend the life of each pair by allowing the spongy midsole to recover. It also lowers your injury risk from the repetitive motion of running all those miles in one type of shoe.

→ **Train yourself to eat and drink on the run.** Taking in calories and fluid while you run can extend your energy, but your system will need to adapt to having liquid sloshing in your stomach and sugar coursing through your blood. A good time to practise is on your long runs. Put a packet of energy gel in a pocket, or pin one to your shorts. You can carry water or a sports drink in a bottle or in a specially crafted hydration device. Or drive your long-run route before you run and stash bottles every 3 miles or so. Ideally, you want to take in 100 to 300 calories during every hour of your training runs and races.

→ **If you're racing for time, you'll want to practise grabbing a cup and drinking while you're running.** Don't laugh: it can be surprisingly tricky. Sometimes you're lucky to get a sip while the rest goes up your nose and down your chest. Set up a table and put out paper

know that you have an exceptionally hard week coming up at work or that you'll be away on holiday, that might be a good time for your rest week. Just swap the week you'll miss with the one before or after.

Find a partner or running group. Training for a marathon is one undertaking you don't want to attempt in isolation, particularly the long runs. You can still do plenty of training by yourself, but running partners and groups make long runs far more bearable. To find partners, think about joining your local running club.

Choose your race carefully. Completing a marathon can make an ordinary runner feel like a hero. Many courses are lined with bands and entertainment. Cities turn out to cheer participants for miles on end. Food, drink, music and a coveted finisher's medal await runners at the finish, along with a supreme feeling of accomplishment. But frankly, all races are not created

cups filled with sports drink. Practise running by and grabbing a cup. To avoid spilling, pinch the top of the cup closed as soon as you grab it, and then drink from the resulting V in the cup.

➔ **Get creative with training partners.** Even runners who like to go it alone find that they enjoy company on the long runs leading up to a marathon. Three hours or more is a long time to be on the road alone. If none of your friends is on the same training plan, schedule your run so that a friend can run part of it with you. Some runners even schedule several friends to take turns joining in on loops of the same run.

➔ **Test the shoes and clothes you'll be racing in.** Whatever you wear in the race should be tested during the long runs leading up to your race. A bra that seems comfortable on a short run might begin to chafe terribly after an hour, and you don't want to wait until race day to find out about it. Never use anything – clothes, food, and so on – on marathon day that you haven't tested during a longer run.

➔ **Eat right, take a good multivitamin and get plenty of sleep.** Marathon training asks a lot of your body. Several studies have shown that long runs can temporarily suppress immunity, making marathon runners more susceptible to colds and flu. Pamper yourself while you're training so you arrive at the big event in optimal health.

equal. When choosing a first-time marathon where the emphasis is on fun, research your choices. Sometimes the best race will not be the one on your doorstep. Consider the following:

✳ Size. In general, the larger the event the more race-related activities and entertainment it will include. Also, more runners mean more company out on the course. (Twenty-six miles can get awfully lonely when there are only 500 other runners spaced out over a long distance.)

✳ The course. City courses tend to have more crowd support. Don't underestimate the power of thousands of screaming fans when the going gets tough. Rural courses are much quieter but often very beautiful. Think about which of the two better fits your personality.

✳ Hills and altitude. Both can make the race much tougher to complete. These are often described on the race's entry form, or you can contact the race organizer to ask about the course.

✳ Average race temperature. The hotter and more humid the race conditions the harder the marathon will feel. Ideally, you want to run a marathon with low humidity and cool weather.

Check out *Runner's World* magazine or www.runnersworld.co.uk/events for information on races throughout the country.

Give yourself plenty of time to train. Depending on your starting point, 5 to 6 months is a reasonable amount of time to prepare for a marathon. The programme offered here assumes that you can run comfortably for 30 minutes 4 times a week. Work up to that point first, if necessary, and then choose a race no sooner than 5 months away.

By leaving a few extra weeks in the plan, you'll allow for setbacks. An old saying goes – the one guarantee in marathons is that nothing is guaranteed. That goes for the training as well as for the racing. But you can minimize the impact of setbacks by giving yourself plenty of time to reach marathon fitness. That way, a week off with a cold, an unexpected business trip or a family emergency won't completely throw your schedule.

If you do miss some workouts, don't try to 'cram' and run extra to make up the miles. If you miss a long run, do not jump up to the next level. Rather, pick up where you left off. If you miss time due to an illness, you may need to spend a week easing back into your schedule with some shorter runs. Then pick up where you left off. If you have planned some flextime into your training schedule, you'll still be on target. If you miss several weeks or a month of training, however, consider rescheduling your race.

Listen to your body, then be nice to it. Staying healthy is perhaps the toughest part of marathon training. You need to train enough to achieve proper conditioning. You should not train so much that the stress leads to exhaustion, injury or illness. It's a fine line. Beginning runners in particular risk overdoing it because they're not as familiar with signs of overtraining. Abnormal aches and pains, a sore throat, difficulty sleeping, a higher-than-usual resting heart rate: these are all warning flags. If in doubt, forego a day's run rather than grind through a workout that leaves you feeling sick, exhausted and demoralized.

Women are notorious for denying their own needs even when symptoms of stress are obvious. They focus on family, work and even friends before themselves. If you want to make it to the starting line, you must make a commitment to taking good care of yourself through the training process. That means eating well, getting enough rest and even taking time for a hot bath or massage when the going gets very tough. Not a bad lesson to learn.

WHEN YOUR GOAL IS TO RACE

Racing a marathon is unlike racing any other distance. Because of the length of the race, a slight miscalculation in pace can be magnified tenfold at the end. Ailments and discomforts can crop up after miles of smooth sailing. Everything from a slight breeze to a wrinkle in your socks can seem monstrous after the 20-mile mark. 'In the marathon, even when the race is going as planned, you will get to the point where you question your existence,' says Willie Rios, who has coached countless women to success in the marathon. 'What you do then is up to you – and the training you've done.'

When you decide to see how fast you can run a marathon, you enter a new realm. Put bluntly, you open yourself up to hitting the wall. Plenty of runners can tell stories of trotting along happily on pace only to tie up around 20 miles, losing 2, 3 or even 5 minutes per mile. That's why the greatest challenge of racing the marathon is pacing. It requires great patience to go more slowly than it feels comfortable at first. It then requires great fortitude to maintain that same pace at the end of the race. And, perhaps most of all, it requires tremendous self-knowledge to figure out what that target pace should be.

'The key to running the marathon is accurately determining the shape you are actually in and running it at an even pace,' says Jane Welzel, five-time Olympic Marathon Trials qualifier and a masters runner with more than 50 marathons under her belt. She explains that determining your target pace takes both practice and intuition. 'On race day, everything goes out the window. It could be hot, cold, or windy, or you might just not be 'on'. So everything at that point must be based on how you feel. And you learn to

Marathon Checklist

A lot can happen during a run of 26.2 miles. The more prepared you are, the fewer things you leave to chance. Use this checklist to make sure your marathon goes as smoothly as possible.

THE DAY BEFORE THE RACE:

➜ Pick up your race number and information. At big city marathons, these are usually available at the race expo, which is a pre-race event that features running-product retailers and organizations. Consult your entry form for information.

➜ Prepare a bag with clothes, shoes, your race number and anything else you'll want the morning of the race. This might include petroleum jelly for toes, underarms and around your bra line; energy bars and gel; a water bottle; sunscreen; a baseball cap and additional warm clothes.

➜ Pin your race number to the top you'll be wearing during the race. Prepare a bumbag with whatever you need to carry for the race, such as toilet paper and energy gel packets, or pin those items to your shorts.

➜ Gather some 'disposable' warm clothes to wear at the start. An old T-shirt and a pair of socks for your hands can keep you warm at the starting line and you can discard these before the race begins or after a few miles when you've warmed up. If it's raining, a large black bin liner with a hole cut in it for your head will keep you dry.

➜ Work out race-day logistics. Where are you going to park? Where will you meet friends after the race? How will you get back to the start? Remember that many roads are closed the morning of the race, so consult your race information and plan accordingly.

➜ Eat a dinner that's high in carbohydrates and not so high in fibre. Don't eat any foods you are not used to.

trust that by practising. In training, I pay attention to how my body feels, learning what it feels like, for example, for my body to know that I can do such-and-such a pace for this distance. It might not be as fast as I thought or wanted, but that's not the point.'

The workout schedule offered here assumes that you are an intermediate-level runner who has been training 3 to 5 times a week for at least a year and

➲ Drink plenty of liquids to ensure that you start off the morning hydrated.

➲ Try to relax. And by the way, a few sips of beer won't hurt you. It might even help you sleep.

THE MORNING OF THE RACE:

➲ Don't panic if you didn't sleep well. (Almost nobody does.) The night before the race matters much less than your sleep habits during the week leading up to the race.

➲ Wake up at least 2 hours before the race. Eat a light meal, such as a banana and a bagel. Don't eat anything unfamiliar. Avoid foods that are high in fibre, or you'll be making pit stops during the race.

➲ Drink some water or sports drink, but stop drinking half an hour before the race. That will give you time to go to the toilet before the start.

➲ Apply a thin layer of petroleum jelly anywhere you have chafing problems. Typical areas are the underarms, inner thighs, under the bra band and toes. Go easy on the toes; too much can make them slippery, which can contribute to blistering.

➲ Jog slowly for just a few minutes, then stretch gently to loosen yourself up before the race starts. Recreational runners needn't do long warmups; they can use the first mile to ease into their pace. Serious racers should still limit their warmup. A mile of jogging and a few strides and stretches are enough for most women. Any more than that is a waste of energy.

➲ Position yourself on the starting line according to your predicted pace. Large races will post signs as guides along the starting area, marked '7-minute mile', '8-minute mile' and so on.

who has some experience with interval and tempo workouts. If you are not, this programme will probably be too difficult. It is very challenging to run fast-paced workouts while you are increasing your distance. If you're not ready for this programme but still wish to challenge yourself, try using the training schedule from the first half of the chapter, each week replacing one of the easy runs with a tempo or interval workout from this schedule.

Concentrate on quality, not quantity. Many women think that if they're going to race a marathon, they must log 60, 70 or 80 miles a week. That thinking is not only untrue but also dangerous. Too many miles can make you ill or injured – or both. 'The whole goal in training – especially marathon training – is to get the most out of the least,' Roben says. 'People become so obsessed with mileage, when the trick really should be how *little* you can do – especially when you have a real life!'

Excellent preparation can be accomplished with 5 days of training a week; 6 is the maximum most women should do. A day or two of rest will allow your body to recover more fully and to come back with strength for the next series of workouts. 'I tell my compulsive types, who absolutely must do something every day, to go for a walk or a swim,' Roben says. 'But make sure that those alternative activities are something gentle. It defeats the purpose to go and cycle your brains out.'

Focus on your long runs. Literally, that is. If you want to race, unlike the runner who just wants to complete the distance, you should *not* treat long runs as 'time on your feet'. 'The long run is something you should really put mental energy into,' Welzel says. 'Even though they're not all at race pace, this is the place you really have a chance to get to know your body and how it will respond in a long race.'

The training programme offered here combines two approaches to long runs – slow and fast – for a number of beneficial results. You'll note that once the long run reaches 14 miles, the weekends alternate, one weekend with a run increasing by 2 miles, the next weekend with a run of 10 to 12 miles. Although the primary reason for this is to avoid overtraining and injury, it also allows you to benefit from two different workout focuses.

The long runs of 14 miles and more should be run at whatever pace is comfortable for completion. Run as slowly as you wish; these workouts will condition your body to handle long distances.

The 10- to 12-milers on the alternating weeks should be faster, about 30 to 50 seconds per mile slower than your goal marathon race pace. The purpose of these workouts is to get your body used to pushing for an extended period and to become comfortable at an effort near your race pace.

The longest run in this programme tops out at 20 to 22 miles. Although some competitive runners like to know beforehand that they can go the full marathon distance, it's best to save your legs for the rest of your training and the race.

Determine your race pace based on training. That might sound simple and obvious, but a common pitfall for marathon runners is to choose a target finish time before they start training and then stick to it no matter what. Such unrealistic thinking can lead to marathon disaster, when you go out at a pace far more challenging than you can handle.

A wiser approach is to begin training and see how your body responds. About midway through training (around the 8-week mark) you'll be ready

Smart Tips

Follow these tips to have fun and run a great race.

➡ Start conservatively. When you think you're at the right pace, slow it down one more notch. Between having rested for weeks and the excitement of the start, you'll be fuelled with so much energy that you're likely to almost fly through your first mile. The biggest mistake you can make in a marathon is to start off too fast. This event is an exercise in patience. Starting 10, 20 or even 30 seconds slower per mile than you'd planned is much better than slowing by several minutes a mile at the end.

➡ Drink small amounts often rather than guzzling at a few points during the race as this can be tough on your stomach. Plan to drink at least a sip or two at each available water stop. Feel free to stop and walk and gauge your thirst, drinking more if you need to.

➡ Work hard to maintain your form. Everyone's body has a natural tendency to tire in a certain manner; some women find that their shoulders hunch, others bend forward at the waist, others start taking tiny strides. This is more than uncomfortable; it's actually counterproductive. The more you allow yourself to deviate from proper form, the harder you're making your body work to move forward. Try using the mile markers as reminders to do a form check. Take this time to relax every part of your body and regain proper running form.

to test the waters. Roben recommends using one of your 10- or 12-mile runs as a time trial, or entering a local half-marathon. The pace you're able to run will be a good approximation of what you'll be able to handle for the marathon 2 months further down the road, when you're in peak shape, fully rested and focused on your big event.

Train at race pace. Many runners neglect this most basic aspect of training. 'I've seen so many women who do track workouts at 6-minute pace and long runs at 8-minute pace, and then they go to the race and say, "I'm going to run 6:30 pace" – and they have no idea what that feels like!' Welzel says. 'You should be able to nail that race pace, any day, any time, whether you're tired or fresh. You need to be comfortable at that pace. You're going to ask your body to do it for 26 miles.'

So incorporate race pace training into your workouts. Throw a mile or two of race pace into the middle or end of one of your long runs when you're on a measured course. Or begin one of your easy runs at the track, timing your first mile and hitting race pace. Go run the rest of the distance, then come back and time the last mile, again hitting race pace.

Roben makes each of her runners go to the track and time 2 miles a few weeks before the race. The runner looks at her watch every 400 metres and comes as close as possible to hitting even splits for race pace. You'll find this workout in Week 15 of the training schedule.

Do some training faster than race pace. Your track sessions, fartlek and tempo runs should be run faster than your marathon pace but no faster than 5-K pace. You don't need to develop sprint speed for the marathon, but you do want to develop enough speed that your marathon race pace feels easy. Follow the guidelines below. (For more information on track, fartlek and tempo runs, see chapters 6 and 7.)

✱ Track workouts. Warm up for 1 to 2 miles. Loosen up with 8 high-intensity 100-metre strides. Then complete 800-metre and 1000-metre repeats at your 5-K pace. Jog 3 to 4 minutes between each repeat. Finish with a cooldown of 1 to 2 miles.

✱ Fartlek. Fartlek incorporates faster and slower speeds into one run that's conducted without stopping. Warm up with 10 to 15 minutes of easy running. Then alternate 3- to 6-minute periods of faster running with slower jogging intervals of 2 to 3 minutes. Aim for a total of 18 to 24 minutes of up-tempo work, and run near or slightly slower than your 10-K race pace. For example, run 6 periods of 3 minutes or 4 periods of 6 minutes. Cool down with 10 to 15 minutes of easy running.

✳ Tempo runs. Warm up for a few miles, as indicated in the schedule. When starting out with the 2-mile tempo runs, aim for your 10-K pace. This pace will slow as the distance of the tempo run increases. Attempt to maintain even pacing throughout the run. Cool down as indicated in the schedule.

Be flexible and intelligent. Perhaps more than any other kind of training, marathon training pushes the fine line between working hard and overdoing it. Studies have shown that runners are more susceptible to colds and flu after long runs and while undertaking hard training. It's more important than ever to listen to your body when you're in the middle of your marathon training. Don't become a slave to your running schedule. If you feel rundown, take the day off. Likewise, if the weather is terrible and you have a hard workout planned, run easy that day and do the hard workout the next day. Be sensible. Nothing is sacred about doing a certain workout on a particular day of the week.

Smart Tips

After the marathon, be sure to follow these tips for a quick and full recovery.

➲ Drink plenty of fluids and eat immediately, being sure to include some protein and carbohydrates in the mix. The sooner you refuel, the better off your immune system and your muscles will be. If you don't feel hungry after the race because of the intensity of your effort, seek out a food that goes down easily, such as a fruit smoothie or milkshake. This is one time that you might want to ignore your body's signals and eat more than you feel like eating.

➲ Get to your warm clothes, or use the race blankets handed out by volunteers.

➲ To ease sore muscles, jump into a cold shower or swimming pool if you have access to one. Although a hot bath might sound good, a cold bath – even one with ice in it – will be better for your legs.

➲ Don't plan to do any running for a few weeks. You've earned a break; now let your body recover.

BEGINNER MARATHON TRAINING SCHEDULE

	MON	TUES	WED	THURS	FRI	SAT	SUN
WEEK 1	Off	30 min	30 min	Off	30 min	Off	40 min
WEEK 2	Off	30 min	35 min	Off	30 min	Off	50 min
WEEK 3	Off	30 min	35 min	Off	30 min	Off	1 hr
WEEK 4	Off	30 min	35 min	Off	30 min	Off	1 hr, 15 min
WEEK 5	Off	20 min	40 min	Off	30 min	Off	1 hr, 30 min
WEEK 6	Off	20 min	40 min	Off	30 min	Off	1 hr, 45 min
WEEK 7	Off	20 min	40 min	Off	30 min	Off	2 hrs
WEEK 8	Off	20 min	Off	Off	20 min	Off	1 hr
WEEK 9	Off	20 min	40 min	Off	30 min	Off	2 hrs, 15 min
WEEK 10	Off	20 min	45 min	Off	30 min	Off	2 hrs, 30 min

	MON	TUES	WED	THURS	FRI	SAT	SUN
WEEK 11	Off	20 min	45 min	Off	30 min	Off	1 hr
WEEK 12	Off	20 min	45 min	Off	30 min	Off	2 hrs, 45 min
WEEK 13	Off	20 min	45 min	Off	30 min	Off	3 hrs
WEEK 14	Off	30 min	45 min	Off	30 min	Off	1 hr
WEEK 15	Off	30 min	45 min	Off	30 min	Off	3 hrs, 15 min
WEEK 16	Off	30 min	45 min	Off	30 min	Off	3 hrs, 30 min
WEEK 17	Off	30 min	45 min	Off	30 min	Off	1 hr
WEEK 18	Off	20 min	30 min	Off	30 min	Off	45 min
WEEK 19	Off	20 min	20 min	Off	20 min	Off	Race

ADVANCED MARATHON TRAINING SCHEDULE

	MON	TUES	WED	THURS	FRI	SAT	SUN
WEEK 1	4 miles easy	1 hr with fartlek	Off	2 miles warmup, 2 miles tempo, 2 miles cool-down	3 miles easy	Off, or a few miles easy	8 miles
WEEK 2	4 miles easy	Track: 4 × 800 m	Off	2 miles warmup, 2 miles tempo, 2 miles cool-down	4 miles easy	Off, or a few miles easy	9 miles
WEEK 3	4 miles easy	1 hr with fartlek	Off	2 miles warmup, 2 miles tempo, 2 miles cool-down	4 miles easy	Off, or a few miles easy	10 miles
WEEK 4	4 miles easy	Track: 4 × 1000 m	Off	3 miles warmup, 3 miles tempo, 2 miles cool-down	4 miles easy	Off, or a few miles easy	12 miles
WEEK 5	4 miles easy	1 hr with fartlek	Off	3 miles warmup, 3 miles tempo, 2 miles cool-down	5 miles easy	Off, or a few miles easy	14 miles

	MON	TUES	WED	THURS	FRI	SAT	SUN
WEEK 6	4 miles easy	Track: 5 × 800 m	Off	3 miles warmup, 4 miles tempo, 3 miles cool-down	5 miles easy	Off, or a few miles easy	10 miles
WEEK 7	4 miles easy	1 hr with fartlek	Off	3 miles warmup, 4 miles tempo, 3 miles cool-down	5 miles easy	Off, or a few miles easy	16 miles
WEEK 8	4 miles easy	Track: 5 × 1000 m	Off	3 miles warmup, 4 miles tempo, 3 miles cool-down	5 miles easy	Off, or a few miles easy	10–12 miles
WEEK 9	4 miles easy	1 hr with fartlek	Off	3 miles warmup, 3 miles tempo, 3 miles cool-down	6 miles easy	Off, or a few miles easy	18 miles
WEEK 10	4 miles easy	Track: 6 × 800 m	Off	2 miles warmup, 5 miles tempo, 2 miles cool-down	6 miles easy	Off, or a few miles easy	10–12 miles
WEEK 11	4 miles easy	1 hr with fartlek	Off	3 miles warmup, 3 miles tempo, 3 miles cool-down	6 miles easy	Off, or a few miles easy	20 miles

ADVANCED MARATHON TRAINING SCHEDULE (CONT.)

	MON	TUES	WED	THURS	FRI	SAT	SUN
WEEK 12	4 miles easy	Track: 5 × 1000 m	Off	2 miles warmup, 5 miles tempo, 2 miles cool-down	6 miles easy	Off, or a few miles easy	10–12 miles
WEEK 13	4 miles easy	1 hr with fartlek	Off	3 miles warmup, 3 miles tempo, 3 miles cool-down	4 miles easy	Off, or a few miles easy	20–22 miles
WEEK 14	3 miles easy	Track: 8 × 400 m	Off	2 miles warmup, 2 miles tempo, 2 miles cool-down	4 miles easy	Off, or a few miles easy	10–12 miles easy
WEEK 15	3 miles easy	Track: 2 miles at race pace	Off	5 miles with 10 × 100-m strides	4 miles easy	Off, or a few miles easy	7 miles
WEEK 16	3 miles easy	Track: 4 × 400 m race pace, with 10 × 100-m strides	Off	4 miles with 10 × 100-m strides	Off, or a few miles easy	2 miles easy, with a few strides	Race

Note: If you are feeling especially tired in your training, you can turn a week into a 'rest' week. Choose a week with a long run of only 10 to 12 miles so you don't miss the longer workouts.
Then run only easy distances for the rest of the week's workouts.

TRAINING LOG

The marathon entered my running vocabulary only because a great number of my friends were planning to travel to the 100th running of the Boston Marathon in 1996. It was to be a huge event, the most significant anniversary of the grandest footrace in the world – in short, a party not to be missed. There was one problem. Unlike most other marathons, an entry form and a cheque aren't enough to get in. Boston has qualifying time standards based on age and sex; that meant I had to run 3:40 in another race first. Fair enough. I started training.

But something funny happened along the way. I found that I relished the weekend's long run. The harder the better. I felt great, held up well under the extra training, and grew stronger and faster. I had found my niche. A friend mentioned casually – jokingly – that a 2-hour, 50-minute marathon would get me into the Olympic Trials. And thus a dream I had laid aside ages ago quietly re-entered my heart. Don't get me wrong. I never believed that I could qualify for the team. But maybe, just maybe, I could qualify for the Trials race, also to be held in the spring of 1996.

My coach at the time warned against disappointment. Not enough time to shift gears in training, he said. I was running only 40 miles a week. Sure, I was doing great, but why not aim for 3 hours, a goal I knew I could reach? Yep, I nodded. Sensible. But when I lined up for the start of the qualifying marathon in the autumn of 1995, I knew that I was running with one purpose: to qualify for the Olympic Marathon Trials. I never wanted to be stuck wondering, *what if?*

For 20 miles, I ran on pace for my 2:50. Then, simply and inexorably, I ran out of gas. I finished in 2:55 – and burst into tears. Faster than I'd ever dreamed – far faster than the required 3:40 – yet not fast enough. My coach, waiting at the finish, could not understand my sobs. Joy or sorrow, he asked, trying to help his exhausted, weeping athlete.

Joy or sorrow? Both. As pure a contradiction and as complete a spectrum of emotion as I have ever felt in my life. Welcome to the marathon.

CHAPTER 10

Solo or Social

For some women, running provides precious, sacred time alone, when they can hear the sounds of their breath and feet, have the freedom to think about whatever pops into mind, and relish the birds, the wind and whatever else nature chooses to sprinkle across their paths.

For others, running becomes the heart and soul of their social lives, where great, looping conversation is punctuated with laughter, where motivation to run comes from the promise of coffee and croissants miles down the road.

Of course, you can always create your own mix, choosing runs and companions to suit your psyche on any given day. Some runs may be social and easy, where the company matters more than the workout. Others are hard training efforts, best done alone or with a familiar training partner. There is no better or worse; it's a matter of personal preference. In the end, the most important thing is to get what you need.

RUNNING ALONE

Running is essentially a solitary sport. No one else will get your legs moving for you. No amount of support from a friend can keep you going when you've just plain conked out. Ultimately, running comes down to you and you alone. Perhaps that's why the sport tends to attract its share of loners. Non-runners have been heard to ask, 'How can you stand being out there alone for so long?' Plenty of runners think that solitude is the very crux of the sport. That time alone is as much the point of running for them as a healthy heart and strong legs.

Not every woman wants to be alone with her thoughts for long periods of time. But for those who do, this time can provide a period of meditation, stress relief and mental cooling off. Because the relaxed state that prevails during a run is conducive to free-flowing thought and creativity, many women also consider it a time for problem solving. More than one work crisis has been solved during a lunch-hour run and its ensuing brainstorm.

Solo runs lend themselves well to all types of training. Because you set the pace, you can ensure that your recovery runs remain easy and that your harder efforts are tailored to your needs alone. When you run alone, you don't have to worry about being drawn into a run that's too long or too fast, or the opposite. And scheduling couldn't be easier: you can go when you have the time, and you aren't beholden to another runner's time demands.

For women, the main drawback of running alone is safety. Although safety during a run is largely a function of location, some women prefer never to be out alone. Others feel fine running alone at night in their neighbourhoods. You'll need to work out your own comfort level and act accordingly. (For information on running safety, see chapter 17.)

Other runners find that motivation is harder to come by when they go it alone. When it's just you heading to the door for a run, distractions and excuses can be more likely to trip you up on your way out. But for the most part, those who like to run solo tend to be highly motivated and won't let anything get in the way of their time alone.

TRAINING WITH PARTNERS

A training partner can help provide the impetus to run when nothing else does. Just knowing that somebody is waiting at the park, or that the group is about to leave, can motivate you on days of lacklustre energy. And there's no denying that chatting during runs makes the time go by more quickly. Some groups initially gather for the running benefits but eventually come to value the socializing every bit as much.

The key to running with others is to find the right 'others' to train with. Just because someone is your best friend doesn't mean that she's cut out to be your training partner. She might be too fast, too slow, too chatty, too quiet, too negative – too almost anything once it's just the two of you out on the road for 30 minutes or more at a stretch. If a non-running friend tends to carry over well into your new sport, it's a stroke of luck.

Smart Tip

To find a running club in your area, contact UK Athletics, www.ukathletics.net/clubs, which lists all the member clubs in the country. This is a good resource to consult if you're moving or if you want to find a group to run with while travelling.

Ideally, running partners should be at similar points in their training. If you're a beginner, running with someone who can understand your struggles and share your triumphs may be comforting. Finding somebody who is also training for her first race, for example, can enhance the experience greatly. A more experienced partner has benefits, too, as she can serve as a mentor. Just be sure she's willing to run your pace: while experience doesn't always equal speed, it certainly might. It is trickier for partners of mismatched abilities to work out together, but it's possible. (The faster runner can do an easy recovery workout, for example, when the other is scheduled for a harder effort.)

If you're training to race and increase your speed, you may appreciate a partner who can challenge you and provide expert feedback. It's also true that to a degree, running with faster runners can make a runner faster, forcing her to rise to the peak of her ability. I say 'to a degree', however, because if those other runners are in another league, the effect might be more discouraging than encouraging, and the physical result might be injury instead of improvement.

The best running partner is someone who shares or at least acknowledges your goals and enthusiasm. This goes for beginners and expert runners alike. 'The people you train with can have a huge impact on your performance,' says runner and personal trainer Ant Smith. 'If you're training with people who are holding you back, think about finding some new running partners.'

One of the pitfalls of running with others is that you're subjected to their mindset, for better or worse. And just as some people can be inspirational and positive, others can be downers. Negativity can take many forms, from subtle discouragement or lack of faith to downright disapproval. It can come from unlikely sources – a close friend who is threatened by her old friend's weight loss, or a husband who suddenly realizes that his wife can beat him soundly in a 5-K.

All such disapproval has the same debilitating effect: it undermines your confidence.

'Self-belief provides that extra bit of energy, grit and determination that you need to cross the finish line,' says Lisa Jackson, co-author of *Running Made Easy*. Having someone tell you that you can't, or that you shouldn't even be making the attempt, is a sure roadblock on the path to progress. If you find you're getting a chilly response from training partners, don't be afraid to find new ones. 'Surround yourself with people who have the same aspirations, or who at least allow you to have those aspirations. If you believe you can attain your goals, you're likely to be proved right,' she says.

RUNNING CLUBS

The best way for novice and intermediate runners to meet potential training partners is to join a local running club. These can range from structured institutions with membership fees to informal groups that meet regularly for workouts. Running clubs are a terrific way to meet other people with similar interests. Members typically represent a broad spectrum, from young to old, speedy to slow. You're almost guaranteed to find a partner at the level you need.

Ros Tabor of London club Dulwich Runners says: 'New members are accompanied by an experienced runner until they find a suitable group to train with. Whether a new member simply wants to run to keep fit or train for races, she'll always find a group to run with.'

You can tailor your involvement in such a group to suit your running needs. Clubs tend to hold organized runs once or twice during the week, but smaller groups often splinter off to meet at other times as well. Some hold track sessions and other harder workouts in addition to traditional easy distance runs. In all cases, you're free to run at your own pace and you can usually find somebody else of comparable ability to run with. Clubs can offer the benefit of training with a common goal in mind, too. Often, a running club will target a local race or a major event to travel to, and then build a workout programme for it and progress towards that goal over several months. The club may also offer coaching assistance, advice and even customized workout schedules.

COACHES

It used to be that only school-age athletes and elite runners used coaches. That's changed, partly because of the omnipresence of running, but also because of a cultural atmosphere that's conducive to professional instruction in general – think life coaches and financial planners. Today, runners of all levels choose to benefit from external instruction and guidance, and it's not unusual for a complete novice to find a coach. So whether you're beginning a running programme, hoping to increase your fitness to a new level or wish to maximize your potential, you can benefit from coaching.

Each coach will have a unique philosophy and training method. As with running shoes, there's no such thing as the best one – there's only what works for you. The key to a good runner–coach relationship is to find a fit, both physically and emotionally, that feels comfortable. Psychology and ideology can be just as important as workout preferences. If you don't respond well to old-school tactics, don't sign on with a coach who barks out orders. If you want to push your limits, don't hire a coach who's essentially conducting a social group. The best coaches don't use a 'one-workout-fits-all' approach; they tailor workouts and schedules to their individual runners.

The more serious you are about your running, the more important it is that you have utter faith in your coach. The wrong training programme can leave you plagued with self-doubt: *Have I run hard enough? Too hard? Long enough? Too long?* Your coach should be willing and able to answer questions about the rationale behind your workouts. He or she should

Running with Dogs

Dogs never whine or complain, miss a workout or make snide remarks about your pace. Dogs make great running companions, especially for women, since they add an element of safety. If you decide to run with your dog, first make sure that Rover is up to the task. 'The same things that hold true for people hold true for dogs,' says Dr Leslie Sinclair, a veterinarian and author of *Ask the Vet About Dogs*. 'Just as you wouldn't start right off on a hard workout programme, you can't do that to your dog.'

Dr Sinclair recommends the following steps for canine safety on the run:

➔ Have your dog examined by a veterinarian. In addition to performing a regular checkup, the doctor should look for any orthopaedic maladies, such as arthritis or hip dysplasia and for heart and breathing abnormalities.

➔ Start off slowly, allowing your dog to become conditioned much as you would need to if you were starting your running programme.

➔ If your dog is a puppy, avoid intense exercise. Some breeds can have problems with developing joints, so talk to your vet about the growth period of your dog's breed.

also be able to set out both long-term and short-term programmes for you.

Recognize that it is possible to outgrow a coach. While some runner–coach bonds last virtually a lifetime, others naturally reach a point of diminishing returns. This can be caused by many things, from changing levels of maturity to a changing body and evolving fitness needs. A good coach won't impede your growth but, hopefully, will offer constructive advice when you're contemplating changing course.

PERSONAL TRAINERS

A personal trainer is different from a running coach in that their expertise is broad as opposed to deep. While they might be certified athletic trainers, note that their knowledge about running per se might be limited. Personal trainers are best for women who are just beginning a running programme and for women who wish to incorporate running into an overall fitness programme. They can also provide guidance for overweight or older women or for those with other challenges who need close monitoring of their fitness programmes. Trainers can be useful in providing a workout

⊙ Pay attention to the characteristics of the breed. Some dogs, such as hunting dogs, were bred for endurance; others, such as pugs, are clearly not athletic.

⊙ Remember that your dog can't say, 'I'm tired,' and he will likely run to the point of exhaustion to keep up with you. 'Just because they will keep going doesn't mean they should keep going,' says Dr Sinclair. Monitor your partner closely, looking for excessive panting. If the dog has lost energy and lags behind, it's a sign to stop.

⊙ Offer your dog water often during the run. Some water bottles have a cup attached that works well for this purpose, or you can train your dog to drink from a squirt bottle.

⊙ Keep an eye on your dog's paws. Make sure that he or she doesn't have broken toenails or cuts before you start. On hot days, choose grass over pavement, or run in the morning or evening when it's cooler. In the winter, make sure that ice and snow don't build up between your dog's toes.

⊙ Brush up on obedience training. Since your dog will be running and there will be other dogs and people around, you won't have as much control as usual. Make sure your dog responds to voice commands.

schedule that combines running and other aerobic exercise with strength and flexibility work.

If you're an expert runner, you might also consult a trainer at certain points in your schedule. He or she can be particularly helpful with tips on strength and stability exercises, and with incorporating this and other cross-training into your schedule. Make sure you tell the trainer that you want a programme to complement your running, focusing on endurance rather than power. Be aware that because personal trainers are well versed in general fitness but not necessarily endurance sports, they can be less likely to recognize signs of injury or overtraining in serious runners.

If you're looking for a trainer, start with your local gym or health club. Most have a variety of trainers on staff, some of whom might specialize in a specific age group, sex, set of activities or even health concerns. You can also check out the National Register of Personal Trainers (www.nrpt.co.uk) for a referral. Interview a trainer much as you would a coach to find one with a training approach and philosophy you feel comfortable with. Some trainers will offer a free consultation before you sign on.

CAMPS

Like coaches, running camps are no longer only for the speedy. A wide variety of camps now exist, with most adult camps welcoming runners at every point on the spectrum of ability. Camps are a great way to learn more about running and to make new friends. They typically mix organized runs with instructional sessions on running form, nutrition, stretching and training, as well as recreation and relaxation. The inspiration gleaned from a few days of soaking in a healthy pastime with like-minded runners can last for months after you head home.

Camps are available around the country, so you can probably find one that's local, although you may need to travel further afield for a more comprehensive getaway. When choosing a camp, if it's important to you to find runners of similar ability, ask about the level of expertise of the other runners attending. Facilities tend to vary greatly – as do prices – so if you prefer hotel luxury to dormitory economy, pick a camp accordingly. Ask yourself whether you'd prefer a single-sex environment or one with men. If you go the mixed route, ask the coach about the atmosphere, which may range from laid back to hard core.

To locate a camp, check out the listing each month in *Runner's World* magazine, or log on to www.runnersworld.co.uk to explore the options both at home and abroad.

Smart Tips

More and more runners are turning to the internet to find both real-life coaches and virtual ones. The Register of Exercise Professionals (www.exerciseregister.org) lists British personal trainers. When signing up for online coaching, be wary of paying more than one month in advance – the site could vanish tomorrow – and make sure a coach asks about your health and running histories. Here are just a few of the coaching options currently available online:

➔ www.runnersworld.co.uk/smartcoach

Input a recent race time into this virtual coaching programme then specify details such as how often you want to train, your current mileage and the day you'd like to do your long run, and you'll receive a free 16-week training plan.

➔ www.fetcheveryone.co.uk

This free website provides peer-to-peer coaching in a community of runners of all abilities. Users can create and edit a training plan for you, which is then delivered to your training log every day.

➔ www.trainsmart.com

Trainsmart creates a tailored SmartZones programme for your goals, and a digital training diary so you can track and analyse your progress. This programme works best in conjunction with a heart rate monitor. There's also an option to receive feedback from an experienced coach.

➔ www.mcmillanrunning.com

This popular website from respected running coach Greg McMillan offers personalized weekly or monthly training programmes with unlimited email feedback. Worksheets are also available to enable you to monitor your progress.

RUNNING WITH MEN

Running is one of the few sports in which women and men compete on a truly level playing field. They work out in the same manner and usually run in the same races. So, unlike in other sports, male and female participants can easily find themselves out on the road together as training partners. Luckily for women, bad encounters when running with men are the exception rather than the norm.

There was a time – a few decades back – when the running world was a bastion of testosterone and women worried about being on the receiving end of snide remarks or other bad behaviour from men. But even in

TRAINING LOG

I grew up as one of the lads. At school, since there was no girls' cross-country team, I ran with the boys. In the 1970s, that had all the makings of a nasty, ostracizing experience, but I was lucky. My older brother, who was also on the team, and his friends essentially adopted me. They made sure that I was always okay. The result: I felt more at home among the relaxed competition and teasing banter of the boys than I ever did when the school finally got around to creating a girls' team. To me, the girls seemed gossipy, not serious about their running and uptight when it came to competition.

Yes, I was biased. It was a blatant case of reverse discrimination. And as soon as I went to university, my bad attitude cleared up and I developed close training partnerships with women whom I valued for their friendship, empathy and understanding. And today's young women grow up every bit the competitors that men are – training and racing are taken for granted for them, and many aren't even aware of the days when girls were new to this subculture.

To this day, though, I enjoy training with men now and then – perhaps as much for the memories as for anything else. And of course I've found along the way that not all men are such easygoing training partners as my brother's friends from school.

There are the men who insist on picking up the pace on easy runs in order to prove that a woman couldn't possibly keep up with them. (With these guys, you're faced with the choice between ruining your 'easy' run or allowing them their smug satisfaction when they prove their point.) There was the running club guy who spouted off about how impressive elite women runners are: they can actually run faster than he can!

the early days of running, most men were supportive of women's efforts.

Ros Tabor joined London club Dulwich Runners in the 1980s. ' From the first club run I was made to feel welcome,' she remembers. 'And I haven't looked back since – in fact I'm now the club chair.'

Today, most running groups feature a comfortable mix of both sexes – they're far closer to 50–50 than they were in the 1970s, and you'll find plenty of locations now where women outnumber men. And group runs tend to break down on the basis of pace, not chromosomes. 'Women today are far less hesitant to run with men,' Tabor says. 'They are not intimidated, and many of the younger ones would rather be in an environment

---

(*Heavens, what a measuring stick,* I thought.) There was the first date, when I mentioned that I'd be doing my 15-miler the next day and the date invited himself along, then got upset when I dropped him. I had told him exactly how fast I planned to run, after all, and he had said, 'Perfect'. At about 10 miles, as he was dying a slow death and I was faced with the prospect of slowing to a crawl, I instead continued on without him (and never saw him again).

But my favourite 'running with the guys' story comes from a trade-show business trip. A major running-shoe manufacturer planned a run early in the morning. All paces were invited, but when I arrived, the organizer said that it was pretty much novices only and that it would be more of a social outing. I told him that I needed to get in a harder workout that day, and he recommended that I trot over to a hotel round the corner, from which the hard-core runners would be departing. As I jogged up, a group of about seven men was just leaving, and I asked if I could join them. 'Sure, whatever,' one muttered.

We proceeded along and they talked their guy talk, basically ignoring me, which was just fine with me. I was just there for the workout anyway. After a few miles the pace quickened, then more so, and more so. Soon we were clipping along a hilly park at a rate that had dropped one man, then two. The chatter had stopped. At the turnaround it was clear that two more runners were about to fall off the back of the pack. 'Hey, she's going to beat you,' called out one of the guys in front. With a mile to go, with two men and me remaining in the lead pack, I was acknowledged for the first time: 'Hey, who are you, anyway?' one asked. *Sweet triumph,* I thought. I'd become one of the lads again.

with both sexes. Then the run becomes a social thing, even a way to meet the opposite sex.'

Still, when it comes to choosing training partners, some women – older women and beginners in particular – might prefer the comfortable company of other females. They feel less self-conscious conversing about their training or about body or scheduling issues with others who can relate to their particular challenges. If you feel this way, you shouldn't rule out running clubs or groups, though: you can still enjoy the social aspects and break into your own group of women for the run.

When the male training partner in question is a husband or boyfriend, the equation becomes loaded with more complex emotional issues. Of course, if both of you are runners, consider yourself lucky. Couples who share sports and fitness pursuits have a shared passion that can become a bond in the relationship, and they'll be healthier physically and emotionally for it. They also have fewer misunderstandings and problems of jealousy when it comes to spending time on their chosen activity.

Some partners, particularly if they are of similar abilities, can train together with no problem, enjoying their runs as quality time together. But running relationships are not always rosy. Some couples find running together to be a source of tension, especially when they are at mismatched levels of expertise. If the man in your life tends to be impatient or even derisive about your slower pace, you're probably better off training separately. Same goes if you're a speedier woman with a mate who tends to become threatened and angry when he's passed by his beloved.

If your paces are mismatched but you like the idea of sharing your workout time, there are solutions. Try leaving the house for your workout or driving to your running spot as a duo. You can warm up and stretch together, then head off for your runs separately. This works well if you're planning to run for a similar amount of time. If you actually enjoy running together but the difference in your paces makes it difficult, try planning workouts once a week that will work for both of you. For example, if he's faster, you can schedule your weekly high-intensity run for a day when he's doing an easy run.

It's not worth it to let 'running fights' permeate the relationship. Some couples just aren't cut out for training together. It's better to train alone or with others than to let the stress harm either your relationship or your running. Consider it your time apart, and enjoy comparing notes when you return from your separate workouts.

CHAPTER 11

The Balancing Act

WE HAVE A NAME FOR WOMEN WHO TRY TO PURSUE A CAREER, a family, exercise, spirituality and a social life. We call them superwomen. But by that measure, what woman isn't a superwoman? We live in a culture that encourages us to want it all – in fact, to insist upon having it all. Sky-high expectations and ever-greater demands on time mean that every day is a balancing act of priorities. For even the most easygoing women, it's a precarious proposition. On some days it's possible to juggle it all with aplomb, while at other times, tugging requirements cause life's fabric to fray at the edges.

Running presents both a solution to the problem and a contribution to it. Finding the time to run adds another line to the to-do list in an already overbooked day. Yet for so many women, running is their salvation, their key to health and sanity. Well-being and perspective justify taking time out to run.

WHY YOU SHOULD TAKE THE TIME

'Exercise is not a selfish thing,' says Susan Kalish, author of *Your Child's Fitness: Practical Advice for Parents*. 'You become a better person, and that ultimately helps your family, your work and everything else. Exercise keeps you young. It helps keep you who you want to be over the years.' Kalish, a mother of two, says that she's known for years that running makes her a healthier, more confident and optimistic person. 'I'd rather give my family an energetic mum who's going to be around a long time than not take the time to run,' she says.

That's an almost radical idea, especially for an older generation of women who are used to taking on the role of the caretaker, and who are used to denying themselves in general. But it's not just Kalish's opinion. Research has shown that a programme of regular running or walking reduces anxiety, stress and depression and increases feelings of well-being and self-esteem. Those things in turn translate into a healthy lifestyle that fosters more energy, better relationships and even a more optimistic outlook on life.

If you're a mum, taking the time to stay healthy also makes you a positive role model for your children. I feel good when my daughter sees the example of her mother taking the time to care for herself in a physical and emotional manner. This self-care also creates a foundation of self-respect that can permeate other relationships. And it inspires confidence in all of life's exploits. 'When you are a strong person, you will be treated as a strong person,' Kalish says. 'And when you go into an environment saying that the sky's the limit, then people will believe that you are capable of that, too.'

WHEN PARTNERS OBJECT

Some partners don't find all of the benefits of running particularly appealing. Reactions in partners can range from the rather silly (embarrassment because it turns out that you're faster than they are) to the frightening (they're threatened by your newfound confidence and discourage you from continuing).

If your partner is less than supportive of your running, try to determine the reason. If they don't run, they might be jealous of your time away, or of your improving fitness or even your independence. In this case, you could encourage your partner to take up the sport with you. The shared pursuit can draw you closer. If running holds no appeal, perhaps another sport might fit the bill for them. Otherwise, it is possible that as you grow more serious about your running, the gap between you and your partner in terms of fitness, lifestyle and time commitment will only grow wider.

Some women have husbands or boyfriends who are runners and still send subtle messages of discouragement or disdain about a woman's running. In this case, it's possible that the partner is uncomfortable with the idea that any woman can keep up with him – or beat him – on the road. If you happen to be with one such man, you can sidestep this affront to his masculinity by running separately. Meanwhile, be sure to inform him that the best women runners can beat virtually *any* man, so he's not in bad company.

Women whose partners never come to accept their running might have a problem that's much larger than disagreement over a workout. Although a partner might complain about the amount of time spent running, the real issue could be one of control. If a healthy pursuit such as running develops into a serious sore spot with a partner, it's probably appropriate to investigate the nature of the conflict with a professional therapist. More than one woman has started running and found that she finally has the strength to run right out of an abusive relationship.

MAKE THE COMMITMENT

Even if you're already convinced that your health – and your running – is a priority, scheduling your runs on a busy day can still be a struggle. You may often ask yourself, *how will I find the time?* The first step toward your answer is simple: change the question. Instead, ask, *how do I make the time?*

To commit successfully to any workout programme, you need to schedule exercise as a priority on a par with work, family and other commitments. If you leave 'finding' half an hour or an hour a day up to chance, odds are that you won't find that block of time. On the other hand, if you wouldn't skip a run any more than you'd skip a day at work, you'll almost always make the time for it.

Here's a look at some of the best tricks of the trade to help you overcome scheduling problems.

Do it first. Run before anything else in the day can interfere, before anyone else encroaches on your time, when interruptions and excuses are least likely. If you have trouble overcoming the temptation to sleep another hour, a good trick is to set your shoes and clothes by your bedside the night before so they serve as a reminder of your commitment come morning. Also leave your blinds or curtains open, so in the summer the sunlight will encourage you to get out of bed. All this makes stumbling out of bed and onto the pavement simpler than hunting around in the dark for the right clothes. If you're scheduled to the max already, you may feel it's impossible to lose another hour in the morning. Hopefully you'll notice your body getting used to the early exercise, and you might even come to enjoy waking up to a run. And, if it's possible, you might consider an earlier bedtime.

Do it immediately after work. A run can help shake out job stress and serve as a relaxing end to the day. But beware of motivation sappers: the sofa, the television, the glass of wine. Instead of stopping at home first, go straight from work to your running location. That way, you're not as likely to be sidetracked by other things. If you run from home, change into your running clothes and head directly out the door. Don't listen to phone messages or check email until you get back from your run.

Use creative scheduling at work. Arrive earlier in the day or work later at night in order to take a midday break. And here's an idea: if the atmosphere allows, consider inviting colleagues to a run instead of the typical meeting. Depending on the nature of your work, you might find this a good fit, as ideas flow and energy rises more than they would sitting around a conference table.

Make your runs more than just exercise. Instead of meeting friends for lunch or dinner, suggest a group run. If there's a non-runner in the group, suggest that she ride her bike.

CHILD-CARE ISSUES

If you have an infant or toddler, you might have plenty of time on your hands – time during which you are captive to the needs of your child and exercise is probably the last thing on your mind. It is possible to carve out running time even with a little one underfoot. Here are some options to help you combine your workout time with family time, which is especially helpful for multitaskers with busy schedules.

Running buggies. These days, it's easy to run with a baby (or even two) in a buggy. Purchase a buggy that's specifically designed for running so it can handle wear and tear from the road. These can be found in running shops, sports shops and running catalogues. Spend what you can comfortably afford – you'll notice the difference in quality in a more controlled ride. If you run on tracks or wide trails, larger wheels will translate into a smoother ride, and a hand brake and wrist strap will give you more control on hilly terrain.

Treadmills. Investing in a treadmill is an instant child-care solution that will last for years. You can run at home and maintain a close watch over your child. (A bonus: you'll be happy to have the machine on hand when the weather turns ugly.)

Pool running. You can take your child along while you run in the deep end of a public pool. Pool running is done with the help of a special flotation belt that's available at www.aqua-running.co.uk. A baby can sleep in a car seat while you keep an eye on him; an older child can play in the pool while you get a workout in.

Babysitting groups. Find or start a group of women runners who have young children. Each woman can take turns watching the little ones on one day while the others run. The number of days you run each week will of course depend on the size of the group. The trade off is a good economic solution for women who would never dream of paying a babysitter just to exercise.

Tracks and parks. When children are old enough to play on their own, you can take them with you to a track, park or other area of limited size. While they play, you can run around the perimeter, keeping an eye on them.

Family fitness. Have young ones ride a bike alongside you while you run.

ON THE ROAD

No matter how disciplined a runner you are, it's tough not to hit a roadblock that sabotages your training schedule when you travel. An out-of-whack body clock, a crammed itinerary, dining out and late-night entertainment all encroach on your best intentions.

If travel is rare in your life, don't worry about missing a few runs while you're on holiday or on a business trip. Sometimes a break from the routine can be welcome and refreshing. But if you're going to a location that's running friendly, by all means pack your shoes. Instead of looking at running as a chore while you're away, view it as another way to see the city or countryside you're visiting. It can be thrilling to wake up early in a new place and explore it on foot while others are still sleeping. You can get your bearings, make a mental note of places you want to check out later in the day and find hidden gems that you wouldn't discover in a rental car.

Business travel is a trickier matter. If you have a career that requires you to be on the road often, look for ways to keep running. I learned the hard way to *always* pack my running shoes no matter how tight the itinerary. After waking a few times at 4:00 a.m. and wishing I could go for a run, I learned that the sleep disruption that comes with constant travel can give me the time to take a quick run on some of those early mornings.

Many hotels now feature a gym or exercise room with a treadmill. While the view and the atmosphere might not be inspiring, at least you can get your blood flowing. Or ask at the front desk for recommendations of where to run; more and more hotels offer maps of local running routes.

JoAnn Scott managed to compete at a nationally ranked level as a masters runner while juggling a career as a flight attendant. She understands the travel challenge better than most. She says while the workouts often leave something to be desired, it's better to get some running in rather than skip it altogether. 'Sometimes you just have to train tired,' Scott says. 'You might not hit the times you want to, but you adjust your expectations and go out and do it.'

Her pointers on running while on the road include the following:

Be disciplined but rational. Don't lose sight of safety concerns. If you're in a strange city without obvious running routes, work out on the hotel's treadmill. If your hotel doesn't have its own treadmill, ask the staff at the front desk about exercise options. Chances are that they have a deal with a local gym.

Drink, drink, drink. Travel can be dehydrating. Limit your intake of coffee, tea and soft drinks, and drink plenty of water, juice and sports drinks.

Try to eat right. Buy fruit to keep in your hotel room. Bring energy bars along to fend off hunger in business settings. By eating healthy foods during the day, you'll be less likely to feel starved and splurge on fatty foods and dessert at night.

Respect jet lag, but don't let it get the better of you. If you're in Cape Town, but your legs still think they're in London, factor that into your workouts. Adjust your mileage and pace accordingly so you don't train too hard.

Get plenty of rest, and limit your late-night entertainment. Scott thought up this effective line to fend off colleagues who implored her to come with them for nights on the town: 'I'll have a glass of wine with you tonight if you get up and run with me in the morning!'

A CHANGING ROLE

To strike a balance, you need to find a place for running not only during your day or week but also within your life. The role of running in your life inevitably changes over time. Your fitness goals might fall by the wayside when life intervenes in the form of work, children, marriage or anything else that puts demands on your time and energy.

If you've become more serious about your running, and especially if you're competitive, it can be hard to accept these changes. 'You have to roll with the punches,' says Susan Kalish. 'You do what you can do, and you set priorities, but then you must be willing to give yourself a break.' For Kalish, it was children who rearranged her priorities. 'Work didn't do it; marriage didn't do it; but boy, kids did it!' she says. She had been competing seriously before the birth of her first child and thought she'd quickly pick up where she left off. 'If you'd asked me before, I'd never have said that I would let that affect my training. But then, 4 months after giving birth, I realized that my expectations had to change.'

It was years before Kalish was able to resolve the anger and frustration of not being able to resume her running career at the same high level. 'I finally realized that I was at a different segment of my life but that I could still have fun with running. My focus now is on building a fit family.

'You just never know which category you'll fall into, whether it will be a piece of cake to run with kids or a job, or whether it will be impossible. And it can change from one experience to the next for the same woman. If you live long enough, you eventually will find balance,' Kalish says.

Many women echo her frustration when they're forced to cut back on their training. They miss the feeling of being at peak fitness and the confidence that comes from pushing limits. They don't like the way their less-fit bodies feel – or look. At times like these, it's helpful to focus on positives. Running can still be a stress reliever, a social outlet, a healthy pastime and a way to get outdoors. For all these reasons, any running is still better than no running. Sometimes it can take months or years to adjust, but all those good aspects are still there when the competitive aspects of the sport are stripped away.

When things aren't going as planned, perspective can be a hard thing to come by. But running itself teaches the importance of patience, endurance and a long-term outlook. Heidi Wilson started to run six years ago to improve her fitness. She was recently selected to represent Great Britain in the IUA 50-K Trophy Final in Palermo, Italy in 2007. 'Running made me realize my mind is a powerful tool and can help me to push beyond accepted boundaries,' she says. 'Becoming injured is frustrating but I cross-train and know that I will return from injury stronger both mentally and physically.'

WHEN ENOUGH IS NOT ENOUGH

While most women struggle to make enough time for exercise, a smaller number find themselves consumed with their running, prioritizing it above all else. For these women, running can become a focus to the exclusion of other things, even family and work. 'I call it the magnificent obsession,' says Dr David Martin, leading exercise physiologist and co-author of *Better Training for Distance Runners*.

Sports psychologists point out that as a behaviour, running technically is not an addiction in the way substances such as alcohol or drugs can be. However, it can certainly reach the point of unhealthy compulsion. When a runner no longer feels a choice in the matter, but feels compelled to run despite the circumstances – sickness, injury or other pressing concerns – she might have crossed a healthy level of engagement.

You don't have to perform at an elite level to fall prey to this obsession. Runners at all levels of competition can lose perspective. Dr Martin says that although researchers are only beginning to understand who might be prone to such behaviour, many agree that the trigger is some sort of success.

TRAINING LOG

One of the toughest but most gratifying times of my life was when I was working as the editor of a national magazine and at the same time attempting to see how fast a runner I could become. I was training twice a day, and I let nothing interfere with my running. That meant sacrificing dinners, trips to the cinema, parties, dates and holidays. Everything. I had told myself that I would never miss a workout because of anything except illness and injury, and I never did. Once, when I was due to depart on a 7:00 a.m. flight for business, I dragged myself out to the track at 4:00 a.m. It was still pitch-dark and my body was still asleep, but I ran my workout.

Now, there are two points to be made here. The first is that – ah, the clarity of hindsight – I was out of balance. I never did qualify for the Olympic Trials that year as I had hoped. Instead I caught flu a week before the race. I was easily fit enough, but I was burned out. Exhausted. Okay, so that's how I learned the lesson that there's such a thing as too much discipline.

But do I have any regrets about what I gave up that year? Not one. My mistake was in the way I went about going for it – without information, without recognizing when enough was enough. My mistake was *not* in 'going for it'.

I kept my bargain with myself, and I know in my heart that I couldn't have given an ounce more than I did. In doing so, I learned that I was capable of far more than I ever thought possible. If I hadn't tried, I always would have wondered.

It was also the right time in my life. I had no children; I wasn't in a relationship. I had the freedom of selfishness.

Balance can mean different things at different times. Plenty of people observing that year of mine – not one trip to the cinema, not one! – would have said that I was out of balance. But I knew that I was grabbing that year for all it was worth. Opportunities like that don't present themselves often in life. Balance? I can now balance out that year of intensity with the years to come, in which my running is the recreation that punctuates the richness and fullness of the rest of my life.

That success is loosely defined – it can mean anything from winning a race to losing a significant amount of weight. 'When a woman runs a marathon and she didn't think that she could do it, or she wins an age-group award, that is powerful validation,' he says. 'This gratification is very appealing.' The seduction can take on many forms, as other people compliment you on your accomplishments, and as you feel better about your body, your performance and your capabilities.

'The obsession comes when normal behaviour goes awry,' Dr Martin explains. 'The more success you have, the more you try to do. That's followed with more success, so you try even more. You literally drive yourself to your limits – and unfortunately, you know your limits only when you have surpassed them.'

Some coaches believe that women are more prone to running obsession than men, but there is no evidence to support this idea. Dr Martin believes that the perception might result from women manifesting such behaviour differently from men. For example, women might feel pressure from a need to prove themselves, from years of being expected to 'do it all', or from women's traditional role of looking out for everyone except themselves. These factors can mean that women are less likely to question a coach about what's expected of them in a workout and are more likely to question themselves.

Some women report using running to fill a void or as a numbing device. By concentrating on running, they can ignore other problems in their lives. When they're feeling so tired from workouts, they don't have the energy to feel much else. If your running has reached this point, it's no longer a positive part of the equation. You need to step back and work out whether you're using running as an unhealthy form of medication. If you feel powerless to control your behaviour, seek counselling from a therapist or sports psychiatrist who specializes in such problems.

As ever, balance is the key. 'It's not bad to pursue excellence,' Dr Martin says. 'Some people say that you should never be obsessed, but that's how you get to be good. I'm sure Beethoven was obsessed. But it's a fine line between obsession and having no other meaning to your life.'

CHAPTER 12

Staying Motivated and Beyond: Mental Aspects of Running

THE LONGER YOU ENGAGE IN A RUNNING PROGRAMME, the easier it becomes to stick with it. In fact, after a few years of the sport, many runners report feeling 'not quite right' after a stretch of inactivity – a feeling that's as much mental as physical. When you reach that stage, motivation is hardly a problem. A run is often the highlight of your day.

But until that point arrives, most runners will wake up to days when staying in bed seems more inviting than the dark, heat, cold, wind or whatever else awaits them outdoors. On these days, working out how to stay motivated is crucial.

Motivation can droop for any number of reasons: boredom, lack of results, stress and a shortage of time are primary among them. Some people are natural experts at finding motivation even in the face of such adversity. But if you're more inclined to fold than to fight, you can still develop motivation, just as you'd develop your muscles.

When you find yourself dreading a run instead of looking forward to it, you should first determine whether your feelings are truly due to laziness or boredom or whether they are instead a sign of exhaustion or an oncoming bout of illness. If the latter, you'd be sensible to listen to your body and modify or skip the workout.

But if you're otherwise healthy, beware the classic signs of lack of motivation: finding excuses not to run, stalling with other projects, or experiencing feelings of boredom or listlessness. When you find yourself in that lazy frame of mind, try some of the tips outlined in the rest of this chapter. And even if you succumb to the sofa one day, don't put yourself down. Instead, just make sure not to let one poor day stretch into a pattern of inactivity. Every day is a fresh start; don't measure yourself by yesterday's troubles. Finally, remember that just about whatever you're suffering from, you'll feel much better after you go for a run.

When boredom strikes, fight back. If you're fighting boredom, it's probably a sign that you could do with some variety and new challenges in your running. Do you always run in the same place? At the same speed? For the same distance? No wonder your motivation is flagging.

Many runners become creatures of habit; they do the same 3 or 4 loops over and over again. When you find that you've dug yourself a rut, shake yourself out of it. There are no rules in running, so go have some fun: leave your watch at home and run just by feel. Drive to a new park for a change of scenery. Plan a run with friends to a café in the next town (drop a car there before you start). When you have time, set out on an adventure, taking every turn your heart desires. Chances are you'll discover a renewed sense of wonder along with a new running route.

Take the first few steps. You can often overcome lack of motivation by focusing only on getting started rather than working up the gumption to take on an entire workout. It's been said that the first step out of the door is the hardest, and any runner will attest to that truth. When laziness strikes, make a deal with yourself that you'll at least give the run a try. Change clothes, head out of the door and start moving. In most cases, the fresh air and circulation will have an energizing effect, stimulating you enough to get through the run. If, after 10 minutes or so, you're still truly trudging, try walking or just call it a day. Maybe you're overtired and your body is trying to tell you that you need rest more than exercise.

It might help to remember that even the best runners in the world have days when their minds and bodies would rather head out for ice cream than for a workout. Jackie Joyner-Kersee, one of the greatest female athletes of all time, admits that she played the just-get-out-the-door game, too, when she was competing. 'I'd tell myself just to start,' she once said. 'Then, even if I couldn't get through it all, at least I'd done something.'

Make running a priority. People don't marvel when you show up for work every day; it's expected. Try giving your run the same type of priority in your schedule. If this seems daunting, try it out for just 2 weeks – enough time to set a new pattern. Think of it as an investment in yourself.

Be social. Set a date to run with a partner. It's harder to miss a run when you know that a friend is relying on you.

Do dwell on the past. Think back to previous runs and how good you felt during and afterward. Chances are that if you're feeling unmotivated, your energy could use a jump-start, and running will be just the thing.

Get your kit ready in advance. Place your running shoes and clothes by your bedside if you run in the morning. If you run after work, set them out next to your desk. Having your running attire in plain view will help motivate you to run.

Set a goal. Without a goal to strive for, working out can seem aimless and pointless. Some runners find it hard to train at all if they don't have a race, social event or other goal to focus on. Anyone can have a goal; it needn't be a fast time in a race. Beginners can aim for running 30 minutes without stopping or just for exercising 5 days a week for a month.

MAINTAIN A POSITIVE ATTITUDE

A big part of motivation is not letting the doldrums creep into our mindset. All runners have days when their legs feel as if they just won't move. They feel sluggish and 'flat', and no matter how hard they try, they can't find a comfortable groove. Some women react with tension when their bodies don't do what's expected. As expectations become loaded and muscles grow tight, running becomes even harder. Motivation can suffer as a result. The cycle, which can go on for days or weeks, can lead to frustration, anger and even depression. Professional runners know that there will always be *those days*. No matter what your running level, you'd do well to keep their wisdom in mind.

Willie Rios, who specializes in coaching women distance runners, drills the importance of staying positive into each of his runners' heads. Rios likes to recount one story of a runner who was having a frustrating workout. 'She was getting angry because her times were so much slower than they had been,' he says. 'By changing the focus of the workout – in this case, to thinking about the triumph of just completing it on a day where it would have been easy to walk away – she had an opportunity to learn something about herself and to experience a success rather than a defeat.'

Within every run, there are successes and defeats. As an advanced runner, you learn that you can make a conscious decision to focus on either the negative or the positive. Sure, you can always find defeats: not going as fast as you had hoped, not feeling light on your feet, not having time to run as far as you expected. But you can always find successes just as easily. Some days, it's going further or pushing harder than ever before. Some days, the success is just getting out the door. Some days – on the really rough days – a success can be as simple as staying in good spirits and reminding yourself that tomorrow is a fresh opportunity to feel better. It's a lesson that, once learned on the run, proves invaluable when applied to other aspects of life.

Rios has been known to admonish women who downplay their accomplishments or find fault after every workout. 'When you beat yourself up like that, you invite every abusive person from your past back into your life. You reinforce any negative message ever heard from a boss, boyfriend or husband,' he says. 'You don't want other people to treat you like that. Why would you do it to yourself?'

A positive attitude can be cultivated. Try some of these ideas:

After every run, find at least one success. Perhaps you allowed yourself to relax and enjoy the clouds. Or maybe you felt tired but didn't let that stop you. The more ways you can find success, the happier you will be with your running.

Write or recite positive affirmations. Negativity often stems from a difference between your perception of where you are and your perception of where you want to be. Instead of dwelling on negative self-talk, replace it with positive affirmation. For example, when you find yourself thinking, *I can't believe I ran that slowly,* try telling yourself instead, *I am lucky to be blessed with strong, healthy legs.*

Build a positive support team. It's important to surround yourself with people who want you to succeed. (That goes for running, but it's sage advice for every aspect of your life.) Professional runners, such as Paula Radcliffe, are experts at creating support systems that encourage their best performance. Detach yourself from running partners, 'friends' and coaches who downplay your achievements, question your goals, deride your weight or make you feel generally miserable about yourself. Find others who boost your confidence and encourage your efforts.

Keep running in perspective. Just as women go through different phases in work and home life, they can expect to go through different phases in their running. Recognizing this can go a long way towards alleviating frustration and allowing only positive forces to flow from the sport.

If you've become used to the daily affirmation of an energizing run, an interruption in the routine can prove devastating. A new job, a return to education, a baby – any number of changes can shift priorities and make running seem more of a chore than a rejuvenation. An ensuing cycle of failed expectations can foster self-doubt and negativity.

Susan Kalish, author of *Your Child's Fitness: Practical Advice for Parents*, went through such a period after the birth of her first child. 'I felt gross and fat and embarrassed,' she remembers. 'I didn't return to fitness anywhere near as fast as I thought I would, and I felt like my running, which had been my good friend, was humiliating me.'

After the birth of her second child, Kalish decided to take a different approach, removing any expectation of a timeline in which to return to her former level of running. The approach worked, and she once again reaped the positive benefits she had remembered. 'I had thought running was letting me down, but it was just changing,' she says.

It is particularly important for women, who are busy with so many responsibilities to others, to keep running in perspective. Remember that running should not become just another source of pressure or expectation. Think of your run as your own personal time to meditate, relax, enjoy and think. You'll be guaranteed to find motivation for this time of the day.

THE MANY BENEFITS OF MENTAL FITNESS

Staying motivated is an aspect of running that you must work at and develop. But there's a flip side to exercising your mental muscle: the mental strength that the sport demands and encourages leads to benefits that extend far beyond the physical. In a way, running gives back as much as – or even more than – it takes. As you work to develop your motivation and as you progress with your running, don't be surprised if you find a positive impact on other areas of your life.

Take this example: sitting down to breakfast the day before a race, a number of female runners were discussing why they ran. *Time to myself,* some said. *Empowerment. Sanity.* When it was one woman's turn to speak, she listed a few reasons. *Stress relief. Fitness,* of course. And then came this: recently, one woman's husband had hit her for the first time. Running was something she could do for herself in order to feel strong and in control.

The women at the table nodded their heads in understanding. Not one of them seemed particularly shocked by this stranger's soul-baring statement. In some way, they'd been there themselves. They hadn't necessarily been victims of physical abuse. But they had needed a sense of strength and control in their lives. Maybe the feeling came when they started a new job. Or when one of their children was troubled. Or when they were suffering from pointed loneliness. Somehow, running had given them strength.

It's something that women runners themselves marvel at. Get them in a group and invariably the subject will meander over to something far deeper than split times and waist sizes. For most women runners, the sport is more than a great aerobic workout; in some way, it fills a corner of their souls. Women speak of running as meditation, therapy, quiet time, an outlet for emotion, a catalyst for growth, a microcosm of their bigger picture. Running takes on these roles and more, often with powerful effects on your whole life.

Anne Audain, six-time Olympic Games qualifier and former 5,000-metre World Record Holder, says that she boils the essence and benefits of running down to one word: *movement*. It's a word that comes up time and again when speaking to women about the impact of their running.

'By movement, I mean cleansing,' Audain says. 'By moving the body itself, you are moving not just air, food and blood but even thought through the body. If you let things sit still, you'll get cobwebs. Movement gives you so much more energy.'

And that means energy for all aspects of your life: physical, mental and emotional. Runners quickly realize that the three are connected. Many women who enter the sport for the health or weight management benefits find themselves continuing for the mental and emotional energy. In a survey of women runners of all ages and abilities, more than half said that stress relief and time by themselves were the main reasons they ran.

Marathon runner Dr Jerry Lynch, sports psychologist and author of bestselling books *Working Out* and *Working Within*, puts it this way: 'A woman who embraces a running programme and the movement that comes with it now has a metaphor for movement in the rest of her life.' Dr Lynch believes that many women who find themselves at a crossroads in life are ripe to discover the integration of body, mind and spirit that running offers. Although these women focus on their bodies as the starting point for change when they begin running, the benefits can't help but move into other parts of their lives as well. Mary, 52, is a great example. After only 3 months in the sport, she decided to run a marathon. 'I'm at a crossroads in my life,' she explained. 'I needed a change; I'm going back to college, and it's all connected for me. If I can take this step with the running, then I can take the others as well.' Now that's motivation.

The Road to Self-Discovery

Many women find that running changes their lives for the better in some way, large or small. These women felt so strongly about the benefits that they made running their life's work.

➡️ 'I discovered running quite late in life in my 50s. I'm so disappointed that it took me so long because it has genuinely changed my life. When I first started running I could hardly manage a mile and I was the slowest person in the group. I'm still not quick but I've progressed from running a few miles to running marathons and beyond. When my husband died in 2002 from prostate cancer I realized how precious life is and how short it is, so I decided to run around the world. I set off from my home in Tenby, south Wales on my 57th birthday in October 2003 with no support crew, very little money but with a deep desire to complete a circle of the earth on foot. It's been the most amazing experience through Northern Europe, Russia and North America and I've met so many wonderful people along the way and it wouldn't have been possible without my discovery of running.'

– ROSIE SWALE-POPE, running author and journalist

➡️ When I started running, I was married and a mother of four. And that's how I saw myself: as a mother and a wife – certainly all those things before an individual. But when I started running, I was surprised to see that the people I ran with didn't care about those other things. They related to me as Diane. It gave me a strong feeling of who I was, separate from all the roles I had. Ultimately, it gave me courage to make changes in the rest of my life, including seeking more supportive relationships.

– DIANE PALMASON, champion 60+ age-group competitor and co-founder of Women's Running Camps

➡️ 'I took up running in 2002 when I gave up smoking, although I was already quite fit because I'd worked in the fitness industry since 1998 as a personal trainer. I loved it from the start, quickly joined a club and started taking part in races, running everything from 10-Ks up to ultra-marathons. My husband and I are both passionate about running so the Running Inn seemed a natural extension of that passion. We now host a range of running and fitness courses for all levels of guests at our Eastbourne hotel.'

– FIONA BUGLER, personal trainer and proprietor of the Running Inn

HOW RUNNING HELPS WOMEN

Almost any physical activity will improve your mental state. A body of research has shown that exercise, particularly endurance-oriented activity, can elevate moods and alleviate stress in both men and women. But speak to women runners, and you'll find more going on than a simple endorphin buzz. The benefits seem to go beyond science and benefits at the cellular level.

See if any of these comments from women runners rings a bell with you:

✽ 'Running has a very calming effect on me; it's a time when I meditate and work out unsolved problems and generate my most creative thinking.'

✽ 'I feel so great about myself and my life after a run.'

✽ 'It's very empowering to feel strong and to have the mental endurance to be by myself for hours at a time.'

✽ 'Running makes me happy and optimistic; it helps me solve problems and get a better perspective.'

✽ 'Running gives me confidence and inner peace. I am stronger and more in tune with where I'm going in life.'

✽ 'It gives me a boost in my self-esteem – it makes me think I can do other things.'

✽ 'I now have a confidence and a sense of competence that has filled all of my life.'

How is it that an act as simple as putting one foot in front of the other can reap such complex rewards? The key might be running's simplicity. The sport lends itself to a meditative quality that's not possible in many other activities. Self-propelled and in touch with the ground, not reliant on or distracted by equipment, the runner finds that her mind is free to wander or focus as she chooses.

'It is something that is unique to running. You see it somewhat in other individual sports, but particularly in running because it is so measurable,' says Diane Palmason, who holds age-group records in distances ranging from 200 metres to 50 miles for women over the age of 60. 'When you accomplish something in running, it is so obvious that it is you and you alone who accomplished it. In other areas of our life, there is rarely an obvious measure. In running, when you achieve a quantifiable goal, you have every right to feel good about yourself.'

When women do achieve goals in running – whether losing 10 kg or breaking 20 minutes for a 5-K – they grow far beyond those results, and sometimes beyond what men would experience in similar situations.

Although men have grown up developing positive self-images through sports, most middle-aged and older women have yet to experience similar affirmation. Women who come to sport later in life find their own playing ground on which to develop confidence and control. With girls today taking part in sports as a matter of fact, future generations of women probably won't have to wait until middle age to make such gains.

Running can have such a positive effect in a woman's life that clinical

TRAINING LOG

I ran in the rain today, a loamy smell escaping the warm spring earth. I ran at first a grown woman, slowly, slowly growing new once more.

I ran through mud puddles on the trail, the cold, thin brew of coffee-and-milk-coloured water shocking my toes awake. I ran until I slipped the world of time and taxes, work and weariness that I had left at my desk just minutes before.

I ran until there wasn't an inch of dryness to be found. Drenched and dripping, giving in, a smile spread across my face. I ran until I was a child.

And the others still out in the rain – the ones who hadn't scurried back inside, who had also given in – they replied with smiles of their own. We were all children out there, running in the rain, no matter our age.

As the rainclouds slipped down the valley and closed in around the trail, I turned towards home.

I imagined myself an old woman, twenty years or so down the road. Still running. Lacing up my shoes and leaving worries and old bones at the door. Slower, to be sure, but still running. Growing young again each day, if only for an hour.

Every run is a work of art, a drawing on each day's canvas. Some runs are shouts and some runs are whispers. Some runs are eulogies and others celebrations. When you're angry, a run can be a sharp slap in the face. When happy, a run is your song. And when your running pro-gresses enough to become the prism through which life is viewed, motivation is almost beside the point. Rather, it's running that motivates you for everything else the day holds.

psychologist Dr Leon Hoffman includes the sport as part of his treatment programme. 'Unfortunately, in today's world, affirmation is crucial,' says Dr Hoffman. 'Some women have problems because they have been trained to be funnels, not cups. For these women, when the applause stops, the depression sets in. But running can fill that. A woman can do it at her own pace, be assertive, try different things, be expressive, enjoy her body. She can give all these good things to herself, and not have to rely on somebody else or have it be in response to a man.'

Dr Jerry Lynch says that running and women are a natural match. The sport requires one to be fluid, or 'soft but strong', which he considers intrinsically feminine characteristics. 'Women tend to find the more spiritual, deeper side of running. It is just natural for women to align themselves with the concepts of courage, companionship and co-operation. Win or lose, when women run a race, at the end they hug, congratulate each other and then talk about how to improve the next time, all the while learning and achieving their goals.'

CHAPTER 13

Eat Right to Run Your Best

WE'RE USED TO IT BY NOW: endless waves of nutrition information hitting the headlines with a frequency that seems to ratchet ever upward. Carbs are good! Carbs are bad! Don't eat so much fat! Eat more fat! Eggs, chocolate, red wine, soya . . . in a few minutes online you can find an argument for and against virtually every food, every diet, every philosophy conceivable. Each week seems to bring a new diet, and with it, a new guru. By the time you've tried one 'miracle', the industry's ready with another.

But it's ironic: as all this research and information bombards us, our food choices, health issues and weight struggles grow worse than ever. Has the simple act of eating become so complicated that we no longer know how to eat? At times it seems that way.

Yet a different message is quietly being spread, one that's easy to comprehend and follow, one that runs counter to the overly analytical diet books that populate bookshelves in shops everywhere. It's simply this: eat real food. Eat food you can recognize. Whenever possible, eat food that doesn't come from cans, boxes or fast-food containers.

'I get frustrated,' says Nancy Clark, author of *Nancy Clark's Sports Nutrition Guidebook*. 'These days people look at carbs, protein and fat, and they forget we need real food.'

Real food. That means food that grows in the ground, is picked from a tree, that lives on the farm. It means buying ingredients like these and cooking at home.

Throughout this chapter we'll look more specifically at what makes for a healthy woman's diet, but along the way you should always keep in mind this mantra: eat real food. If you have to remember one thing, that's it.

THE ACTIVE WOMAN'S DIET

Running places demands on your body that require you to pay more attention to healthy eating. It increases your energy requirements, which translates to a need for more – and better – calories and nutrients. 'When you're exercising regularly, it's vital to eat a healthy diet,' explains Anita Bean, author of *The Complete Guide to Sports Nutrition*. 'Your diet not only has to keep you healthy, it also has to meet the tough demands of your training. If your diet lacks energy (calories) or a particular nutrient, you risk illness, low energy levels and a drop in your performance. A poor diet will have greater consequences when you're active.'

Since you can't be cavalier about nutrition when you're a runner, it's a good thing that running often makes your body start craving healthier items. This nice side effect might be Mother Nature's way of making sure that you're taking care of yourself.

The other good news is that eating well doesn't have to be complicated. It doesn't require extra hours spent in the kitchen or supermarket. By understanding your body's needs and making smart choices, you can easily eat for optimal nutrition, fitness and weight management. While diets go in and out of vogue, the true foundation of proper nutrition remains constant – and simple. You can start by ignoring all the diet books and gurus. Forget extremes and strive instead for balance. Your primary goals should be to balance your caloric intake with your energy expenditure and to balance your meals in a healthy manner.

A HEALTHY BALANCE

Some runners subsist on pasta, bagels and bananas because they believe that eating plenty of carbohydrates is the key to success. They tend to exclude more calorie-dense foods, which are often high in protein and fat, from their diets. Other runners swear by protein: they'll eat plenty of lean meats and avoid refined carbs such as bread and cereal.

Who's on the right track? That's been a subject of great debate. There are proponents of just about every imaginable ratio of carbohydrates, protein and fat. And over time, the scales have tipped in all different directions. Generations ago, runners would eat a hearty meal of steak and eggs before a race. In the 1970s and 1980s, carbohydrate depletion followed by carbo loading was common practice before events. In the late '90s, high-protein diets were once again in vogue.

Strip away all the hype, however, and what you should be eating as a runner is pretty much what everyone else should be eating. 'Basically, you don't want to go too heavy or too lean on anything,' says nutritionist Susan Kundrat, author of *101 Sports Nutrition Tips*. She points out that the high-protein diet adopted by so many athletes might be counterproductive: 'As a diet fad for women starting a running programme, that can be detrimental. That might not be providing enough quick energy – carbohydrates – for running. It's especially important to avoid following a fad diet when you're starting to run. Otherwise, if you don't feel good, you run the risk of thinking that it's the running that's not working for you – that you just don't have enough energy – when in fact the pitfall might be the diet.'

A more current way to think about the balance of carbs, protein and fat is something called nutrition periodization. The concept recognizes that our bodies and training change throughout the year, and our nutritional needs change along with them.

'The wave of the future is to change based on physical goals,' says Bob Seebohar, author of *Nutrition Periodization for Endurance Athletes: Taking Traditional Sports Nutrition to the Next Level*. While Seebohar works with athletes who are highly focused on their performance, all runners can learn something from this balanced system. In it, a runner shifts the balance of her diet and caloric intake slightly based on the needs of her body. A typical breakdown would look something like the following:

Base-building phase (think springtime, returning to training, building endurance with mileage): Carbohydrates should be fairly high so that you're fuelling yourself to train; protein intake is moderate; keep fat consumption fairly low.

Intense training season (probably during summer, when you're running intervals and track workouts): Maintain higher carbs, but bump up protein since there is more muscle breakdown due to intense exercise. Fat intake is low to moderate. Your calories can increase a bit overall since you're at the peak of your training.

Competition season (or leading into a big race): Moderate to high carbohydrate intake; bring down protein to low–moderate; fat intake is low.

Off-season (recovery period, winter, or after a marathon or long racing season): Carbs decrease, protein increases, fat stays low. Because of the drop in carbohydrates, overall calories decrease slightly, with a goal toward avoiding weight gain.

You can see that there are no hard and fast percentages. Rather, balances shift somewhat intuitively based on the demands placed on the body. That makes a lot of sense for most women. After all, when's the last time you sat in your kitchen calculating percentages? For those who insist on following the numbers, a safe baseline for runners is to take in roughly 60 to 65 per cent of calories from carbohydrates, 25 per cent from fat, and 10 to 15 per cent from protein.

What's really more important is following commonsense guidelines as opposed to fads and fast fixes. The foundation of your diet should be grains and grain products: bread, rice, cereal and pasta, the less refined the better. After that come fruits and vegetables. Be sure to get a good variety of both, since they provide different vitamins and phytochemicals (literally, plant chemicals – a variety of substances found in plants that can help fight cancer, heart disease and stroke). Eat meat, fish, eggs, nuts, beans and dairy products in small portions, as accents to your meals, and use sweets and fats sparingly.

Few women – few people, for that matter – eat such a balanced, healthy diet. Women tend to fall into two camps: those who eat too many carbohydrates to the exclusion of fat and protein and those who eat too much fat and processed food, denying themselves healthier complex carbohydrates. Most such patterns come from misguided notions that certain foods are good and others bad. Beef, eggs and dairy products are just some of the foods that have had a bad reputation over the years. In fact, there's a place for all of these in a runner's diet.

Today, nutritionists believe that one of the keys to any healthy diet is to consume a wide variety of foods. A number of studies have shown that people who eat a wider variety of foods on a daily basis consume more vitamins and minerals along the way than their counterparts who eat a limited number of items day after day. Excluding foods or entire food groups can lead to nutritional deficiencies, not to mention periods of rebellious bingeing.

SPECIAL CONCERNS FOR WOMEN WHO RUN

Adhere to the basics outlined above and you'll be well on your way to good nutrition. Following is a more detailed look at some of the items of special concern to women runners.

Protein

Many good protein sources are also high in fat. That fact has made many runners remove beef, cheese and nuts from their shopping lists. But you need these foods to repair the muscle breakdown that comes from exercise.

Perhaps the best and simplest recommendation is that you consume some protein-rich food with each meal in the day.

Sure, you can find formulas, but will you really follow and measure out

Supplements and Performance

Never mind health, some runners say. What about a magic pill to help me run faster? No matter how much excitement surrounds any given supplement, the fact is that when research catches up with the buzz, it tends to debunk the idea of gaining performance benefits from supplements.

One particular focus for endurance athletes has been the area of so-called antioxidants. The antioxidant vitamins, it was theorized, could be taken in larger doses by athletes such as runners in order to improve performance.

A review of research published in the *Journal of the International Society of Sports Nutrition* in 2004 concluded there was scant evidence that either of these benefits was the case:

➜ Vitamin C, it reported, showed benefits only in those individuals who were deficient but did not enhance performance in those with general standards of nutrition.

➜ Vitamin E can enhance oxygen utilization, but the conclusion was that this is not the case at sea level, only at altitude.

➜ CoQ_{10}, an antioxidant found in separate pill form in plenty of runners' medicine cabinets, has also been thought to improve utilization of oxygen (it's used therapeutically in the treatment of cardiovascular disease). But according to the ISSN report, this effect is not seen in healthy athletes, and it might even lead to muscle tissue damage.

your protein grams? (If you are that rare creature, aim for .5 grams to 1 gram of protein for every pound you yourself weigh.)

Protein is available in plenty of healthy foods, including eggs, beans, fish, soya products and low-fat dairy products. And don't forget the importance of variety and moderation in eating: if you're active, you can feel free to dine on beef, cheese and nuts as long as they don't make up the foundation of your diet.

Fat

The very mention of this three-letter word can make almost any woman cringe. Most women see fat as the enemy, something to be eliminated at all costs – from your body and your diet. But for every woman who rigorously

---

Although the evidence remains inconclusive, it does point toward the possibility that supplementation might be beneficial to older athletes, whose own protective mechanisms have begun to slow down.

Runners looking to maximize their performance also empty their wallets at the herbal-supplement counter. In this area, too, little proof exists for the many claims.

A 2006 review of scientific literature published in the *Journal of the International Society of Sports Nutrition* runs down the list of the most popular hopefuls, leaving little to get excited about:

➔ *Ginkgo biloba*, shown to improve aerobic endurance in elderly patients with arterial disease, shows no such effect in healthy athletes.

➔ Ginseng, also supposed to promote aerobic endurance, shows no conclusive result when put through rigorous scientific testing.

➔ *Tribulus terrestris*, sold as a purported testosterone booster, fails to increase hormone levels and measures of strength.

In the end, supplementing with *health* in mind – rather than performance – is probably the best thing you can do to run to your optimal ability.

strips her diet of every iota of fat, there's another who merrily orders another cheeseburger with fries. Neither approach is optimal for health or fitness.

Too much of the wrong type of fat in your diet can contribute to heart disease, not to mention the health problems that accompany being overweight, such as diabetes.

But eliminating all fats to a drastic degree has its own set of health con-

The Carb-Loading Conundrum

Ladies: here's your excuse to load up on pasta . . . .

For decades, distance runners have engaged in a practice called carbohydrate loading before competition to boost performance. The idea is this: the body typically begins to run short on muscle glycogen after about 90 minutes of endurance exercise, leading to inevitable fatigue. Loading up on foods rich in carbohydrates, such as pasta or brown rice, boosts the body's glycogen stores heading into a race, delaying the fatigue and improving race times. Traditionally, this was accomplished by first skimping on carbs for two days – the glycogen-depleting phase, when the diet consists of only 40 to 50 per cent carbs), then heavily weighting the diet towards carbs for 3 to 4 days (up to 70 per cent carbs, resulting in glycogen loading of the muscles).

Does it really work? It seems so; evidence shows that performance is more or less consistently improved, if not all the time. But here's the catch: much of the original research on the subject that draws this conclusion was conducted on men. And it turns out that men and women process carbohydrates differently, probably due to hormonal differences.

Now the benefit of carbohydrate loading for women has been investigated, and the result is fairly ambiguous. According to a 2006 research review in the *Journal of the International Society of Sports Nutrition,* women might see some gains in performance, but they must ingest significantly more carbohydrates proportionately than men to see any effect. So while men can simply switch their pre-race diets to 65 to 70 per cent carbs, women must do the same – *and* increase their overall food consumption by about 30 per cent for 4 days to see any results.

Is it worth it? I'm sceptical. By the time you're 3 to 4 days out from your big race, you should be tapering off your training and running fewer miles. The idea of eating *more* than usual when you're easing off and

sequences. Some types of fat are actually good for your health – especially if you run. Depriving yourself of these good fats can even affect your skin and hair and leave you perpetually hungry. 'When women severely restrict the fat in their diets, they have more of a tendency to binge and, in turn, develop other eating problems,' Kundrat says. 'Also, when women have a real fat phobia, their intention might be to eliminate calories, but they end

expending less energy sounds unappealing at best, and it's somewhat counterintuitive.

This is one of those cases where I'd leave the science in the laboratory and stick to common sense. By eating plenty of complex carbs the days before the race, you can ensure that your muscles are well fuelled with glycogen. Here are some guidelines:

➡ Research has established that the glycogen-depleting phase isn't as critical as the glycogen-loading phase, so you needn't forego carbs for days beforehand.

➡ Be sure to consume carbs in the 2-hour window after any training session, when the muscles are best able to absorb their nutrients.

➡ Even better, it turns out, carbs are optimally consumed in a steady stream of small amounts. Avoid having one large meal right after a run, and instead have half a bagel with peanut butter, and then follow that with a small bowl of porridge half an hour later. After that, sip on a smoothie made with plenty of fresh fruit and yogurt over the next half an hour.

➡ Look for good, healthy sources that offer plenty of nutritional benefit – whole grains like porridge, brown rice, potatoes and sweet potatoes – as well as the ubiquitous pasta.

➡ As with any race strategy, only you can tell what works for you. The best way to learn is by experimenting gently with your body during training to see how you respond.

And by the way, you needn't worry about any of this for a 5-K or 10-K. Remember, we're talking about races that last more than 90 minutes; for most of us, that means half-marathons and up.

up avoiding protein, calcium, magnesium, zinc and plenty of other important nutrients because a lot of the foods that contain fat are also good sources of these other nutrients. What might start as a well-intended low-fat diet can snowball into an unintended nutritional problem.'

How can you tell the difference between good fat and bad fat? Here's an overview:

✻ **Monounsaturated fats.** These are found in avocados, nuts and olive oil. Make them the predominant fats in your diet.

✻ **Omega-3 fatty acids.** Found in fish such as salmon and mackerel as well as in flaxseed, these fats can prevent heart disease and cancer. They might even help you lose weight and reduce muscle soreness along the way. Try to eat fish once or twice a week. Use flaxseed oil on salads, and add ground flaxseed to your favourite recipes.

✻ **Polyunsaturated fats.** These fats are found in most cooking oils. Treat them as neutral: they neither help nor harm your health.

✻ **Saturated fats.** Found in most animal products, saturated fats encourage heart disease. Limit them as much as possible.

✻ **Trans fats.** Found in margarine, many baked goods and many processed foods (such as cakes and biscuits), trans fats are even worse for your health than the saturated fat in bacon and butter. Limit them as much as you can.

If you need to cut back on your overall fat intake, don't drastically try to change your eating habits overnight. Instead, gradually adjust what you eat so your body and appetite don't rebel. Try making a few minor changes each week. Substitute a baked potato for chips. Try low-fat cheddar in your sandwich.

Just as important, switch to eating healthier sources of fat most of the time. Choose olive oil over butter, fish over beef. Remember, moderation is the key. If you love the taste of butter on your toast, you don't have to give it up. Just make sure that the rest of your day isn't filled with similarly saturated fat sources. If, on the other hand, you have a fat phobia, sneak nutritious sources of fat into your regular recipes: toss some walnuts or almonds into your cereal or pasta. Sauté veggies lightly in olive oil.

Coffee and Caffeine

Coffee's reputation has risen and fallen over the years. Sometimes it's portrayed as the villain, sometimes as the hero, and neither depiction is utterly

Now Is a Good Time to

→ Take a realistic look at your eating habits. Try keeping a food journal for 3 days. Write down everything you eat and drink. You might be surprised by the results. Often, women overestimate the amount of protein and vegetables they eat, or they underestimate their intake of sweets and junk food.

→ Have an expert review your diet. Most health clubs have nutritionists on hand for consultations. There are also many websites that offer nutritional analysis.

→ Keep your kitchen cupboards well stocked. Keep plenty of healthy, convenient foods available for times when you have to eat in a hurry. Beans, tuna, rice, frozen vegetables, nuts and dried fruits are all good staples to keep on hand.

→ Make changes slowly. If you find that your diet is out of balance, don't try to overhaul it overnight. Make a few healthy changes each week to give your body a chance to adapt without rebelling.

---

unfounded. On the downside, coffee can interfere with iron absorption, cause stomach distress and lead to the jitters. On the upside, it's a stimulant that clearly boosts energy, focus and concentration, plus it has high levels of antioxidants. Some of the worst fears about coffee – that it contributes to osteoporosis and heart disease – have yet to be proven. And now it seems that even one of its more benign side effects, dehydration, might be far less a factor than previously thought. 'We shouldn't be as scared of drinking coffee as we've been in the past,' sums up dietician Seebohar.

Caffeine has long been thought a performance enhancer for runners, and in fact, it used to be banned in high doses by the International Olympic Committee. But it was removed from the list of banned substances in 2004, and besides, research has cast doubt on (or at least not proved) the ironclad assumption that it conveys a clear benefit. One study in particular showed that caffeine reduces blood flow to the heart, a factor that was exacerbated during exercise. On the other hand, numerous studies have documented a performance improvement for athletes who have consumed caffeine.

Nancy Clark points out that some research suggests that caffeine functions primarily as an energy enhancer because of its effect on the brain, as opposed to any direct effect elsewhere in the body. In other words, exercise may seem easier after a dose of caffeine, but in fact, physical function remains unchanged. Other studies suggest that caffeine encourages fat burning, which can in turn spare your body's glycogen reserves on the run.

So what's the bottom line? If you like coffee – or tea – it's perfectly safe to indulge to a degree. Three servings or fewer a day is a good rule of thumb. But it would be a stretch to start hitting Starbucks just to improve your running. All the research in the world doesn't change the fact that caffeine's impact will vary dramatically from one woman to another. Although some runners won't leave for a workout without downing a cup of coffee, others won't go near the stuff – for them, it brings on a racing heart, dizziness, nausea, dehydration and diarrhoea.

Some runners wonder whether they should avoid coffee before races because of caffeine's diuretic effect. If you're a regular coffee drinker, foregoing a cup on race day is likely to do more harm than good, bringing on side-effects of withdrawal that can include headaches and jitters. Just keep your consumption at the typical levels you're comfortable with to avoid digestive difficulties – don't double your dose under the assumption that more will be better.

And by the way, if soft drinks are your preferred caffeine delivery system, that's a whole different story. It's hard to find any compelling argument in favour of soft drinks, particularly cola which has been shown to have a negative impact on bone health in women. The calories in full-sugar soft drinks take away from healthy calories you could otherwise be consuming, and diet colas are chock full of sugar substitutes that are questionable at best. If you must indulge, aim to keep it to one can a day.

Calcium

Calcium is one of the most important minerals in a woman's diet, yet it's not atypical for a woman to take in only half the amount she requires on a daily basis. Women who monitor calories and regulate their eating to control their weight often do so at the expense of calcium-rich dairy products.

But calcium is essential throughout a woman's lifespan in order to maintain healthy bones. Bone mass peaks by age 30, which is to say that up until that age a healthy body is actively building bone density and strength. That means calcium is essential for girls and young women to

Smart Tips

Eating a healthy, balanced diet doesn't have to be an exercise in tedium. You don't need to carry around a kitchen scale or calculate calories from package listings. Strive to take in a sampling of healthy fat and protein every day along with a larger dose of complex carbohydrates (grains, fruits and vegetables) with each meal. Often you can accomplish this with creative additions to old favourites. Little adjustments throughout the day add up. Here are some tips to help you begin. Once you get the hang of it, you'll naturally think of others.

➔ Spread toast lightly with natural peanut butter instead of butter. Unlike butter, which contains high amounts of artery-clogging saturated fat and virtually no vitamins and minerals, peanut butter contains heart-healthy monounsaturated fat and a good dose of vitamin E.

➔ Add fresh fruit and yogurt to cereal and porridge. The fruit will provide lots of phytochemicals, which are healthy for your heart and fend off muscle soreness. The yogurt supplies appetite-suppressing protein and a good dose of bone-boosting calcium.

➔ Mix steamed vegetables into your pasta. On its own, pasta contains few nutrients. The veggies add plenty of the vitamins you need.

➔ Add frozen vegetables or a can of chopped tomatoes when cooking rice. Rice supplies plenty of energizing carbohydrates. But like pasta, white rice is weak on nutrients.

➔ Crumble tofu into your pasta sauce. Soya products contain isoflavonoids, which may ease menopausal symptoms, boost bone health, lower heart disease risk and prevent breast cancer.

➔ Add greens and tinned beans to soups. Both supply plenty of appetite-suppressing fibre.

➔ Add tinned tuna, nuts and chickpeas or other beans to salads. All provide quality sources of protein with no artery-clogging fat.

build bone, and also critical for middle-aged and older women in order to maintain that bone mass and prevent weakening. Calcium's role in bone health takes centre stage, but the mineral might also prevent high blood pressure and colon cancer, though recent studies have cast some doubt on the strength of this connection. If you need more convincing, there's this: runners who don't consume enough calcium are more susceptible to muscle cramping.

While women have been admonished in the past to supplement their diets with calcium pills no matter their individual situation, research has shown that these supplements don't necessarily have a clear benefit. Sports nutritionist Clark has a simple take on the matter, saying that if a woman eats a proper diet mindful of calcium sources, she can certainly get enough calcium in her diet.

Energy Bars and Gels

Energy bars were originally created to provide easily digestible fuel for athletes during and after strenuous workouts. Now used by everyone from busy executives to marathon runners, they have become a multimillion-pound industry.

Although there's certainly no harm in these products, nutritionists point out that they don't contain anything you can't get from ordinary food – at a far cheaper price, to boot. Such supplements are really not necessary for low-mileage runners who work out for less than an hour a day. But energy bars are convenient. 'If it's the bar or nothing at all, then it's a fine alternative,' says Tammy Baker, a sports nutritionist and author of *Eating for Energy*. 'It depends on your lifestyle. For junk-food junkies, this might be the healthiest thing they eat all day.'

Sports nutritionists caution you to read labels. Be sure that what you're getting from an energy bar fits into your overall dietary profile for the day. Originally, energy bars contained primarily carbohydrates with a small amount of protein. These kinds of bars are best for consumption before or during runs. Many newer varieties, in the interest of improving flavour, contain a whopping number of calories from sugar and fat. Some are really sweets masquerading as sports fuel in order to capitalize on the fitness craze. They're fine – if you're looking for sweets. Other

'If you're eating cereal with milk, some cheese with your sandwich at lunch and a decaf latte in the afternoon, you'll have your three servings of dairy,' she points out.

It all goes back to the point made at the beginning of the chapter. Eat real food, eat real meals, eat low on the food chain and you won't have to worry about supplementation.

Dairy products are the most concentrated and convenient source of calcium. Low-fat milk and natural yogurt in particular are excellent choices. Although other foods such as vegetables and fish do contain some calcium, you'd need to eat a very large amount of those foods to get the necessary daily dose. If you're a vegan or if you're allergic to dairy products, consider adding calcium-fortified products such as orange juice and soya milk.

You should take in a total of 1,000 milligrams of calcium per day if you're

bars attempt to deliver a full range of nutrients, carbohydrates, protein and fat. Often high in calories, they can serve as meal replacements at a pinch. All energy bars are best washed down with water for easier digestion.

Gels and jelly beans are another form of quickly digestible energy food. Both provide easily transportable, quick bursts of fuel. They don't sound or look particularly appealing. Gels taste a lot like cake frosting and slide down easily. Sports jelly beans taste worse than the sweetshop variety but are arguably more palatable than gels for most people. Both are intended for competition and long workouts – you certainly wouldn't want to be snacking on them for any other reason.

Both gels and sports beans consist primarily of carbohydrates and are readily absorbed by the digestive system. For high-mileage runners, they can be a godsend during a workout. Many marathon runners now count on them and stash a packet or two in their shorts. If you've never tried them before, be sure to experiment on some long runs before your race. Try eating a gel packet or some sports beans after an hour or so of running and another one every 30 minutes thereafter. In races, plan to eat them before water stops, since they're best digested when chased down with a few sips of water.

under 50, or 1,500 milligrams if you're over 50. Since your body can absorb only about 500 milligrams at a time, spread out two or three servings of calcium-rich foods throughout the day.

Iron

Few women take in enough iron, and this can lead to anaemia. Anaemia can easily go undetected because the symptoms – extreme fatigue, dizziness and shortness of breath – mimic those of exhaustion. To prevent anaemia, most women require about 15 milligrams of iron a day. Although the iron recommendation isn't any higher for runners, taking in that basic amount becomes even more crucial. Iron helps to combat the increased breakdown of red blood cells caused by exercise, Tammy Baker explains.

Although plenty of foods are fortified with iron these days, the type of iron they contain is poorly absorbed. Lean cuts of red meat remain the best source of iron around. So, if you don't eat red meat, you'll have a difficult time getting enough iron, says leading sports nutritionist and presenter of the film *Understanding the Food Guide Pyramid*, Dr Kristine Clark. Clark says that women runners should take a daily vitamin and mineral supplement and take a second look at red meat. 'To stay away from red meat [for fat purposes] is a ridiculous concept for athletic females,' she says. 'Not only can you now buy very lean red meat, but in some cases it's leaner and lower in fat than poultry.'

If red meat is not a part of your diet, you need to be especially vigilant about your iron intake. Chicken and fish are sources for non-vegetarians. Dried fruit, beans, leafy greens such as chard and kale and fortified cereals are all good sources. Also consider taking a multivitamin with 100 per cent of the recommended amount of iron.

Vitamin and Mineral Supplements

Reputable nutritionists often repeat the following mantra: try to get all the nutrients you need from real food, not from pills. That's good advice for several reasons. First of all, your body absorbs the nutrients present in 'real' form – from foods – better than those found in supplements. What's more, research shows increasingly the importance of micronutrients that are present in foods such as fruits, vegetables and whole grains, and science has only just begun to identify and understand these compounds. Supplements don't come close to offering the benefits of nutritious foods.

Having said that, most women don't eat optimally on any given day. And strenuous exercise makes the presence of basic vitamins and minerals even more essential. So there's nothing wrong with taking a supplement. You can think of a multivitamin as insurance and peace of mind. But do consider this a supplement to your healthy eating habits – not licence to cheat on the rest of your diet.

What should you take? One simple women's multivitamin that bases its dosages on standard intake amounts is all you need – really. A handful of horse-size pills with doses several times the level that's proven safe can be dangerous. Fat-soluble vitamins can accumulate, because they're stored in body fat. Even water-soluble vitamins (such as the B-complex elements and

Timing Is Everything

The more you run, the more you'll want to concern yourself with the relationship between what you eat and when you exercise.

If you run for half an hour or so a few times a week, this is a fairly simple proposition. Eating a healthy high-carbohydrate snack, such as a banana, and sipping a glass of water shortly before a run will fend off hunger, dehydration and any related tiredness.

If you're a more competitive or high-mileage runner, things get a little trickier. Since it can take a day or more to replenish fully liquids lost during high-intensity workouts, keeping hydrated becomes a full-time proposition. You should drink throughout the day and before you head out for a run. Eat a good-size snack, such as a banana and a couple of pieces of toast, an hour or so before running to help ensure that you'll get through a longer workout.

After a rigorous run, you need to replenish energy as quickly as possible. Several studies have shown that your body is most receptive to rebuilding glycogen stores within a 30-minute window immediately after exercise. If you eat soon after you complete your run, you can minimize muscle stiffness and soreness. You'll mostly want to eat quickly absorbed carbohydrates such as fruit, but don't ignore protein altogether. According to Kristine Clark, the combination of protein and carbohydrates enhances the transport of glucose to the muscles. She recommends a ratio of 1 gram of protein to 3 grams of carbohydrates. Eat a bagel spread with peanut butter or drink a shake made with fruit and yogurt.

vitamin C) have come into question in large doses. According to Dr Winter Griffith, author of *The Vitamin Fact File*, excessive intake of vitamins and minerals beyond the recommended upper limit can result in everything from gastrointestinal distress (from vitamin C) to bone pain and hypertension (from vitamin A), as well as other complications.

In fact, safe upper limits are now being spelled out. For more than 50 years, the term RDA (Recommended Dietary Allowance) has been a trusted guide for people wanting to know how much of a supplement to take. Now a newer, more accurate system has evolved to solve inadequacies of this one measure being applied and possibly misinterpreted across an entire population. New Dietary Reference Intakes (DRIs) provide a range of numbers intended to address not only the minimum amount of a substance required to avoid nutritional deficiencies, but also the optimal amount to avoid chronic disease and, yes, upper limits to avoid negative effects. The National Institutes of Health Office of Dietary Supplements offer specific information and tables on their website, http://dietary-supplements.info.nih.gov/Health_Information/Dietary_ Reference_Intakes.aspx.

Water

Ah, water. How can such a simple thing be the source of such complication and confusion? The question of how much to drink to stay properly hydrated for runners is one that has seen a pendulum swing of opinion. Luckily, at this time, that opinion seems to be settling in a middle ground of common sense.

Before explaining the most recent thinking on fluid intake, here's a little history: when running first became popular as exercise for the masses, participants were encouraged to drink. And drink. And drink. Dehydration was the enemy, a serious risk for novice and expert alike. Before this time, ranging back for centuries, athletes typically didn't drink at all when running, as it was thought to interfere with the body's performance and cause all sorts of trouble.

The advice to drink was based on the assertion that thirst was a poor indicator of hydration. Experts told us that by the time we're thirsty, we're already dehydrated. Further, we were told, this was a problem because any level of dehydration put both health and performance at risk.

Runners were encouraged to replace *all* the fluids lost during a run, and were encouraged to weigh themselves before a run and after to make sure they finished the run at the same weight. Formulas encouraged runners to calculate and consume fluids to the maximum of their tolerance.

By the late 1990s and early 2000s, this thinking was starting to be called into question as something called hyponatraemia raised its head. Sometimes called overhydration or water intoxication, hyponatraemia is an imbalance of electrolytes caused by drinking too much water. It rocked the running

TRAINING LOG

Reading books and magazines is one way to learn the importance of proper fuelling. Having the pavement rise up and smack you in the head during an afternoon run is another. Although such a dramatic demonstration packs a potent punch, I'd advise you to learn from others' mistakes . . . okay, *my* mistake.

It happened when I was notching up my training before for a marathon. I was running twice a day most days of the week. I was also working 10 hours a day, which left precious little time for luxuries like, say, eating. I'd run a long track session in the morning, then have a sandwich and coffee at work.

Now, it's not as if I was ignoring my diet. In fact, I was pretty proud of myself: I'd stashed a jar of peanut butter in my office to make sure I had some protein and fat in that sandwich. And on the day in question, I'd grabbed a banana before leaving home, for good measure. So I ate my sandwich and banana at my desk, worked most of the day, and headed out in the early afternoon for my second run, which was supposed to last an hour.

Ten minutes into the run, I felt fine. After 20 minutes, I was becoming dizzy and weak. After 25 minutes, I turned around, worried that I'd have to walk in order to get back. Next thing I knew, I had to sit on the ground. The walk back to the car was one of sheer determination, during which I cursed my idiocy. Let's see: a sandwich, 400 calories; peanut butter, 200 calories; a banana, 100 calories. That's less than I should have had all day if I hadn't run at all, much less after running more than 10 hard miles in the morning!

When I reached the car, I fumbled around in the glove compartment and sucked down the two packets of energy gel I had stashed there. I felt better within a few minutes. Except for the residual embarrassment, that is. Amazing. Calories out, calories in. Energy out, energy in. What a concept. It's one I haven't ignored since.

world when a few fatalities hit the headlines. Suddenly it was clear that runners could – and did – in fact drink too much.

What's more, women are at higher risk than men, as we tend to sweat at a lower rate. And relatively untrained women running a marathon are at the highest risk of all. That's because a slower runner is capable of consuming more liquids while burning through less. Some experts also anecdotally point out that women are at greater risk because of their greater propensity to listen to advice and to take care of their bodies: thus, when told to drink, they do so – as opposed to men, who might be more cavalier and macho and go without. So a woman jogging a marathon at 12-minute pace can actually end a race weighing *more* than when she started because of fluid intake, something faster runners would have a hard time accomplishing because of their higher level of exertion and the unlikelihood that they'll slow down to drink enough.

What's a runner to do? Here's where it gets refreshingly simple: drink when you're thirsty. Don't if you're not. Guidelines adopted by the IMMDA (International Marathon Medical Directors Association) in the US in 2001 changed the hydration prescription when they counselled runners to drink *ad libitum* – according to thirst. The guidelines also gave an upper limit of consumption (no more than 400 to 800 ml per hour), as opposed to offering minimum requirements and admonishments to surpass those to the greatest degree possible.

For most runners, water or juice is an adequate hydrator. If you log a lot of miles, you might want to replenish your electrolytes by drinking one of the many sports drinks available. For the average recreational runner, these drinks aren't necessary. In fact, for women who are simply jogging half an hour a day, guzzling sports drinks before and after a run could easily replace all the calories burned during exercise – not exactly the result many novice runners are looking for.

CHAPTER 14

Slimming Down:
The Runner's Weight-Loss
Programme

MANY WOMEN COME TO THE SPORT OF RUNNING WITH THE GOAL OF LOSING WEIGHT. They've come to the right place. If reducing the number on the scale is the goal, just about any regular exercise programme can help, but running is one of the most efficient sports for weight loss, burning an average of 100 calories a mile. That's a lot more than most activities.

Compare running to walking, another favourite of women who want to regulate their weight: for a woman who weighs 68 kg, half an hour of walking at 3 miles per hour (mph), or 20 minutes per mile, burns about 120 calories. The same half-hour of jogging at 6 mph (twice as fast, 10 minutes per mile) burns roughly 350 calories. (The precise figure varies depending on speed, size and fitness level.)

When it comes to the overall number of calories required, cross-country skiing provides a comparable workout and is one of the few activities that generate such a high calorie burn, but how many women can pop out the front door and go skiing any given day of the year?

Running can melt off the pounds faster than most other activities, because simply put, running takes more energy than most other sports, exercises or activities. For one thing, during a run you alone are fully bearing all your weight. That means you don't have the benefit of, for example, a bicycle or the buoyancy of water to support you. Also, and partly because of that, running uses more of the body's muscles than just about any other activity. Your legs, of course, get a full workout, but when you stride across the ground, you're also putting your arms and trunk to work.

When you begin to run, weight loss becomes easier in other ways, too. The aerobic exercise tends to moderate the appetite, especially during the window of time immediately after a run. Many runners report that the activity encourages a general shift to a healthier lifestyle, too; they crave healthier foods and are less likely to engage in self-defeating behaviour, such as bingeing on junk food. The gains in fitness bring more energy and a less sedentary life overall.

While running itself encourages weight loss, your eating habits obviously have a big influence on the process and results. You can help ensure safe, healthy and comfortable weight loss by following these basic principles.

RELEARN HOW TO EAT

The most important step you can take on the road to weight loss has nothing to do with finding a miracle slimming food; it's not about some magic ratio of carbohydrates to protein; it's not about denying yourself the foods you love. The most important thing you must do in order to stabilize at a healthy, comfortable weight is to change your attitude towards food.

Women with a tendency towards being overweight often have developed an understandably antagonistic relationship with food. Food has become the enemy. It's fattening and tempting, a necessary evil to be battled every day.

Does that sound familiar? If so, imagine thinking of food in this way: *Food is pleasurable and nurturing. Food is a source of energy, joy and resilience. It is an enjoyable and essential part of a happy, healthy and balanced life.*

It sounds good, doesn't it? Do you believe it? When you do, you're half of the way towards healthy eating and therefore a healthy weight.

Thinking of food as inherently fattening and therefore bad is a set-up for a nasty relationship with eating that is endlessly defeating.

'People see food as fattening. Or they make up excuses, they say, "I don't have time to eat,"' says Nancy Clark, author of *Nancy Clark's Sports Nutrition Guidebook,* now in its third edition. 'No. Food is fuel. It's really life sustaining and life promoting.'

Clark goes on to point out that the relationship between women and food ultimately must be one of respect. By eating well and healthily, we are

How Many Calories Do You Burn in a Day?

The UK Department of Health recommends that women consume 1,940 calories a day to maintain their current weight. Active women, however, need to consume more. Use the following formula to calculate how many calories your body uses in a day:

1 Multiply your body weight in kg by 34 to find the number of calories you need if you lead an active lifestyle. For example, if you weigh 60 kg, you'll need to consume 2,040 calories a day.

2 To determine how many additional calories you will expend running, add around 100 calories per mile.

3 Add together the figures you arrived at in steps 1 and 2 to determine your total daily calorie expenditure.

---

respecting our bodies. After all, we wouldn't expect our car to run without fuel. 'People just aren't responsible with their food,' she says. 'They think, "If I skip a meal, I'll lose weight."'

In fact, it's the opposite. Studies have repeatedly shown that people who skip breakfast tend to be overweight, and that calorie restriction during the day often leads to overcompensation at night. Clark points out that studies also illustrate a correlation between dieting itself and being overweight: the very act of dieting exacerbates the problem. The way she puts it sounds downright radical: 'When people eat, they tend to be thin. People who diet are overweight.'

For women, that's good news. It's a reason to give yourself permission to eat, to eat well, to eat healthily.

If your goal is to lose weight by running, here are some further guidelines for sensible weight loss and optimal overall health.

Follow the training programmes in this book. There's no magic training programme for weight loss, no different way of exercising. If your goal is to lose weight, follow the training programmes in this book for either the beginning or the intermediate runner, depending on your experience level. The same programmes that help you get in shape will also help you gradually take off pounds.

Consistency is the most important aspect of training when it comes to losing weight. Try to run or walk/run 3 or 4 times a week, and supplement your programme with other active pursuits on your days off. Although it's true that longer or faster running will burn more calories, you shouldn't try more strenuous workouts without first working up to them with the more basic training schedules. Taking on extra workouts to lose weight faster presents the same pitfalls as any rapid increase in a training programme: increased risk of injury and burnout.

Don't starve yourself. Some women think that because they're burning calories while running, they can double their rate of weight loss by also cutting back what they eat. But severely restricting calorie consumption while running is not a recipe for successful weight loss. In fact, it can have the opposite effect. Taking in too few calories can leave you feeling weak, tired and irritable, diminishing the amount of energy and willpower you have to run. By dropping your consumption below what your body requires to function, you can also cause your metabolism to slow down.

'Women who cut way down on calories at the same time they increase their exercise intensity run the risk of injury and exhaustion and won't see the benefits of a running programme as quickly,' explains Susan Kundrat, a sports nutritionist and author of *101 Sports Nutrition Tips*.

Kundrat, who specializes in working with female athletes, advises women to adjust their eating habits gradually. 'A lot of women who start exercise programmes want to make sweeping changes in diet at the same time because they are very motivated, but it's important not to make those changes all at once,' she says. 'Rather, let your body get used to the changes that come with exercise. Make sure that you're getting enough fuel. Then, once you are feeling good with your workouts, you might want to assess where you are, determine what your goals are. You might wish to lose body fat or get stronger. Then you are in a position to make changes that can complement your exercise routine.'

If you're running primarily to lose weight, let the exercise do its work gradually. Eat consciously, without being too restrictive. Listen to your body, eat when you're hungry, stop when you're full and make wise and healthy choices when you do eat. By doing this, you'll ensure that you have enough energy to run. Follow this formula and you're more likely to lose body fat gradually, in a safe, conservative manner. That means you'll be more apt to keep it off, too.

Watch your calorie intake. Although I just told you not to *severely* restrict your food intake, you should pay attention to your overall calorie consumption. That's because it's the total number of calories consumed that has the greatest impact on your weight. Fad diets continue to offer all manner of formulas to achieve weight loss, but the bottom line is that whether you eat grapefruit or steak, the total number of calories you consume will determine the weight you gain or lose.

You can watch your calories in a general sense by recording what you eat each day and by not overindulging in high-calorie treats or huge portions. If you prefer a more precise method, use the formula in this chapter to determine your daily caloric requirement. By eating this number of calories each day, you should roughly maintain your weight. In order to lose weight healthily while running, restrict calories by no more than 10 to 20 per cent of this number.

Once you've reached your target weight, the calories you burn while running can negate many sins of overindulgence. In fact, plenty of runners who have been at the sport for years say that one of the great bonuses is that they're able to eat more.

Make wise food choices. Sports nutritionists usually frown upon categorically restricting or relying on certain foods – the basis of most formalized diets. But that doesn't give you the freedom to eat willy-nilly, grabbing anything you want. Healthy food choices are of the utmost importance for anyone trying to lose weight.

Follow the guidelines for healthy eating outlined in chapter 13. Make your choices wise ones, optimizing the use of the calories you do take in. That means minimizing junk foods, fast foods, and empty calories from soft drinks and the like. It also means relying on unprocessed foods such as whole grains and fresh vegetables and fruit as the foundation of your meals. If you make good choices a habit, an indulgence now and then needn't be cause for concern.

Eat out less often. You probably know that fast food is filled with hidden fat and calories. You probably *don't* realize just how much extra butter, oil and sugar is tucked into a typical restaurant meal. Chefs tend to add far more fat and sugar than we ever would at home: they make almost anything taste better!

By eating at home, you maintain control over what you eat and what goes into every dish. You'll also be less tempted to indulge in fattening starters and desserts, and more likely to eat a reasonably sized portion. When you do eat out, don't be afraid to make special requests, such as ordering salad dressing on the side or vegetables without butter.

Treat yourself. If you make wise food choices, you can still indulge occasionally. When you give yourself permission to indulge a craving now and then, you'll be less likely to feel deprived and eventually binge. Remember, you aren't supposed to be dieting, but rather making changes that you can maintain as a long-term lifestyle choice. How likely is it that you'll be able to give up cheesecake for the rest of your life? Go ahead and have a small piece – just don't make it an everyday occurrence.

Follow the 90/10 rule: make healthy choices 90 per cent of the time, and

TRAINING LOG

Okay, I'm thin. Running for decades will do that to you. It's funny, though, how many women, after seeing how much and how freely I eat, will say, 'It must be your genetics. You must be naturally thin.' I don't know about that. My mother was always quite skinny, but I also know she denied herself food to the point where she was probably borderline anorexic. Meanwhile, my father and his entire family tended to be overweight. So what would my 'natural' weight be if I didn't run? Who's to say?

I do know that by now, I have become naturally thin. By that I mean that I feel in balance at this weight, neither denying myself nor controlling my food intake to stay at my current weight. I attribute that largely to my *outlook* on food as opposed to any diet specifics.

I prefer to think of eating well as health management rather than weight control. That way the focus is not on deprivation or a loss of something, but on benefits and gaining something. Maintaining an appropriate weight feels good, increases energy and allows me to be my healthiest self. When I eat lots of vegetables, I do it because I know they're nutritious, not because I'm focusing on their low calorie count.

And while I definitely am conscious of what I eat and make healthy choices much of the time, I'm hard-pressed to think of a time I've really denied myself anything. Part of that is because when you truly start to eat healthily, you rarely desire truly unhealthy food. Oh, I love a cheeseburger and chips as much as anybody, but I don't really crave one more than once a month or so. Certainly not every day. And I love sweets as much as any woman. But years of healthy eating has 'trained' my body to appreciate home-made, quality items – made with healthy milk, nuts and wholesome ingredients – over some processed, packaged treat.

When you look at eating this way, denial isn't really an issue. In fact, fresh, nutritious foods become positive indulgences. Like summer's strawberries with muesli. Or an autumn curry of sweet potatoes and carrots. Treats like these are every bit as sinfully delicious as a gooey dessert. But instead of feeling guilty after eating them, you can relax knowing that you've indulged in a different kind of luxury: caring for yourself.

allow yourself a splurge during the remaining 10 per cent. The simple idea that you don't have to be perfect will help you make better choices more consistently and not get depressed or fall back into old patterns after you've eaten a biscuit or two with your afternoon latte.

Fuel yourself throughout the day. Distribute your calories evenly, as if you were parcelling out medicine and attempting to keep a constant dosage in your body. This steady course of fuel will keep your energy levels strong and hunger pangs at bay, so you'll consume fewer calories in the end. Peaks and troughs of fuel can do the opposite: skipping breakfast and foregoing lunch are notorious for leading to bingeing later in the day.

Take this notion a step further and you'll be even better off: be sure to have some extra protein with every one of your meals, even the smaller ones. It's protein that results in a full, satisfied feeling that lasts. So instead of having just porridge for breakfast, top it with some yogurt or nuts; add some almonds, cheese or chickpeas to your lunch salad; and have a peanut butter sandwich, not a croissant, when those afternoon hunger cravings hit.

Eliminate the concept of snacking. Close your eyes – I'm going to ask you a question. What types of food come to mind when you hear the word 'snack'? Nutritionist Dr Kristine Clark has a hunch that you were thinking of something sweet, possibly salty, probably highly processed.

Clark is all for the idea of spreading calories throughout the day, but, she says, 'We should take the word snack out of our vocabulary'. This is because it results in poor choices.

Clark prefers to refer to a small afternoon meal as a 'second lunch'. When you refer to it that way, you're more likely to grab balanced and healthy items – a slice of pizza, yogurt and muesli, a peanut butter and honey sandwich – as opposed to biscuits, pastries or crisps. By the way, the same goes for your children if you have them: think in terms of a 'second lunch' for after school and you're bound to make better choices for them, too.

Supplement running with strength training. File this in the 'rich get richer' department: the more muscle you have, the more calories you'll use even during rest. Conversely, if you have a high percentage of body fat, you'll burn fewer calories. That means that by building muscle, you can boost your metabolism and burn more calories, facilitating weight loss.

Strength training is the most straightforward route towards building muscle, and it's a good complement to any running programme. As an added boost, it will visibly tone your body – a nice visual motivation to maintain both your healthy eating and running.

CHAPTER 15

Body Image Issues

IT IS THE BEST OF TIMES AND THE WORST OF TIMES for women's bodies. Why the best? Acceptance of women's participation in sports and fitness activities has changed the manner in which the female body is viewed. Women are no longer held up to an ideal of beauty that's rooted in fragility and helplessness. Muscle, strength and athletic ability are celebrated, as is variety among body types.

Which brings us to the worst: relentless media images of ever-increasing perfection skew the standards of beauty. The particularly au courant look – a lean body with large breasts – is a genetic impossibility for all but a few women. Yes, muscles and strength are acceptable, as long as they come in an attractive package. In fact, the fitness craze has upped the ante, since now women needn't just be trim, but toned, too. Fat is, as ever, taboo.

Compounding these expectations is a damning belief that a woman should be able to create any body she chooses – the self-help craze run amok. She just needs to work out hard enough and demonstrate enough discipline – or have enough money. Stubborn pockets of the body that resist the effects of training can be enhanced or made to disappear, thanks to cosmetic surgery. The message to every woman: if you're not happy with something, you can change it.

That message is a dangerous one. Striving for a healthy body and seeking perfection are very different things. Not understanding the distinction is a recipe for frustration. Sure, abdominal crunches will flatten your abs, running will tone your thighs and liposuction can trim the rest, but nothing will alter your fundamental body type, bone structure and height.

LOVE YOUR BODY

For the vast majority of women, the increased physical fitness and awareness that come from running counteract negative messages and contribute to a healthy body image. 'Exercise can help a woman develop a body in which she feels in control: strong, powerful and toned,' says Dr Carol Otis, co-author of *The Athletic Woman's Survival Guide* and founder of www.sportsdoctor.com. Through running, you'll start to see your body as a finely crafted mechanism. You'll learn to appreciate your strength and abilities. Running, for so many women, is the answer to a lifetime of body battles.

Coming to terms with your physical self can, in turn, contribute to a sense of well-being. Women runners, when compared with their sedentary counterparts, are typically less depressed and less anxious and have more energy and greater self-esteem, according to Dr David Brown, a behavioural scientist, in his research in the journal *Medicine and Science in Sports and Exercise*. And indeed, many women who began running later in life can pinpoint a fairly obvious shift in outlook that occurred once they took up a more active lifestyle.

For a smaller number of women, however, exercise becomes a double-edged sword. These women take the positive elements of fitness one step further, into the dangerous realm of unrealistic expectations. *If I'm this fit now,* they wonder, *then how much more will I gain by losing a few more pounds? Or by running still more miles? Look,* they say, pointing to thighs, hips and tummies, *I still have fat to lose!* Suddenly a healthy pastime becomes a knife of obsession with which they attempt to carve a better self.

'When women use exercise to reshape their bodies, it can be a form of punishment,' says Nancy Clark, author of *Nancy Clark's Sports Nutrition Guidebook*, who has worked with a wide spectrum of female runners on body image issues. 'Someone who runs for more than an hour a day might be training for a race, which is fine. If not, it might be a mode of punishment.' These women come to view their bodies as 'the enemy', as objects that need reforming.

Clark says that if you're one of these women, it's important to realize that the problem doesn't lie with your body at all. 'Your body is perfect the way it is. It's your relationship with your body that's not perfect. You want to work on loving yourself from the inside out.'

Body dissatisfaction tends to be more prevalent in women than in men, in younger women than in older women, and in women who participate in sports such as gymnastics and rock-climbing, in which a certain look or weight is beneficial to performance. Because of this correlation, some say that some sports actually contribute to self-critical thinking and behaviour. But today, it's largely accepted that personality traits – not particular sports – are the cause of such body image issues. 'If these women didn't run, they'd be beating themselves up in some other way,' Clark says. 'They'd be the ones saying, "My hair is the wrong colour", or, "I'm not pretty enough".'

When women have profound body image dissatisfaction, it can manifest in many different ways, including excessive exercise and restrictive eating. Such beliefs and accompanying behaviours are now considered symptoms of a psychological problem that lies elsewhere. 'Such behaviours are smoke alarms that mean there's a fire somewhere else,' Dr Otis says. 'It's often the case with the compulsive runner or the person who uses exercise as punishment that there are family issues, relationship issues or a history of abuse.'

Extreme body image dissatisfaction and its ensuing behaviours can be episodic, coming and going depending on the stage of a woman's life. Times of extreme stress and changes in relationships with family or partners can exacerbate the psychological factors that lead to body image dissatisfaction. So can times of transition, such as when a girl enters puberty, when a young woman leaves for college or when an older woman's children leave home.

One factor that can exacerbate such tendencies is what Dr Otis calls a sport-body misfit. This is especially prevalent in activities that put a premium on a certain look, such as ballet and gymnastics, but it can also be seen in runners. 'When a woman is born with a shot-putter's body and she wants to be a good distance runner, that's a sport-body misfit. It puts her at greater risk for body image dissatisfaction.'

Dr Otis says that this phenomenon is most prevalent in a level of runner sometimes called the sub-elite. Recreational runners don't have a problem because they don't focus on performance, and top professionals in the sport tend to have bodies that lend themselves to success. But because sub-elites are attempting to achieve high marks in a sport for which their bodies might not be built, chances are scant that they will be able to break through to the uppermost levels of competition. That serves to compound their frustration and determination, adding to body-related unhappiness. And in fact, Dr Brown confirms that the self-esteem benefits of running begin to drop off among high-mileage, competitive women runners, who actually have an increased rate of mood disturbance. 'For someone who's born with the apple-like endomorph's shape, all the running in the world won't turn her into Grete Waitz,' Dr Otis says, referring to the Norwegian marathon great. 'If you are born with a short, stocky frame, exercise won't change that. But you will develop a strong, toned body that matches what your inheritance is. It's important for women to recognize more images of what "normal" is and for them to choose role models from this wider range.'

BURNING MOTIVATION

Women don't have to be competitive to suffer from unhappiness with their bodies. Many recreational runners enter the sport in order to lose or stabilize their weight. Some of these women never get past this mindset. To them, physical activity is little more than a calorie burner. These women may also carefully measure and restrict what they eat and calculate how much they're losing on the run.

But what they are losing is far more than weight. These women, who are essentially restricting themselves to negative motivations, may also be losing out on everything else that physical activity has to offer: greater self-esteem, relaxation, pride of accomplishment and more.

Furthermore, they might not even be accomplishing their weight-loss goals. If a woman restricts her eating severely, she won't have enough energy to run. Chances are that she'll feel lousy during her workouts; she may even need to slow or stop early. As her body tries to conserve precious energy, her metabolism will slow down, meaning that she'll burn fewer calories throughout the day. She could be setting herself up for failure, should her body not respond in the manner she had hoped or as quickly as she had planned. If weight loss is the only motivation, then this kind of disappointment can even end a running career.

Though it's fine to use running as a method of weight control, ideally it shouldn't be the sole source of motivation. If you're one of those women who equates every run to calories, consider focusing on a gentler relationship with your body. You might also seek out other, healthier motivations and goals for your running. For example, other similar reasons to run that have a healthy twist might include:

❋ To be as healthy and strong as possible
❋ To encourage healthy forms of socializing
❋ To indulge in a pastime for your own pleasure

* To get to know your body better
* To develop your mental and emotional fitness

By taking a more holistic approach to running, you can open yourself up to the entire range of benefits that the activity has to offer. Increased self-esteem, discipline and well-being add up over time to a lifestyle that's conducive to healthy weight management without negative self-criticism.

EATING DISORDERS

Although headlines about anorexia and bulimia are alarming, the overall percentage of female runners who suffer from a clinical eating disorder remains small. Numbers are highest among competitive secondary school- and college-age athletes. Eating disorders are illnesses with serious health consequences, and they should be treated professionally. Left untreated, an eating disorder can lead to potentially life-threatening malnutrition, heart trouble and bone loss.

Anorexia nervosa is an intense fear of fat that is diagnosed technically when a patient weighs significantly less than the normal amount for her height and frame. A person with anorexia severely restricts her caloric intake and suffers from a distorted body image, continuing to feel fat even when she's emaciated. Without successful treatment, the anorexic will eventually suffer from symptoms of starvation. In what amounts to a dangerous and vicious cycle, ensuing lethargy and feelings of worthlessness make her less likely to seek treatment.

A person with bulimia, although she also may restrict calories and exercise obsessively, indulges in binges in which she rapidly consumes large amounts of food. She also displays counteractive behaviour, such as self-induced vomiting and the use of diuretics or laxatives. Bulimia can go undiagnosed and unrecognized by friends and family because women who suffer from it typically are not underweight and therefore do not fit the expected profile of a person with an eating disorder. A person who suffers from bulimia will eventually develop telltale symptoms, including worn tooth enamel, tooth decay, puffiness in the face and a chronic sore throat.

Compulsive exercising is now also recognized as a form of purging and is therefore considered a symptom of bulimia. Women can manifest this compulsion in many sports; however, running is a popular outlet due to the high number of calories burned. Women who undertake this form of purging can be acting in an attempt to burn off calories or to punish themselves for eating or for having the wrong body type.

'It is important for family and coaches to pay attention,' says Dr Steven Ungerleider, a sports psychiatrist and author of *Mental Training for Peak Performance*. 'Often, people who are close to the runner will suspect something but be in denial. Parents might hear through the grapevine that something isn't right. If I hear, for example, "My girl's doing great, but she's so tired and not looking good and her coach expects more," those are red flags.'

Healthy Body Image

If you think you're obsessing about your body, take these steps, as outlined by Dr Carol Otis, co-author of *The Athletic Woman's Survival Guide*.

➔ Resist comparing yourself with anyone else.

➔ Emphasize health rather than weight.

➔ Understand what your body type is. Look at people in your family to get an idea of what a realistic goal is for you.

➔ Understand what it means to be healthy for your body type. For example, some women will naturally become very lean when they run, while others retain more body fat. Both types can be at optimal health while at different weights.

➔ Choose 'body-appropriate' role models. If you have a larger frame, instead of hanging a picture of a very thin cross-country runner on your wall, find a shot of a woman who represents your body type in its fit stage.

➔ Emphasize the positive. Instead of loathing your thighs and pinching for cellulite, recognize how strong your quadriceps are.

➔ Choose clothing that's appropriate for your body and for your comfort level. You don't have to wear tights or skimpy shorts. Try looser trousers and longer shorts.

➔ Practise yoga or engage in a stretching programme. Both have been shown to make women feel good about themselves.

➔ Start to get outside help early. If you feel that you'd be fitter or faster if you lost some weight, work with a sports nutritionist. Consultations are available at gyms and on many websites, or you can call a specialist where you live.

Where to Turn for Help

For further information about eating disorders, support groups, and programmes, contact these organizations.

➔ National Eating Disorders Association
www.b-eat.co.uk

➔ Eating Disorder Expert
www.eatingdisorderexpert.co.uk

Women who suffer from eating disorders tend to be perfectionists and might come from dysfunctional families. Their behaviour often begins as an attempt to control or numb psychological pain by blocking it with physical pain. Many suffer from depression. 'In a way, eating disorders and compulsive exercise are an attempt to self-treat depression or poor body image,' Dr Otis says. 'These people do need psychological help to deal with these issues.'

Today, most experts agree that horror stories about coaches bringing on eating disorders with off-the-cuff comments about a runner's weight are largely mistaken. Although an athlete herself might claim that such an event was a trigger, experts will agree that other psychological factors have made her prone to an eating disorder in the first place. Nevertheless, coaches, parents and others close to the athlete should be cautious not to contribute to a problem by applying additional pressure for performance.

If you believe that you or someone you know has an eating disorder, seek help from a doctor who specializes in such issues. Increasingly psychotherapy is recommended in order to understand what has triggered the eating disorder, to correct distorted body image and to change obsessive behaviours. Nutritional counselling is advised as well, in order to learn healthy eating patterns. Doctors may prescribe antidepressants and other medications to combat depression, boost self-esteem and reduce obsessive–compulsive behaviours.

DISORDERED EATING

More common among the general population of athletic women than full-blown clinical eating disorders is what has come to be known as disordered eating. This term refers to a wide spectrum of ineffective and potentially harmful eating behaviours. Nancy Clark explains it this way: 'Normal eating is eating when you are hungry and stopping when you're content. Hunger is seen as a simple request for fuel. But a disordered person will respond to that request by saying, "Oh no, I'm hungry. I'm going to get fat."'

Although they don't suffer from anorexia or bulimia, these women are inordinately concerned with their eating habits. They tend to restrict calories, banish certain foods from their diets, fast for periods of time, weigh themselves often, worry constantly about weight loss and fit their social and eating patterns around these concerns. Sometimes, disordered eating habits will develop into a clinical eating disorder, but not necessarily.

In some cases, disordered eating results from a lack of education about nutrition. Clark says that she often sees women runners who diet at breakfast, diet at lunch, 'blow it' at night – and then do it again the next day and the next. 'That's because they don't know that it's okay to have 600 calories each for breakfast and lunch. They have a flake of cereal for breakfast and a piece of lettuce for lunch. They don't know that the signs of what they see as an eating problem are actually hunger.'

In more serious cases, disordered eating is a symptom of other psychological difficulties, much the same as with more severe eating disorders. 'It's not that these women don't know how to eat, but rather that they have other issues going on, and this is how the problems are manifested,' Dr Otis says.

It can be difficult for some runners to determine the difference between a healthy concern about performance and disordered eating. Dr Ungerleider recalls experiencing such problems himself. 'When I was training for marathons, there were times when I'd come back from a long run of 18 miles and still be very picky about what I'd eat – and I had a background in sports psychiatry!' If you think that you are developing patterns of disordered eating, Dr Ungerleider recommends becoming educated in sports nutrition and taking the following steps:

❋ Honestly assess your current situation. Are you spending more time thinking about food than you used to? Have you changed your eating habits? Are you going through an especially stressful time?

❋ Examine any training and weight-loss goals to make sure they're realistic.

❋ Check in with somebody who is close to you: a coach, training partner or parent. Talk about your concerns and see whether they have noticed any potentially harmful behaviour.

TRAINING LOG

It was Saturday morning, and we'd just run an 18-miler. Our group – my coach, two male runners and three females – headed to a bustling breakfast place to refuel, rest and socialize. The guys ordered the breakfast special: eggs, potatoes, veggies, cheese, and plenty of other goodies on the side. One of the women ordered a plain bagel. The other two ordered croissants without butter or preserves. After 18 miles. This prompted one wise young man to comment: 'What's with you women, anyway?'

What's with us, anyway? We were women in our 20s and 30s, a group of local- to national-level competitors, not particularly elite but quite serious about our training. None of us was suffering outright from bulimia or anorexia. We ate several times a day, usually making healthy choices, and didn't binge or purge.

We did, however, constantly restrict our food choices, constantly limit our calories, constantly monitor the sizes of our thighs and constantly compare our bodies with those of other runners. (Perhaps not unrelated, most of us were constantly grumpy.) And we were not alone.

A professional female runner in her 40s once told me that she doesn't know a single competitive woman who hasn't had 'issues' with food. I had no trouble believing her.

My own flirtation with disordered eating didn't last long – I love food far too much to deny myself of it for any length of time. It reared its head for the year-and-a-half in my mid-30s during which I became very serious about my training. But looking back, it's clear to me that it wasn't the running that brought on my hypercritical diet. Rather, it was my own struggles with body image brought to the surface in a culture of thinness that we women runners perpetuated and secretly admired. 'Eat, eat,' we would urge each other on. 'You're looking too thin.' But the speaker of such thoughts would never be caught in her *own* infraction of consumption. It was a silent game of diabolical one-upmanship. *She just wants me to get fat and slow,* the thinking went. *I'll show her.* Thus the plain bagel.

Every woman's experience is different. For every problem I had withholding dessert and agonizing over the heredity that gave me puffy inner thighs, I had equal and greater triumphs of body image. As a runner, I'd come to love the strength and endurance of my body, and, for the most part, I liked the package it came in. When I dropped my plans to compete, I suddenly gained perspective. When I dropped my miles and gained a little padding, I didn't mind feeling curves in new places. I was more than just a machine built for speed; I was a woman built for a dozen different roles and challenges. Seeing my body in a new light, I blinked at the darkness of the tunnel I'd been in – even if just for a brief while – before.

✳ Consult a sports nutritionist or doctor. Make sure that your diet is adequate for your level of activity.

The bottom line for every woman: treat your body with the respect it deserves. For some women, that may mean becoming educated; for others, it might mean getting help. For all of us, it means loving, nurturing and feeding the legs and lungs that carry us through our lives.

CHAPTER 16

Caring for Your Body

YOUR BODY TALKS TO YOU CONSTANTLY. It checks in during every footfall of a run. It warns you of the Achilles tendon that's feeling the beginnings of a strain, of the shins that are suffering from too much impact, of the heel that's starting to throb with displeasure. If you learn how to listen to these subtle messages – and lots of runners don't – you can avoid many running ailments.

The longer you run, the more adept you'll become at interpreting your body's attempts to communicate. Experience will help you figure out the difference between everyday discomfort and impending injury. 'The key to detecting injuries is to know how your body feels when it is functioning normally,' says Dr Roger Henderson, a runner and GP. Your body offers subtle messages, such as a twinge in your thigh, or a pain in your shin or a slight burn on the bottom of your heel. And because running injuries are almost invariably overuse injuries – meaning that they stem from the same action repeated many times, as opposed to acute injuries, such as a stumble that results in a twisted ankle – they do indeed send warning signs your way before becoming full-on injuries.

If you sense such messages and react right away, you can stop many injuries in their tracks. A combination of corrective strengthening and flexibility exercises, proper shoes and corrective insoles can solve many problems.

But left untreated, the same injuries can lead to severe discomfort and tissue damage, eventually requiring a break from running or even surgery.

The lesson? Don't ever try to 'run through' an injury, ignoring symptoms until they become debilitating. Even when your pain diminishes on a run – which it sometimes does, as the injured site warms up – don't consider it licence to ignore your body's plea for help. Dr Lewis Maharam, a member of the International Marathon Medical Directors Association, goes by this rule of thumb: it's okay to self-treat an injury as long as the pain does not alter your stride. When pain makes you limp, see a doctor.

If you've been injured before, you know that seeing a doctor isn't always as easy a solution as it sounds. Running injuries are complicated. Some doctors, especially those who don't run or exercise themselves, will be unable to get to the bottom of your sports-related problem. Or you might end up getting advice that doesn't work.

To avoid frustration, seek out a doctor who specializes in sports medicine or, better yet, in running. Practices where physiotherapists, masseurs, chiropractors and osteopaths are available under one roof are becoming more and more common in the UK. To find a good specialist, ask long-time runners for recommendations or enquire at your local running club.

Some running injuries are cut-and-dried; others defy diagnosis. You can increase your chances of getting a proper diagnosis by providing honest, accurate information about your training. If you don't feel satisfied with the information or attention you receive from one doctor, look for another.

To prevent an injury from happening again, make sure that you understand the underlying cause. Many problems arise because a runner never deals with inherent biomechanical challenges or alignment issues. Other injuries are caused by improper training: running too far too soon or increasing intensity before developing a proper base. Running in shoes that are too old and have lost their cushioning ability, as well as running in the wrong type of shoes, can also lead to injury.

If your doctor tells you to stop running but doesn't offer any tips to correct the problem so that it doesn't recur, get another opinion. When you stop running, your symptoms might go away. Odds are, however, that your injury will only rear its head again when you start running again.

If you have a stress fracture, for example, you'll have to stop running – or run in a swimming pool – until the fracture heals. But you should also work with your doctor, following through with bone-density tests and an analysis of your diet and hormone levels. Only then will you learn why the fracture occurred in the first place.

Massage

Sports massage serves a different purpose than traditional relaxation massage. A good sports massage therapist can loosen up tight muscles, finding potential trouble before it turns into an injury. This kind of body work is typically deeper than other forms of massage and it can cause greater discomfort.

For best results, look for a massage therapist who specializes in sports massage. Some even work primarily on runners. These therapists will know the trouble spots that plague runners, and they can give you the most comprehensive massage. A good massage therapist will ask how much pressure you're comfortable with. You should never be afraid to speak up if something hurts.

If you aren't used to deep massage, your body may feel sluggish and sore the day after the session. This feeling should dissipate within a few days, and it will become less noticeable with ensuing sessions.

Always communicate with your massage therapist about your running schedule. That way, you can get the right type of massage at the right times.

With all injuries, take the following precautions.

Reduce your mileage. You can continue to run with certain injuries. Indeed, in a backlash against doctors' predictable admonishment to stop running, it's become a popular notion that many injuries can be 'trained through'. But this can be counterproductive. Think about it: if running caused the injury you're trying to heal, why do you want to re-stress the area constantly? At least reduce your training to the basics: plan to cut back by half or one-third of your total volume and do that running at an easy pace. Avoid terrain such as hills, which can exacerbate biomechanical problems. Also avoid hard surfaces such as concrete and extremely soft surfaces such as sand.

Train smart. You might have managed to get away with not warming up or cooling down until now, but the time has come to break that bad habit. Precede each run with a gradual warmup and follow it with a cooldown and stretches.

Stretch lightly. Be cautious not to overstretch the injured site. Over-stretching is a common mistake that can worsen an injury. Don't stretch to

Just before and after a tough workout or race, for example, your massage therapist should never go deep. A deep massage before a race can make you feel sluggish. A deep one right after can actually cause more harm than good. But a light rub that warms up your muscles is perfect. You'll usually want to leave at least 3 days to recover from an intense massage before a race.

If you're a competitive runner who trains heavily, consider having a massage every week if time and money allow. On the other hand, if you put in fewer miles, you may wish to schedule a massage only when you've stepped up your training or when you've taken on new workouts that have left you sore or tight.

You can also try self-massage. Using your hands or specially designed massage devices, apply gentle pressure where your muscles are tight. Applying friction by rubbing horizontally back and forth across the muscle can help loosen up knots. You can even hire a sports massage specialist for a session or two to teach you how to best self-treat your trouble spots.

the point of pain, and don't jerk. Slowly ease yourself into a stretch, and hold it for 15 to 20 seconds.

Take painkillers with caution. Anti-inflammatories can often speed the healing process, but never take them before a run. If you do, you'll cut off important physical messages, essentially gagging your body's ability to tell you when you've done too much. Take anti-inflammatories only after a run.

Cool it off. Icing an injury after a run is one of the simplest yet best therapies to reduce inflammation. A bag of ice cubes works fine; strap it on with an elastic bandage to free up your hands and go about your business. Or try an old runners' stand-by: a bag of frozen vegetables, which conforms well to your body's curves. Or fill a polystyrene cup with water and freeze it. Just peel away the edges as needed to massage the ice into your sore muscles. It's easy to hold and control, thanks to the foam insulation.

Consider seeing a physiotherapist. Physiotherapy is an often-overlooked but important part of treatment for most running injuries, says Dr Thomas Shonka, a podiatrist and internationally recognized expert in gait analysis. Dr Shonka points out that a good physiotherapist will do more than just

Does Fitness Affect Sexual Performance?

Anecdotal evidence suggests that some runners experience increased sex drives as their fitness levels increase. 'In women, sex drive is far more psychological than hormonal,' says Dr Mona Shangold, author of *The Complete Sports Medicine Book for Women*. Some research has shown a temporary increase in women's levels of testosterone – which contributes to sex drive – during a run. But the effect is short-lived, Dr Shangold says, and it's unlikely to contribute to increased libido. Increased feelings of well-being and improved body image, however, can make a world of difference, as can simple energy levels. Since runners often report these positive side effects, it's quite possible that you could feel a surge in sex drive as your fitness improves.

---

administer treatments such as ultrasound or electrical stimulation. 'They can be the ones to crack the whip and be sure you do the flexibility and strengthening exercises you need,' he says. 'It's not exactly glamorous stuff, and lots of runners won't do it at home left to their own devices. But that's the important work that will get you back on track and keep you healthy down the line.'

Cross-train. If you have to cut back on your running (or worse, stop altogether) your mood can easily plummet. It's not uncommon for injured runners to feel angry or depressed. Maintaining a positive attitude can be the most challenging part of injury rehabilitation. To keep your mood up, find some form of exercise to maintain your fitness. The type of injury will dictate what type of exercise you can do safely. Consider running in a swimming pool, cycling or swimming. You can also use your downtime to work on strengthening with weights, to focus on rehabilitative exercises that your physiotherapist has recommended or just to take a relaxing break.

Resume your training slowly. After your injury has healed, resume running gradually. The last thing you want is to undertake a sudden leap in training intensity that wreaks new havoc. After a prolonged layoff, your muscles, tendons and bones will need to readapt to the stresses of the sport. Carefully monitor your injury's progress, backing off if the pain resumes. If you've been cross-training, you can start your training again by alternating days of running and cross-training. This will minimize stress on your body.

How much you run when you resume training will depend on how much time you've had to take off. Use these guidelines.

One week off: Resume at previous distance.

Two weeks off: Resume at half of previous distance.

Three weeks off: Resume at one-quarter of previous distance.

Four weeks or more off: Start from scratch, alternating jogging and walking until your body has had a chance to adapt. You'll progress more quickly than a true beginner, but you'll still need to take the time to ease back into your full workout schedule.

Adjust your expectations. The big race you were training for might have to wait. The personal bests you were hoping for might have to come next year. Stubbornly maintaining goals and accelerating a training schedule to get 'back on track' can lead to a cycle of disappointment and further ailments. Injuries, much like races that don't go as planned, usually contain lessons. Heed them and you'll become a wiser, healthier runner.

A GUIDE TO WHAT AILS YOU

The following list includes most common running injuries and considerations, especially those that affect women in particular.

Achilles Tendon Pain

Most runners call it tendinitis, but doctors now call it tendinosis or tendinopathy. Regardless of the name you use for this degenerative condition, the result is the same: frustrating pain that can hinder your running and hang around for years.

Achilles tendon problems typically begin as an inflammation of the lining through which the tendon glides, eventually involving the tendon fibres themselves. Chronic inflammation and deterioration in the tendon area can weaken the fibres, eventually leading to partial or complete rupture.

Pain and inflammation are the first signs of Achilles tendon trouble. Eventually, the tendon area will become tender to the touch and visibly swollen. Upon movement, it may elicit a crunching feeling like that of packing snow.

Cause: When your calf muscles are tight, you exert too much force on your Achilles tendon, which connects the calf muscles to the bones of the foot. The more speedwork and hill training you do, the more strain you apply.

Treatment: At the first signs of Achilles aggravation, stop doing hills and speedwork. See a podiatrist to get a heel lift for your shoes. Warm up and cool down thoroughly during every workout. (More advanced cases of tendon deterioration may require a break from training to allow the tendon to heal.) Ice, anti-inflammatories and ultrasound (administered by a physiotherapist) can promote healing. Massage can accelerate blood flow to the area and break up adhesions from the scar tissue that develops as you heal. Future maintenance should include flexibility exercises, particularly for the lower leg. One to try is the wall lean: face a wall, standing an arm's length away, and place your hands on the wall. Step back with one leg and hold that leg straight while you lean into the wall. For an optimal stretch in your calf, keep your weight on the outside of your foot.

Acne

Women runners can be plagued by skin breakouts on the face, hairline, upper back, chest, upper arms and behind.

Cause: Sweat production combined with hair follicles or friction from rubbing clothes are a formula for acne. Increased temperature and humidity worsen the problem, as do products such as sunscreen and makeup, which sweat off onto the skin and clog pores.

Treatment: To fend off exercise-induced acne, follow these steps from Dr Wilma Bergfeld, author of *A Woman Doctor's Guide to Skin Care*:

✻ Minimize use of makeup and hair-care products before running. Although special makeup products are being developed for and marketed to women who exercise, the best makeup for running is no makeup at all. If time allows, wash your face before running. After running, wash your face again before reapplying makeup.

✻ Use a sunscreen specifically formulated for the face on your face and neck. Choose a gel or lotion for the rest of your body, instead of a cream-based product.

✻ Wipe acne-prone areas with an astringent pad or towelette immediately after running. (Once your body's natural oils cool, they harden, leading to plugged pores.)

✻ Change out of sweaty exercise clothes immediately after running, and shower or bathe as soon as possible.

✻ Cleanse acne-prone areas thoroughly. Gentle exfoliation can help, but don't scrub to the point of aggravating your skin.

✳ If you're prone to acne, consult with a dermatologist about the use of prescription medication.

Allergies

The sneezing, coughing and watery eyes of seasonal allergies can make you feel like taking a nap instead of running outdoors. Fortunately, there's a new prescription medication arsenal that can stop allergies without making you feel drowsy or hurting your performance.

Cause: Specific irritants – such as pollen or dogs – trigger an immune system reaction, resulting in allergy symptoms.

Treatment: Avoid allergens whenever possible. Run early or late in the day, when winds and pollen counts tend to be lowest. Weather patterns and pollen differ in every location, so ask a local allergy expert when it's best to be outside in your area. If rearranging your schedule doesn't provide sufficient relief, see your GP. Prescription medication can alleviate most symptoms, and for most people it's preferable to over-the-counter medication, which tends to cause drowsiness.

Asthma

Exercise can reduce asthma symptoms because it improves lung capacity. But since running and other vigorous exercise can serve as a stimulus for asthma attacks, you need to take precautions during workouts.

Cause: When a person with asthma encounters cold air, smoke, pollution or other irritants, an inflammatory reaction causes airways to narrow.

Treatment: Thoroughly warm up before going into a run or training session, advises Dr Roger Henderson, a runner and GP. 'Cooling down can also benefit here,' he says. Plan to jog very slowly for 5 to 10 minutes before and after your workout. If the air temperature is very cold, cover your face with a bandanna or scarf to warm and humidify the air before it enters your lungs. Finally, ask your doctor about prescription asthma medication. As with allergies, prescription medication is preferable to over-the-counter drugs.

Back Pain

If you have back pain, you might be suffering from more than tight, overworked muscles. When pain radiates down into your buttocks or one of your legs, you've probably aggravated the sciatic nerve.

Cause: Sciatica can be caused by any number of mechanical stresses on this nerve, which runs from your lower back through your pelvic area and down your legs. Such stresses can result from bad biomechanics, damaged vertebrae or even osteoporosis – any of which can put pressure on the discs in your spinal column.

Treatment: Strengthening and flexibility exercises for your trunk and legs can sometimes help eliminate the causes of sciatica, as can attention to biomechanics with proper shoes and inserts. Do the back extensions, crunches and hamstring stretches offered in chapter 18, being especially careful not to strain your back. In some cases, chiropractic adjustments may also help. If you suspect that you have sciatica, see a sports medicine specialist, physiotherapist or chiropractor.

Birth Control Side Effects

Researchers disagree about the impact of hormone-based birth control methods, such as the Pill, hormone patches and IUDs that contain hormones, on athletic performance. IUDs contain such minimal amounts of hormones that any effect is probably negligible. Though most studies have shown that birth control pills and hormone patches have no effect on performance, some research indicates that women on the Pill may have a slight reduction in aerobic capacity, but a large review, published in *The British Journal of Sports Medicine* did not find any evidence that this translated into impaired performance. 'The study also concluded that the advantages of the Pill for sportswomen outweighed any potential disadvantages,' says GP and runner Dr Roger Henderson.

On the other hand, some runners feel that birth control pills might help performance by reducing menstrual symptoms. Some runners prefer to customize their intake of birth control pills, controlling and timing their cycles so that they don't have to race during their periods. Manipulating the timing of your periods by altering the pill cycle is still controversial. Some experts are not convinced of the long-term safety of such a practice; others feel that, if nothing else, removing one's menstrual cycle from the calendar points to priorities that might be out of balance, depending on the circumstances.

Cause: The same hormones that birth control pills (and other hormone-containing birth control methods) regulate to prevent pregnancy can affect the way your body feels and functions. As with the Pill's side effects, this effect is highly individual.

Treatment: Ultimately, you need to decide for yourself whether birth control pills or other hormone-containing birth control methods make sense for you. For each runner who swears by the convenience of the Pill, there is another who insists that she feels and performs better without it. If you run recreationally, you probably don't have to worry about any athletic impact of the Pill, a patch or an IUD. But if you race competitively and don't want to risk sacrificing aerobic capacity, you might consider using a barrier method of birth control, such as the diaphragm. If you wish to stay on the Pill, talk with your doctor about getting a very low-dose version to minimize side effects.

Black Toenails

Often surfacing after a race, especially a marathon or one with lots of downhills, black toenails are largely an unsightly nuisance. These typically are a sign of shoes that are too small or otherwise fitted improperly; it's perfectly possible to run and race without ever having damaged toenails or foot ailments of any kind.

Cause: Repetitive trauma to your toe causes a blood blister under the nail. Since the blister can't breathe, it takes much longer to heal than a blister elsewhere on your body.

Treatment: Make sure that your shoes fit properly. Keep your toenails trimmed. If you do a lot of downhill running, try to lace your shoes tighter along the tops to prevent your feet from slipping forward.

Blisters

Although they're not exactly genetically predisposed, some unfortunate runners seem to be plagued by blisters, while others can run merrily mile after mile without generating so much as a hot spot on their feet. The culprit is often improperly fitted running shoes.

Cause: Friction, typically between skin and sock.

Treatment: Buy shoes that fit. Then buy socks made specifically for running. Look for socks made of synthetic fabrics such as Teflon and CoolMax, which wick moisture away from your feet, preventing the sock from bunching up and causing blisters. Also, look for socks with no seams and a smooth surface. Some runners prefer double-layer socks specially created to deter blisters. (The idea is that any friction occurs between the two sock layers instead of between your skin and the sock.) Blister-prone women can also spread petroleum jelly or a specially made runners' lubricant on problem areas. Just go easy: too much will leave you sliding around in your shoes.

If it's too late and the blister has raised its nasty head, take the following steps: leave the skin covering intact, since it serves as protection. You can drain extremely painful blisters to alleviate pressure. Synthetic skins (now sold over the counter specifically for this purpose) can be placed over the blister to protect against infection and to provide a layer of cushioning. These pads might also speed healing. If possible, run in a different pair of shoes until the blisters calm down, to avoid aggravating the same spots.

Bone Bruises

Technically speaking, bone bruises are deep contusions. They commonly occur on the outer covering of a bone. Runners will often use the phrase to describe a pain, typically in the foot. But in fact, *bone bruise* is not usually the technical medical diagnosis. The actual injury can be anything from plantar fasciitis to a stress fracture.

Cause: True bone bruises are caused by impact with an unyielding object. Trauma typically occurs when the bone is not padded with overlying tissue – think of bashing your shin on a table. In runners, the cause is usually stepping on a sharp rock.

Treatment: Again, actual bone bruises are rare in runners. If you feel a deep pain in your foot that doesn't improve within a few days, see a podiatrist. What you think is a bruise might be a symptom of another injury. The treatment for a true bone bruise is time away from running. If you can run without altering your stride, continue training. Otherwise, cross-train or pool-run until the pain subsides.

Breast Discomfort

Running, or more precisely, the bouncing action that occurs from impact during running, is associated with breast pain in up to 72 per cent of exercising women, says Dr Joanna Scurr from the Department of Sport and Exercise Science at the University of Portsmouth. 'The pain is thought to be caused by support tissues stretching, which can lead to reductions in performance and reluctance to exercise,' says Dr Scurr.

Cause: The skin that supports your breasts is susceptible to stretching over time from gravity and motion. Running exacerbates this stretching – but only when your breasts are not adequately supported.

Treatment: Wear a properly fitted sports bra. The larger your breasts, the more support you will want in a bra. For more on choosing a sports bra, see chapter 2.

Chafing

When your clothing doesn't fit correctly, it moves around as you run, slowly wearing away small bits of skin. At the end of your run, you're rubbed raw. Chafing most often occurs around the bra line, on the inner thighs and under the arms.

Cause: Repeated motion – specifically, skin rubbing against loose fabric or other skin. In humid climates, the constant presence of sweat can exacerbate the problem.

Treatment: Use petroleum jelly or one of several specially formulated runners' lubricants. Spread a thin layer of lubricant on the affected area before you head out for a run. Wear only sports bras made of synthetic materials such as CoolMax that wick moisture away from your breasts and dry quickly. Look for sports bras with smooth seams. Jump around in the shop when trying on sports bras to make sure that the seams don't rub against your skin.

Colds and Flu

Studies have shown that runners are more susceptible to colds and flu when they're training heavily and especially after they've completed a strenuous, long-distance event such as a marathon.

Cause: A weakened immune system is easier prey for the common cold and flu, both of which can result after you inhale or come into contact with a virus.

Treatment: Whether you run when you're ill should depend on the severity of your symptoms and on your own judgment. If your nose and head are stuffed up, an easy run can help clear your congestion. If you have a fever, if your muscles ache or if congestion has moved into your lungs, you're better off taking a break until these symptoms subside. Some doctors refer to this as the above-the-neck test. If symptoms remain in your head, go ahead and run. If symptoms reside lower in your body or all over your body, give it a rest. Most important, know yourself. If you're poorly, chances are that your immune system has been weakened from stress or fatigue. A day or two of rest might be just what the doctor ordered.

Corns and Calluses

Some runners like to show off ugly feet as a sort of battle scar of training. But there's no need for roughing it, and with a little attention even runners can have beautiful feet.

Cause: Skin toughens as a result of friction and pressure from repetitive motion in running shoes. Ill-fitting shoes make the problem worse.

Treatment: Keep corns and calluses under control by going over hot spots with a pumice stone in the shower. For overall comfort, slather on a foot-massage product after running or before bed. Look for products specially formulated for athletes; they're meant to cool burning feet and rejuvenate aching muscles.

Damaged Hair

Your hair might not seem to be at risk from running, but exposure to the elements can take its toll over time. A few precautions can ensure that your locks stay as healthy as the rest of you.

Cause: Your hair reacts to the elements much as skin does, meaning that it can become dehydrated and damaged due to sun and wind exposure. And, much like skin, fair hair is more susceptible to damage than darker hair.

Treatment: Protect your hair from negative environmental effects by wearing a cap when running. Putting long hair in a pony tail or cropping hair into a short style can help keep tresses healthy. Treating your hair with protein- or silicone-enriched products can rejuvenate and strengthen it to some extent. Minimize the use of styling products before running, though, since these tend to sweat off onto your face, blocking pores and contributing to breakouts.

Dehydration

The thinking on dehydration has shifted significantly in recent years. When running first grew in popularity, participants were admonished to drink endlessly, whether or not they were thirsty. Dehydration was viewed as a significant threat to health and as a detractor from performance. Thirst, we were told, is a poor indicator of hydration, not to be trusted. So successful was the push to drink up that some runners literally drank themselves to death, pointing out a different danger: hyponatraemia, or overhydration. Yes, drinking too much can put you at risk of a life-threatening electrolyte imbalance. Symptoms of dehydration include headache, dizziness, nausea and cramping. Symptoms of overhydration are similar on many counts. Both ends of the spectrum sound alarming, and the fact that they can be hard to tell apart is certainly confusing. Luckily, with a little common sense, it's not hard to stay hydrated without overdoing it.

Cause: Inadequate replenishment of fluids during exercise.

Treatment: The most recent guidelines for hydration during exercise boil down to a simple formula: drink when you're thirsty. That's a huge relief, and a lot easier than following some formula of litres consumed and miles run. For runs shorter than 60 minutes long, most runners will be just fine drinking a glass of water half an hour before the run, then sating their thirst afterward. If you run for longer than an hour or if it's especially hot and humid on shorter runs, you might want to consider carrying some water with you and drinking it as your thirst dictates. As the length of your runs increases, particularly for marathon training, switch to a sports drink that's intended for drinking during exercise, which will replenish electrolytes as well as replace fluids.

In addition, concern yourself with proper hydration at all times of the day, not just during or after a run. Drink plenty of water or juice, ditch the soft drinks and pay attention to your thirst. Don't drink to excess just for the sake of it, but be sure to give your body the water it craves. (For more on hydration, see chapter 13.)

Diarrhoea

If you have to make frequent pit stops during your run, you're not alone. It's not unusual for runners to be afflicted by diarrhoea and other gastrointestinal distresses.

Cause: Troubles usually occur during lengthy or strenuous exercise, when blood is pulled to the muscles, leaving an inadequate supply in the intestinal tract. These problems are more common in untrained runners than in highly fit athletes. The bad news: research has shown that women are afflicted more often than men. The good news: a little pre-emptive attention can alleviate most problems.

Treatment: Maintain proper hydration; dehydration exacerbates reduced blood flow. During marathons and long runs of several hours, consume a sports drink to keep up your electrolyte levels. Don't eat foods that are high in fibre before working out: fruit, vegetables, legumes and whole grains are notorious troublemakers. If you must have coffee or tea – both of which pack a double whammy of diuretic and laxative effects – try to give yourself half an hour before running, which should allow time to go to the toilet before hitting the road. Finally, avoid non-steroidal anti-inflammatory drugs, such as aspirin and ibuprofen, which can also exacerbate alterations in blood flow to the gut.

Frostbite and Hypothermia

Despite what your mother might have told you, your throat and lungs will not freeze when you run in extreme cold. Since your body generates significant heat during aerobic activity, you can work out comfortably in most climates throughout the winter. Ultrarunner Richard Donovan, who operates marathons at the geographic North Pole and in the Antarctic, says runners have been able to negotiate both courses without any acclimatization. 'I advise competitors to train as they would for any other marathon and this suffices in meeting the challenges of polar running,' he says. But adequate protection and preparation are a must. Cold air can leave you at a higher risk for frostbite, hypothermia and strained muscles.

Some women are more susceptible to cold than others. Fat provides thermal resistance, meaning of course that it keeps us warm. A runner's individual surface-to-mass ratio also comes into play, so smaller individuals have more trouble retaining heat. In addition, the older we are the less tolerant we become of the cold. Finally, women who suffer from circulatory conditions, such as Reynaud's disease, are particularly at risk in even mildly cold weather.

Cause: Mother Nature.

Treatment: Think about protecting both your extremities and core: wear a hat to cover your ears and wear mittens to cover your fingers. Consider wearing a thin pair of long johns under your running tights or a windproof layer over them. In addition to your base and outer layers, consider adding an additional vest layer; keeping your trunk warm can go a long way toward making your entire body comfortable. Petroleum jelly can help protect exposed parts of your face.

On extremely cold days, monitor your fingers, toes, ears and nose. They should warm up after a few minutes of running. You can help them along by wearing special winter running socks made partially or completely of wool and by tucking disposable heat packets (sold in sports shops) into mittens.

If you become wet from rain or are soaked through with sweat while outdoors in cool temperatures, you'll have an increased risk of hypothermia, a lowering of the body's temperature. This can occur even in temperatures above the freezing level. To stay as dry as possible, wear proper wicking fabrics that will help keep sweat off your body while running. Do not hang around outside if you're damp; change your clothes and get warm as quickly as possible.

Finally, use common sense. If the weather is so cold that you can't run comfortably, you're at greater risk of pulling a muscle. Warm up slowly and run at only an easy pace on very cold days. Save the hard workouts for the coming thaw. Beware of ice on the pavement and road. When you've finished running, head indoors and change out of your wet clothes immediately.

Heat Illness

Running in hot or humid weather increases your risk of heat injury, otherwise known as hyperthermia. There are three levels of hyperthermia, listed here in order of increasing severity:

✻ **Heat cramps** are felt as muscle spasms. Hydration and rest are usually adequate to treat this level of hyperthermia.

✻ **Heat exhaustion** is typically felt as a headache, weakness, dizziness and a decrease in coordination. Although your body temperature will be elevated, your skin will feel cool to the touch. Treatment entails rest, hydration and cooling your body with water.

✻ **Heatstroke** symptoms are the same as those of heat exhaustion, except that instead of being cool, your skin is hot and dry. Because your body temperature can rise dangerously, if you're suffering from heatstroke, you should be taken to Accident and Emergency, where you'll be treated with intravenous fluids and cooling methods.

Cause: Hot or humid weather that creates conditions in which your body can't adequately cool itself. While anyone is theoretically at risk of suffering from heat stroke, some runners and conditions are more likely to cause concern: less-trained athletes and those with a greater body mass are at greater risk than well-trained whippets, since heavy people simply generate more heat. Also, counter to commonly held perception, runners are at greater risk when competing hard in shorter races, such as a 10-K, rather than a marathon, since their exercise intensity is greater.

Treatment: To avoid hyperthermia, run in the morning or evening on days that are very hot or humid. According to Dr Maharam, runners should be particularly cautious when the temperature exceeds 30°C and the humidity exceeds 85 per cent. Additional tips are to wear loose-fitting, lightweight clothing and to stay properly hydrated; drink as your thirst dictates.

It's worth noting that for years, runners were advised to drink to the most tolerable upper limit as a way of combating heat illness. Current thinking recognizes that hydration alone cannot sufficiently fend off hyperthermia, however, and it's dangerous to think it can. For one thing, overdrinking can have its own serious consequences (see 'Dehydration', on page 200).

Furthermore, while proper hydration is required for the body to cool itself, the most significant determinants in the risk of heat illness are instead the rate at which you produce heat and the environment's ability to absorb that heat. That means that heat and humidity coupled with a hard running effort carry a warning sign that can't be ignored, no matter how much you drink.

Heat Rash

These tiny, itchy bumps that typically appear on the trunk usually occur when you're overheated and dehydrated.

Cause: Your body temperature has increased, and your sweat glands are failing to equalize it.

Treatment: Though not harmful in itself, heat rash is a signal from your body that it's time to cool down and hydrate. Cortisone cream, sold over the counter, can help if the bumps persist after you've cooled off.

Iliotibial Band Syndrome

The iliotibial band is a long span of muscle and connective tissue that runs from your hip to your knee. As with so many biomechanics-related running injuries, iliotibial band troubles tend to come on slowly. Increasing pain outside your knee is a cue to take action.

Cause: When it becomes tight or overstressed – often the case in runners who overpronate or underpronate – friction and tension result where the iliotibial band attaches to the outside of the knee. This causes pain and inflammation.

Treatment: Ice, anti-inflammatories and physiotherapy such as ultrasound can alleviate pain and inflammation. Although the iliotibial band itself does not stretch, you should regularly stretch the muscles around it. Stand with a wall to your left. Cross your left foot in front of your right; then, keeping your right leg straight, lean from your hip into the wall and hold this position. Change sides and repeat the stretch on the other side. Proper shoes and orthotics are a must to fend off the problem once and for all. Until the pain dissipates, reduce your training to steady distance. Hills, speedwork and long runs can all exacerbate the problem.

Incontinence

Women are more prone to incontinence than men because of our anatomy. You can take some comfort in the fact that it's a very common condition – it's estimated that about half of all women experience some level of urine leakage – but that doesn't change the fact that it's annoying, inconvenient and disconcerting.

Cause: Women who suspect that they experience more trouble while exercising may be correct. Although running does not cause incontinence, the activity – as well as that of other exercises and sports – can induce urine leakage in women who are already prone to it.

Treatment: Many women find relief by strengthening the muscles in the pelvic area with pelvic floor exercises. To do these, contract your pelvic muscles as if you were attempting to stop a flow of urine. Hold for a few seconds, then release for a few. Repeat for up to 5 minutes. For the greatest effectiveness, do these exercises in a variety of positions: sitting, standing, lying down. There are also several devices, both over-the-counter and prescription, that help control leakage. Talk to your doctor about what method might work best for you.

Medication Side Effects

A running programme should generally have no effect on either prescription or over-the-counter medications, according to Dr Maharam. On the other hand, some medications might have an effect on running performance. Typically, these effects are minimal and of peripheral impact – for example, affecting weight, appetite or energy level as opposed to directly affecting strength or endurance.

Cause: Drugs that seem to be affecting your desire or ability to exercise. As with any medication, any such impact will be highly individual.

Treatment: Speak to your doctor if you are concerned about the effects of any drugs you're taking.

Menstrual Issues

Although some women complain of discomfort during their periods, it's generally accepted that menstruation does not negatively affect running performance. In fact, the menstrual cycle overall is believed to have limited impact on exercise performance. Women have run well, set records and won championships at all phases of the menstrual cycle. Clinical studies have found no change in heart rate, strength or endurance during the female cycle. Although some research has shown a slight decrease in aerobic capacity during the latter portion of the monthly cycle (after ovulation), the significance of the finding is questionable.

Cause: Menstrual symptoms are the result of hormone changes that occur with the female reproductive cycle.

Treatment: Exercise can improve your feelings of well-being before and during your period. Some doctors even prescribe exercise for women who suffer discomfort at this time of the month. Research has shown that moderate exercise can alleviate physical premenstrual symptoms, including breast tenderness and fluid retention. Working out regularly is also thought to relieve anxiety, depression and other mood disturbances characteristic of premenstrual syndrome. (Some research shows that these benefits tend to become less pronounced in women as they approach menopause, due to ovarian hormonal changes.) Exercise can also contribute to changes in the menstrual cycle itself, most typically resulting in a shortening of the luteal (postovulatory) phase.

Another potential problem for runners is the cessation of menstruation. Women who run strenuously can be at higher risk of experiencing irregular or absent periods. The term athletic amenorrhoea has even been coined to describe the phenomenon.

Irregular periods

Cause: In years past, intense exercise was considered a possible sole cause of menstrual disturbances. But today, exercise is thought to be just one piece of a complex puzzle that typically involves a multitude of emotional and physical stresses. Training stress, performance pressure, low levels of body fat and inadequate intake of calories and nutrients are all possible contributing factors.

These elements and others create an equation of energy balance, and when the equation tips toward the negative – whether from running itself or from associated stresses – some women will experience menstrual irregularities. Young runners, those who train at intense levels and those with a history of menstrual irregularities are most prone to disturbances in their menstrual cycles. Other women are able to train at high levels and never experience such problems.

One of the most serious health consequences of amenorrhoea is osteoporosis. It happens because female hormones, which help protect the calcium in bones, are in shorter supply during amenorrhoea. An early onset of osteoporosis can lead to a greatly increased risk of stress fractures and acute fractures. And since decreased bone density is not easily reversed, those serious implications might last for the rest of your life.

An additional concern women runners might face is a lack of ovulation. Because a woman can menstruate even when she's not ovulating, the mere presence of a period is not a sufficient gauge of a healthy menstrual cycle.

Lack of ovulation

Cause: Lack of ovulation can signal insufficient levels of progesterone. A progesterone deficiency can lead to overstimulation of the uterine lining, putting you at risk for endometrial cancer. (Researchers disagree as to whether lack of progesterone alone also leads to loss of bone mass.)

If you suspect that you're not ovulating, track your temperature as if you were trying to get pregnant. A woman's body temperature is generally lower at the beginning of her monthly cycle and higher for the final couple of weeks. The increase in temperature occurs at the time of ovulation. To track this cycle, take your temperature first thing in the morning – before rising – with a basal temperature thermometer. (These are made for tracking the menstrual cycle and are sold in pharmacies.) If your results don't follow the above pattern, chances are that you are not ovulating. Complete lack of premenstrual symptoms, such as breast tenderness and cramping, is another clue. If your condition points toward any such abnormality, consult your GP to determine the cause and a course of action.

Treatment: If you suffer from any kind of menstrual disruption, whether amenorrhoea or lack of ovulation, investigate the cause with your gynaecologist. 'Athletes can never assume that menstrual problems are due to exercise,' says Dr Mona Shangold, co-author of *The Complete Sports Medicine Book for Women*. 'They are not immune to other problems. There might be other serious causes that have serious consequences.' Any condition that causes abnormal periods merits investigation, regardless of whether it's exercise related or not.

Although cutting back on training can help to restore some women's cycles, this shouldn't necessarily be your first or only response. If you're experiencing any menstrual abnormalities, consider the following steps:

✻ Track your periods, recording dates, duration of flow and any accompanying symptoms.

✻ Evaluate your diet, preferably with the help of a nutritionist. Make changes in your eating habits to ensure that the bulk of your calories are coming from healthy food sources, not from junk food. Be especially careful to take in enough calcium, protein and fat.

✻ See a gynaecologist to determine or rule out causes of menstrual irregularities not related to exercise. Discuss with your doctor whether hormone replacement therapy is an appropriate option for you.

✴ Evaluate your training to ensure that you're getting adequate rest and recovery and to make sure that you aren't showing other signs of overtraining, such as slowing times, mood disturbances, trouble sleeping and weight fluctuation.

Muscle Cramps

Muscle cramps can feel like anything from a slight twinge to a severe and debilitating bunching of a muscle. They can occur almost anywhere in your body.

Cause: Cramps are believed to be caused by a combination of dehydration, low electrolyte levels and possibly a lack of flexibility.

Treatment: Thoroughly warm up before and cool down after workouts. Stay well hydrated, drinking a sports drink that contains electrolytes if you are engaged in workouts that last more than 60 minutes. Engage in a regular stretching programme.

Osteoporosis

Running is a double-edged sword when it comes to this common and serious health issue for women. On one hand, weight-bearing exercise, such as running, can help build and maintain bone levels in women. On the other hand, thinness in general is a risk factor for osteoporosis, and women who run tend to be thin. Also, women who exhibit abnormal menstrual cycles, which can result from the combined physical and mental stresses of overtraining and disordered eating, can find that any positive effects on bones can be negated.

Cause: Several studies have shown that women who have disrupted menstrual cycles suffer more stress fractures than their counterparts with normal cycles. These women also typically exhibit lower levels of bone mineral density. Although it's generally accepted that hormone disruptions and premature loss of bone density are linked in female athletes, the cause-and-effect relationships are not clear. For example, some researchers theorize that the type of girl or woman who is drawn to intense athletic performance is more likely to experience and exhibit increased stress in all areas of her life and thus that her hormone levels might be affected even without the exercise. Similarly, women with lean body types might be more drawn to strenuous activity; they, too, might be prone to hormone fluctuations even without exercise.

Treatment: Experts agree that women must act to protect themselves from early-onset osteoporosis, which can leave a 20-year-old athlete with bones as brittle as those of a 50-year-old woman. It is particularly important because it's generally accepted that, once she is past her mid-30s, a woman can no longer build bone but only maintain her reserves.

If you train at an intense level, you should take every precaution to ensure that you're not losing bone mass. Eat a properly balanced diet: in addition to consuming all the important nutrients and calcium in particular, you should make sure that you're eating enough overall fat and calories to sustain your level of exercise. Also, monitor your menstrual cycle, watching not just for irregularities in your period but in ovulation as well. If you have abnormalities, consult your GP. He or she might recommend hormone replacement therapy.

It's also a good idea to have a bone-density test. New technology has made quick, simple screenings possible at a wider range of locations – from health fairs to race expos – and at a lower cost. These screenings, while fine for a general indication of bone health, should not be considered a replacement for a comprehensive analysis, which involves X-ray technology and must be done at a hospital or doctor's office.

Plantar Fasciitis

Most people can go their whole lives never knowing what a fascia is. Lucky for them. Plenty of runners learn all too painfully about these fibrous sheets of connective tissue, thanks to the ones in their feet. Plantar fasciitis manifests itself as pain on the bottom of your foot, usually directly under the heel. Although it starts slowly, the condition can become so debilitating that even walking becomes difficult. Pain tends to be worst in the morning, particularly during the first few steps out of bed.

Cause: The plantar fascia is a sheet of tissue that runs underneath the length of your foot and connects to the bottom of your heel bone. Because the fascia is not elastic, problems arise when other forces tug on it, meaning that something has to give. 'The plantar fascia is not designed to stretch,' explains Dr Shonka. 'It's a strong, thin band that is meant to help support your arch.' This means, he says, that when excessive pronation or an overly tight Achilles tendon and calf exert force, 'the plantar loses this tug of war'. The pain and injury come into play when the fascia is actually tugged away from the bony attachment at the bottom of your heel, causing degeneration of the collagen. In advanced cases of plantar fasciitis, X-rays show a spur extending from the heel bone where scarring has built up bony deposits.

Treatment: Once plantar fasciitis has set in, stretching, ice, anti-inflammatories and ultrasound can promote healing in the inflamed area. Also consider using a night splint. This device holds your foot in an upward flex while you sleep. Many runners once hobbled by the injury swear by this device, which works by keeping the calf stretched. It also eliminates the most damaging tugs on the foot early in the day.

Meanwhile, take action to reduce the root cause of the problem.

✽ Consider buying new shoes. Your old ones might simply be worn out and no longer provide adequate cushioning and protection, or you might require a model with more motion control to cut down on pronation.

✽ Have your biomechanics checked out by a podiatrist; you may need orthotics.

✽ Long-term treatment should include flexibility exercises for the calf of the afflicted foot, especially for its lower section. Take care during this therapy not to further tug and aggravate the fascia. When doing the against-the-wall calf stretch on page 230, relax your back foot and roll it to the outside, then lean into the wall to stretch the calf. It's important to keep the weight on the outside of your foot and not to let your foot roll inward. If it's done correctly, the stretch should be felt in the lower leg, not in the foot.

More serious treatments are available for stubborn cases of plantar fasciitis. Shock wave therapy, approved only a few years ago, has proven largely successful. However, it is painful, expensive and does carry a slight risk of nerve damage. Other more radical treatments such as corticosteroid injections and surgery should be reserved for the last resort if the other treatment options offer no relief after several months.

Razor Bumps

Irritated skin around the bikini line is an annoying side effect of running that some women seem more prone to than others.

Cause: Bumps or inflammation in this area usually result from plugged hair follicles, which are exacerbated by sweat and rubbing.

Treatment: When shaving this area of your body, always pull the razor *with* the direction of hair growth, recommends Dr Bergfeld. 'Shaving against the grain can bury skin detritus and other blockages in the follicle,' she explains. Regularly exfoliate the bikini area with a loofah to keep hair follicles clear.

If that doesn't work, investigate other forms of hair removal. Depilatories and lasers have the benefit of keeping hair away for longer periods of time.

No matter what method of hair removal you use, wait at least several hours or overnight before running, in order to allow any trauma to the skin to settle down.

Runner's Knee

You'll feel this discomforting ache around, under or in front of your kneecap.

Cause: Poor biomechanics is the primary cause of runner's knee, which is medically known as chondromalacia patella. When your kneecap is properly functioning, it glides up and down in a smooth groove of cartilage. When your kneecap gets pulled out of that groove and tracks improperly, the underlying cartilage is aggravated and begins to degrade. Overpronation of the foot is a leading cause of this mistracking because it leads to an internal rotation of the lower leg. Some sports medicine specialists believe overpronation – and thus runner's knee – can be particularly problematic in women, due to the greater quadriceps angle that results from their wider hips. An imbalance in muscle development can also contribute to the problem.

Treatment: Act at the first sign of trouble. Although at first it might seem possible to run through the pain, the discomfort eventually can become severely debilitating and repeated motion can make the injury worse. If it's detected early, runner's knee can almost always be solved with physiotherapy and proper attention to biomechanics. Since damaged cartilage does not heal, however, some advanced cases can require surgery.

Have a podiatrist perform a gait analysis to see if you need orthotics. Changing your shoe – typically to a more supportive model – and temporarily reducing intense training may also help. Don't run on cambered road surfaces; their slant can exacerbate pronation. Use ice and anti-inflammatories. Stretch your outer thigh using the thigh stretch on page 230, and strengthen your inner thigh with the squat exercise on page 240, to keep your kneecap tracking correctly.

Shinsplints

Much like the term *bone bruise*, *shinsplints* is a catchall slang term, not a real medical diagnosis. Runners use it to describe any pain between the knee and the ankle.

Cause: Rapid increases in training intensity. Shinsplints are most prevalent in less-trained and younger runners. Tibial fasciitis is one of the most common medical diagnoses when such shin pain does occur. This results from a tugging on the outer covering of the bone when the connecting muscle-and-tendon unit is overworked.

Treatment: Alleviate inflammation with ice. Stop doing speedwork and other intense training until the shin pain subsides. Pay attention to your biomechanical needs. That means getting orthotics if your feet tend to overpronate. Don't increase your training mileage or intensity too rapidly. It's also crucial to maintain flexibility throughout your calf and Achilles area. 'The interplay of calf and Achilles and foot arch are critical,' Dr Shonka explains. The tighter the calf and Achilles, the greater the tugging on connecting muscles and tendons.

Side Stitches

Sharp pains in your side or abdomen can come on suddenly and are usually felt just under the bottom of your rib cage as a sensation that makes it difficult to breathe. Stitches occur most commonly in novice runners and in more highly trained runners when they're exerting themselves to a point that exceeds their fitness level.

Cause: Side stitches are typically caused by cramping in the diaphragm.

Treatment: Stitches can almost always be alleviated immediately by stopping your run. If you don't want to stop, slow your running pace. Use your fingers to press into the stitch. Exhale forcefully when the foot on the opposite side of your body from where the pain is strikes the ground. (Inhale for three steps, exhale on the fourth, then inhale for three steps again, and so on.) To avoid stitches, warm up properly, breathe deeply from the belly while running and leave half an hour between eating or drinking and working out.

Skin Damage and Wrinkles

Left unchecked, environmental and physical factors can take their toll on your appearance. Skin cancers should be a serious consideration for any runner.

Cause: Sun and wind are the main factors you face that contribute to the ageing of skin, says Dr Bergfeld.

Treatment: You can minimize negative effects with these proper skin-care steps.

✳ Always wear sunscreen when you are running. Look for a product with an SPF of at least 15, UVA and UVB blocks, and water repellency so that sweat doesn't melt the sunscreen off your skin. If you're prone to acne, seek out gels and lotions; creams contain more oil.

✱ Moisturize with a good lotion after running and bathing. New products containing alpha-hydroxy acids, vitamins and retinols have been shown to reduce visible signs of wrinkling.

✱ Try to maintain a stable weight.

✱ Stay hydrated.

✱ Run early or late in the day, when the sun's rays are the least powerful.

✱ Wear a mesh baseball cap to reduce your face's exposure to sun.

✱ Look for running clothing made from new, high-tech fabrics that are formulated to provide extra sun protection. Check the label.

Stomach Upset

This is typically the bane of the beginning runner, but any runner can suffer from gastric distress from time to time. Although they're not dangerous, such stomach troubles can be painful enough to stop a run.

Cause: Stomach upsets usually result from eating the wrong foods or from eating or drinking too much shortly before a run.

Treatment: Although you can solve the problem by abstaining from food and drink for several hours before running, such fasting is ultimately not healthy, especially for runners who are doing workouts or races of several hours in duration. You can train your stomach to tolerate food and drink better, though. Start by abstaining from eating and drinking for several hours until you're able to run without trouble. Then gradually reintroduce food an hour or so before running. Start with only a few bites of bread and a few sips of water. Increase this amount incrementally until you're able to drink a glass of water and eat a small meal, such as a bagel or an energy bar, without gastric distress. Avoid spicy foods and those that are high in fibre.

Stress Fractures

Stress fractures in runners are found most commonly in the lower leg and foot, but they can also occur as high up as the pelvis. Although the metatarsals (the long, slim bones that make up the midsection of the foot) are most prone to fracture, any bone in the foot is susceptible.

Cause: Stress fractures tend to occur when training intensity is increased too quickly. 'Bone is constantly remodelling according to the stresses placed upon it,' explains Dr Shonka. 'When a runner gradually ramps up her mileage, bone strength increases in response to that stress. But when she does too much too soon, she can exceed the ability of her bone to adapt to stress.' Women with low bone density as a result of poor nutrition or irregular menstrual cycles can be at higher risk of stress fracture.

Treatment: In most cases, stress fractures begin as a break in the outer covering of a bone. Left unchecked, this can spread and eventually result in a complete fracture of the bone. Therefore, it is crucial to diagnose a stress fracture at the earliest possible time. Typically you'll sense a gradual onset

TRAINING LOG

My first serious running injury was a textbook case – not only the problem but also my reaction. My knee had become progressively more painful, but I didn't want to stop running. So I didn't. I simply ignored the problem, hoping each morning that it would be gone. It wasn't. My knee finally froze so completely that I could no longer run. That's when I got depressed. (Shocking!)

It's not uncommon for runners to react poorly to injury. Our fix has been taken away, and nothing else will do.

At the time, my injury seemed interminable. But doctors quickly diagnosed runner's knee, fitted me with orthotics to control my overpronation problem and got me up and running again. When I resumed training gradually, I was free of pain.

Having learned from that experience, I'm now prepared to be a better patient when the sidelines beckon. Rather than hoping for divine intervention, I take action. I cut my mileage at the first sign of trouble. I ice. I get massages. I see a doctor and then follow up with whatever treatment is necessary to solve the problem. In the meantime, I stretch, I swim, I lift weights.

But there's one more thing. Once I know that I'm doing everything possible to solve the problem, I let it go. I don't count the days until my next run. Instead, I garden. Read. Clean the house. Have lunch with a friend. In short, I do all the things I never have time to do when I'm training hard. Because as much as we'd like them to, fretting and sulking don't heal tissue and bone. Believe me – I've tried.

The interesting thing is that all of that activity and action make it hard to be too down, anyway. Taking control of the healing process blunts the sense of loss that typically comes with injury. And pursuing other activities is a healthy reminder that there is life beyond running. When I finally get around to training again, it feels that much sweeter.

of pain when you're developing a stress fracture. At the first sign of symptoms, consult with a podiatrist to confirm the presence of a fracture. Although a stress fracture generally won't show up immediately on X-rays, after approximately 10 to 14 days, evidence of bone growth on the injured site will be visible. Bone scans can confirm the injury right away, but the expensive process is not readily available and thus best left to runners who compete at a very high level.

The only cure for a fracture is time and rest, but that doesn't mean that you have to become passive and out of shape. Cross-training can maintain your fitness, provided that the exercise doesn't mobilize or exert force on the injured area. (Pool running is usually good because it generates no impact.) Be sure to eat properly, since inadequate nutrition – especially a lack of calcium – can slow healing.

Vaginal Itching

Some runners seem plagued by discomfort in this area, while others never have trouble.

Cause: During exercise, your groin area produces a large amount of sweat. Because it also tends to be poorly ventilated – think tights and cycling-style shorts – it is a prime location for bacteria production.

Treatment: As soon as possible after exercise, change out of sweaty running tights or shorts and shower with soap. Look for shorts and tights that have wicking fabric in the crotch panel. Try synthetics, such as high-tech forms of nylon and polyester, as opposed to cotton, which tends to hold onto moisture.

CHAPTER 17

Safety

SAFETY PROBABLY ISN'T THE FIRST THING ON MOST WOMEN'S MINDS WHEN THEY RUN. That's not necessarily a bad thing because despite one or two high-profile attacks on female runners in the UK over the last decade, your risk of such an encounter is reassuringly low. But you can further reduce your risk by being a smart runner. 'I want to encourage women to run, but I want them to be aware that there are potential dangers of running outdoors as a lone woman,' says Jo Walker from the Suzy Lamplugh Trust, a charity that campaigns to raise awareness about personal safety. 'It's important not to be complacent about those dangers. The more aware you are the safer you are likely to be.'

The issue of personal safety is controversial: no one wants to discourage anyone from doing something that is such a positive addition to their lives, but with more and more women running it's not something you can ignore. Most of the incidents women encounter while out running are verbal in nature, leading to no physical harm. But even catcalls and leers can contribute to a feeling of vulnerability, a feeling that women can and should work to minimize.

No activity is 100 per cent safe. And there are no actions that can create an absolute guarantee of security. According to Walker and other experts, though, a little precaution and a lot of common sense go a long way toward ensuring your safety on the run. As with every other activity you undertake, you'll make choices and judgment calls. Ultimately, those choices will depend on your own comfort level.

Most women still prefer to run alone, choosing not to sacrifice their personal time for the potential safety of running with a partner. They take other precautions, however, including varying their routes, carrying a personal alarm and making sure someone knows where they are running. 'We all take chances every day, and we all make choices every day,' Walker says. 'In the end they are not "right" or "wrong" but personal decisions. You can't go through any part of life without common sense, and that's what it boils down to.'

STACK THE ODDS

Here's a look at some of the most important precautions you can take when running.

Follow your intuition. Your first line of defence when faced with a questionable situation should be to follow your instincts. 'That feeling that something is wrong is there for a reason – it's there to protect you,' says Mike Finn, a former Metropolitan policeman and martial arts expert.

Use some common sense. Avoiding most incidents requires little more than basic common sense. You may have run around your local park a hundred times first thing in the morning, but is the same run a smart idea at 10 o'clock at night? 'Think about where you'd like to run and when. Then think again,' says Lee Sansum, a martial arts teacher and former bodyguard of Diana, Princess of Wales. 'Carry out a risk assessment of your run and think of yourself as a potential attacker would.' If you think it could be dangerous, it probably is.

'We're all conditioned to be polite at all costs,' Finn says, 'but if the hair stands up on the back of your neck, you should trust and act on that.' That means not being embarrassed to take action when something concerns you. If you're uncomfortable about somebody following you, change course, cross the road or pop into a shop.

Project a confident attitude. Your demeanour can become an important part of the safety equation. 'If you project a confident attitude that shows that you are aware of what is going on, you are less likely to become a victim,' Finn says.

'Potential attackers will detect vulnerability and weakness; they are looking for a victim they think will be an easy target. They are less likely to pick on someone who looks like they will be put up a fight. A lot of that is to do with attitude,' says Finn. He advises making eye contact with people you run past rather than running with your head down. A lack of eye contact could make you seem weak and vulnerable and it tells a potential attacker that you probably won't be able be identify them in a line-up because you didn't get a really good look at them.

Although some situations might call for a different response, it's generally important to look people in the eye so they know that you have seen them. Pay attention to details and identifying marks. 'You are not so much staring them down as you are basically looking at them as if to say, "I can identify you,"' Finn explains. More extreme measures might even involve action (moving away from a person) or verbal contact (telling somebody to move away from you). 'But being confident is the first step that might avoid everything else beyond that,' Finn says.

Pay attention to logistics. Of course, no matter what your demeanour and level of alertness, you should do everything possible to eliminate opportunities for trouble. Run during daylight hours, stay away from lonely areas and run with partners whenever possible. Avoid overgrown trails, and leave plenty of distance between you and bushes or parked cars.

Ditch the headphones. Okay, at least turn down the volume. Safety experts continually warn that one of the worst things you can do is run with headphones. By cutting off your sense of hearing, you put yourself at a disadvantage and eliminate your ability to react quickly.

Don't believe it? Experiments have been done in which a stranger was able to run up to women listening to their headsets and touch them from behind; the runners had no idea that a person was coming up behind them. 'With headphones, you are not aware of anybody approaching you,' says Finn. 'You can't hear a potential attacker or, for that matter, a dog or oncoming traffic. You have five senses; why cut one off? Would you run with a blindfold on?' That said, plenty of women would no more think of running without their music players than they would without their sports bras. If you must run with headphones, keep the volume low enough that you can hear what's going on around you.

Leave contact information. Tell someone in your household where you plan to run, or write down your planned route in your log. Carry identification and money or a credit card for a phone call while you run.

Run in familiar areas, but alter your route pattern. If you run the same route every day, your predictable pattern could be an invitation to an unwelcome interruption. Also avoid a pattern in which you run the same routes on the same days of the week – a pattern in which, for example, Tuesday is the day you run the park circuit. It's better to add more variety.

Leave the jewellery at home. This is especially true when travelling in new cities where you're not certain of the environment where you'll be running.

Ignore verbal harassment. It's very tempting to respond with a smart one-liner, but resist the temptation. Let catcalls and any other remarks go unanswered. Responding could escalate the situation.

Run against traffic. This is not only safer in terms of avoiding cars, but it also allows you to observe the passengers in oncoming vehicles and to spot trouble early.

Carry a personal alarm. Don't rely on these to bring help but they could scare off a potential attacker or provide the vital seconds you need to escape.

Be proactive. Report suspicious behaviour to the local police station. Your intuition can help determine when somebody is up to no good. 'There will be something that indicates to you that all is not right with the picture,' Finn says. It might be an out-of-place vehicle parked in the same spot for days, or a man watching people on the bike path, or somebody dressed for running who is not exercising.

'You hate to be suspicious of everybody, but, here again, you should trust your intuition,' says Finn. It might save somebody else a troubling incident down the road.

Learn to defend yourself. As in life, there are no guarantees of safety when you are running. Even if you follow all the preceding advice there is a still a possibility of being a victim of violent crime, albeit a very small one. If the worst should happen you should be prepared to defend yourself.

'You have to use all your physical tools to your advantage,' says Finn, 'running away should be your first thought to avoid the encounter because running is what you've trained to do. Even if that isn't possible keep that in front of your mind. Defending yourself doesn't mean fighting your assailant, it means disabling them long enough to make an escape. A well-aimed kick to the groin or knee would generally suffice but anything that creates that vital second or two you need is a good idea.'

Finn believes that completing a self-defence course is a good idea just to give you confidence although he's doubtful about the practical benefits of such a class. To be able to react in the right way quickly enough, you would need to commit to really learning a martial art. Lee Sansum agrees.

'When adrenaline floods your body, your fine motor skills are lost. You can't rely on quick moves you've learnt in a self-defence class,' he says, 'it has to become a habit.'

Finn further suggests that where you run and what you shout if attacked is important. 'Don't shout HELP, be specific about what's happening, and when you're running, run towards other people and activity not away from them. It's surprising how many people instinctively do the opposite.'

OTHER THREATS

Potential attackers might seem like the scariest threat, but in fact, you're statistically far less likely to encounter such a threat than you are to have a close call with a fast-moving car. The most likely potential hazards are so mundane we often don't stop to think about them. Here's a look at some of the most common threats and how to handle them.

Animals

Most of the time when you cross paths with a dog while you are running, the dog isn't likely to bite. He may annoy you by barking and destroying your serenity or by following too closely and making you feel as if he's going to trip you. But most dogs don't attack.

The problem is that you have no way of knowing when a barking annoyance will turn into a snapping menace. So the last thing you want to do is escalate the situation. Never yell or physically attempt to threaten a dog, says Dr Leslie Sinclair, author of *Ask the Vet About Dogs*. 'If you make a threatening motion, some dogs will back away, but others will escalate the aggression. And you never know which kind of dog you are dealing with.'

Dr Sinclair suggests that you take the following steps when dealing with a threatening dog.

✽ If you are approached, don't run away. It could prompt the dog to give chase.

✽ Stand still with your hands down at your sides.

✽ Back away slowly, still facing the dog.

✽ Avoid direct eye contact, which the dog might perceive as a threat, but do keep watch on him.

In most cases, a dog will lose interest, Dr Sinclair says. Should an attack occur, roll up into a ball on the ground. This action should help the dog lose interest and can protect you from harm. A personal alarm can be useful in alerting others that you need help.

Drivers

Try to avoid heavy traffic when possible. Besides the safety hazard, it's just plain unpleasant to breathe in vehicle emissions and to have to worry about cars. When you do find yourself faced with traffic, don't count on cars to do the right thing. Too many drivers are so busy doing other things –

talking on mobile phones, eating or looking at the scenery – that they don't pay attention to runners or other pedestrians until it's too late.

Some runners talk about running offensively as opposed to defensively. This means that you must be the one to make the first move to avoid trouble, rather than relying on a driver's judgment. Whenever possible, run facing traffic so that you can see what oncoming cars are doing. In addition to facing the oncoming traffic, you should keep an eye out for particularly hazardous driving manoeuvres – for example, when a car is aggressively overtaking another car by moving onto a road's shoulder and not looking out for runners. Or when a car is turning left and the driver looks only to the right, not seeing a runner coming from the other direction. Also be wary of people backing out of drives or pulling out of car parks and into traffic. Finally, wear reflective materials if you must run at night or in low-light conditions.

Terrain

Run cautiously when you're on uneven surfaces. Trails with rocks and tree roots can lead to twisted knees and ankles. Be especially careful running downhill on trails; acceleration can make it difficult to control your foot placement. Keep your eyes focused several feet in front of you so that you can anticipate the next few footfalls.

Be especially cautious when running on ice. Choose snow-covered sections of road when possible; they offer more traction than slick pavement. If you live in a place where the climate makes winter running predictably treacherous, consider buying some slip-on cleats for your running shoes (they're available at specialist running shops).

Although it might feel pleasant, it's best to avoid running barefoot, even on the grass or on the beach. Glass and other litter present a threat to your feet.

Weather

In many parts of the country, weather can be highly unpredictable. Since runners can be out on the road for several hours, it's possible for you to head out for a workout under sunny skies and end up in a hailstorm several miles from home. Even a small amount of protection can help keep you warm and dry if you get stuck in or decide to wait out a storm. If it's a season of changeable weather, tie a lightweight jacket layer around your waist before you leave the house. A baseball cap is a simple, easy bit of protection that can keep your eyes and face free of rain, hail and snow.

Should conditions turn downright dangerous, follow the common-sense rules that you would whenever you are outdoors.

TRAINING LOG

I do not feel 5 feet 2 inches tall when I run. I do not feel as if I'm 103 pounds. I do not feel like a red-haired freckle face. Okay, that's what I am. But inside I feel tough, and if someone decides to infringe on my revelry with their hostility, sometimes I feel like what I've instantaneously become: an angry runner.

For whatever reason, it's not hard to get an attitude when I run. I've seen my share of suspicious creatures, and when I do, I'd like to believe that I look at them as if to say, 'You've found the wrong target.'

Does this help? Who knows? I wonder myself. When it comes to safety, experts say that attitude has much to do with what comes your way. It's probably true to an extent.

That said, I've had my share of trouble: items thrown from moving cars, doors opened onto me from oncoming traffic, and yes, a man on the side of a deserted road exhibiting inappropriate behaviour. (For the record, none of these things happened in a large city or while I was travelling and running in unfamiliar terrain. They all happened on runs from home, in what would be deemed fine neighbourhoods.)

There's no doubt, such things can ruin a nice run. But I won't let them ruin my running.

I run smart, I pay attention, I run proactively, keeping an eye out for trouble and trusting my instincts. I vary my routes, I take note of number plates when something makes me nervous. But I don't follow all the rules. I have run at night – alone. I have run in strange cities, exploring unfamiliar areas. I have run with my iPod, although I don't crank the volume. I am fully aware as I do these things that I have increased my risk. And that, should real danger rear its head, all the attitude in the world may not help a 5-foot-2-inch freckle face.

The risks that I take are by choice and with understanding. I take them because without a certain level of choice in my life – whether in my running or in any other pursuit – I could not feel free. My choices might seem brash and foolhardy to some; to others they might seem prudish and meek. But they are right for me.

In the end, we must all find our personal level of comfort. We must be smart, educated and aware and take the precautions we choose. And then we must walk out the door and run to our heart's desire.

✳ **Lightning.** If lightning is still far off in the distance, try to get home by as short a route possible. If lightning is already near by, stop running. Take shelter in a building or under a roof. Do not stay outside in the open or under a tree, which could be a target.

✳ **Hail.** Although you can run through a brief shower of light hail, you'll want to take shelter if the storm turns ferocious. Hailstorms are usually brief, so you can probably take shelter for a few minutes and then run home when the storm eases up.

✳ **Ice storm.** When rain freezes underfoot, running can become dangerous. Should the footing become too treacherous, chances are that it won't be getting better anytime soon. Your best bet is probably to call it quits. Walk home if you are close, or use a nearby phone to call a friend for a lift. Don't discount ice as a mere nuisance – plenty of runners have suffered broken bones from falls on icy runs.

CHAPTER 18

The Well-Rounded Runner

ONE OF THE DIFFERENCES BETWEEN NEW RUNNERS and longtime runners is in their degree of devotion to the sport. When women first start to run, they find it understandably difficult to remain dedicated to a programme that has them running four times a week, week after week. But there's an invisible hurdle of regularity that runners eventually clear. For some women it only takes a few months, for others it might be a year or more before a run becomes as natural a part of the daily routine as showering. But natural it can become, and once she's cleared that hurdle, a runner might find that any other exercise tends to pale in comparison.

I mention this because plenty of serious runners simply stop engaging in other types of exercise altogether. Running is convenient, efficient, a great full-body workout. Once you become comfortable doing it, it's easy to feel as if running is the only exercise you want or need.

So why do anything else? You could just run. But it is healthier both physically and mentally to mix things up a bit, to become if not a multisport athlete, at least a well-rounded runner.

Spicing up your running routine with other sports and activities can stave off boredom, boost motivation and inspire you to take on new challenges. 'There's no reason to do the same thing over and over,' says biomechanics specialist and seven-time Ironman Triathlon champion Ray Browning. Browning says that he once added up all the activities he could do around the house that counted as 'working out' and arrived at more than 70. 'Some women like to work out in the gym with a trainer or with friends,' he says. 'For them, a more structured environment is great. Others tend to come from another perspective; they prefer to do exercises on their own and be creative.' For these women, cutting a hedge or mowing the lawn might develop all the upper-body strength they need.

It turns out that variety is actually good for us on a number of levels. Running is a terrific full-body workout, but our bodies tend to adapt to things quickly. That means that if all you do is run for 40 minutes 4 times a week, the gains you see in fitness eventually will level off. It also means you stand to benefit from a variety of activities: it's sort of like doing a new crossword puzzle every day to keep your mind sharp. New motions and activities keep your body constantly building muscle and modelling bone in new ways, even staying smart about balance.

The process of learning a new skill can prove to have value beyond the obvious physical aspects. 'To learn another skill, you really have to pay attention to how your body moves and think of what you're doing,' Browning explains. 'You then carry that same psychology back to running.' A runner often can't tell that she is tight in the shoulders, for example – even when her shoulders are scrunched up around her ears. But when the same runner takes up swimming, she can feel that tightness in the new activity. 'It boils down to the fact that we're more receptive when we're learning something.'

And then there's the fact that running itself provides less variety than a lot of other activities. When you run, you execute the same motion over and over again. There's little sideways movement, little up-and-down explosion. Meanwhile, there's plenty of tightening of the hamstrings and sometimes a weakening of the quadriceps. Abs get weak and backs get stressed. If your stride is less than biomechanically perfect – which is the case for most of us – little imperfections are multiplied thousands of times: feet roll in, knees bow out, hips tilt forward. All this can strain an assortment of muscles, tendons, ligaments and joints. Eventually that can lead to pain or even injury.

Complementing running with other activities – cross-training, strengthening, stretching and drills – can decrease your risk of injury by developing supplementary muscles and systems and also giving these overly taxed systems a break.

In addition to preventing injury, becoming more well-rounded will improve your performance and make running *feel* easier. Women runners often suffer from weak midsections, for instance. By shoring up core muscles with other activities, you can avoid slumping forward at the waist – a common mistake when fatigue sets in. Such an improvement in posture will not only keep lower-back, neck and shoulder pain at bay but will also enable superior pushoff for an optimal running stride.

So how well rounded do you need to become? *How much time will this take*, you might ask, glancing at your watch. It depends on your goals. All runners could stand to do some flexibility work year-round. Recreational runners could benefit from 2 strength workouts a week, while competitive runners might want to boost that to 3 and also add some drills. As far as cross-training, everyone could stand to mix it up with some other activity at least 1 day a week. Here's a closer look at each of those elements.

STRETCHING

Runners are notorious for barely being able to touch their toes, thanks to the tightening effects of the sport. But it's not inevitable that we deteriorate into an ever-progressive scrunch. Regular stretching improves flexibility and thus your range of motion.

Now, will this make you a better runner? Not necessarily. It's interesting that research has failed to prove conclusively a benefit from stretching in terms of actual injury prevention or improved race performance.

Nevertheless, most coaches and trainers do believe that stretching helps runners recover faster from workouts, reduces the incidence of injuries, and improves a runner's stride due to increased flexibility. Besides, the actual benefit of some things – think acupuncture, massage, dark chocolate – can be awfully difficult to quantify, but that doesn't mean they don't feel right. Ask any ageing runner – or any elderly individual, for that matter – if they wished they were more flexible, and you'll hear the same reply. Stretching is one of those things, as any cat would tell you, that just *feels* right.

The stretching programme in this chapter was developed in conjunction with four-time Olympian Colleen De Reuck, who recommends a similar programme to the women she trains. De Reuck believes a little time spent stretching is something that pays off over the long term: 'If we do more of it when we're younger, it will help us when we're older.'

She points out that runners are notorious for not stretching, admitting that she herself wasn't exactly diligent during her long successful racing career. That's why as a coach, she recommends a fairly quick series of stretches like the ones listed here, which can be done in almost any conditions. 'You can do these outside, right before and after the run,' she explains.

Before a run, stretching should be quite light and gentle as a preparation for 'cold' muscles. After a workout, when your muscles are warmed up, it's safer to engage in a deeper, more comprehensive stretch. When stretching, do not bounce and never force yourself beyond the point of comfort – stretching should never hurt. Rather, maintain a position at which you feel slight tension. If this becomes painful or difficult, back off slightly until you reach a point at which you can hold the position.

If you're injured and suspect you've pulled a muscle, don't try to stretch it. That will only make matters worse. Let the muscle rest for a few days before stretching that part of your body.

De Rueck recommends whenever possible during a stretch to alternate the stretch with a brief contraction of the muscles involved. 'It allows for a deeper stretch,' she explains. For example, you might hold a stretch for about 10 seconds, then contract the muscles or push against a point of resistance, and once more return to the stretch for another 10 seconds. In the exercises listed in this chapter, we've identified some places you can do this.

Once you're in a position, you'll often find that moving slightly to the left or right, higher or lower, stretches a slightly different muscle. The key is to maintain good form; otherwise, you won't be stretching the desired body part at all. For example, try to keep your back straight, but not rigid, when stretching your hamstrings and buttocks. Finally, listen to your body. Stretching should never be painful. If it is, you're pushing too far and running the risk of a pulled muscle.

Calf Stretch

Stand about one stride's length away from a wall. Put your palms against the wall. Position your left leg close to the wall, bending your left knee, and extend your right leg back. First, keep your right leg extended with knee straight and your foot pointed forwards. Lean into the wall. Make sure that your rear foot stays flat on the ground and that your ankle does not collapse inwards. Hold for a few seconds. Then, staying in position, raise up on your toes, and lower again, holding the stretch once more.

Next, slightly bend your right knee; you will feel the stretch lower down on your calf.

Switch legs and repeat.

Hamstring Stretch

Lie on your back. Raise your right leg off the floor as high as you can while keeping your knee straight. Gently use your hands to pull your leg towards your head. Do not raise your lower back off the ground. You should feel the stretch along the back of your upper leg. Hold with the muscle relaxed and stretched for about 10 seconds, then contract your hamstring to push against your hands for a few counts, and once more relax the muscle and stretch.

Switch legs and repeat.

While doing this stretch, you can also move your raised leg slightly to the left and then to the right to stretch different areas of the muscle. Some women like to wrap a rope or towel around the foot and gently pull on that for better control.

Thigh Stretch

Many runners stretch their quadriceps in a standing position, but they end up arching their back to a great degree, defeating the purpose of the stretch. This position ensures the stretch targets your quad muscles.

Roll onto your right side. Bend your bottom leg at the knee, bringing it towards your chest (1). Bend your upper leg at the knee, bringing your foot behind you. Holding that foot with your upper hand, gently pull it towards your bottom (2). Keep your back and trunk as straight as possible. You should feel the stretch in your quadriceps, along the front of your *top* leg. Hold for 10 seconds, then tighten the muscle of that top leg and push out against the resistance your hand is providing for a few counts. Relax once more and stretch for about 10 seconds.

Switch sides.

Hip and Buttocks Stretch

Sit on the ground with legs bent at the knee, feet on the ground. Place your arms behind you for balance, your palms flat on the ground pointed behind you. Raise your right leg and cross it so that your right ankle rests just above and on top your left knee(1). Now push your bottom up off the ground (2), bending at the waist and using the weight of your body to adjust the stretch.

Switch legs.

Hip and Core Stretch

Position yourself in a lunge, so that your left leg is in front of you slightly bent at the knee and your right leg is extended straight behind you, your foot flat on the ground. Your left kneecap should be positioned directly over your foot. Lift your right arm, stretching it up and also rotating slightly towards your left side, opening up your core and hip area. (1)

Lower your arm, and place hands on the ground on either side of your forward foot. Allow your back leg to slide further back and gradually lower your hips towards the ground. (2)

Switch and repeat with other side.

Buttocks and Lower-back Stretch

Lie on your back, bending your right leg at the knee. Cross your left leg in front so that your left ankle rests above your right knee (1). Keep your foot on the ground, but slowly drop both legs towards the right (2). Keep both shoulders on the ground and try to keep as much of your back flat on the ground as possible. Switch legs and repeat on your left side.

Inner Leg and Groin Stretch

Sit on the floor with your knees bent and feet with soles pressed together. Hold on to your feet with your hands, and drop your knees towards the floor. Lean forwards at the waist, keeping your back straight, to intensify the stretch.

Hip and Waist Stretch

Stand with your arms at your sides and your legs spread about 1 metre apart. Bend at the waist towards your left and slide your left hand down your leg gradually as far as it can comfortably go, meanwhile raising your right arm straight towards the sky. Keep your body aligned facing forwards, bending neither forwards nor backwards. Switch sides.

Abdominal Stretch

Lie on your stomach on the floor, with your legs hip width apart. Place your palms down on the floor just outside your shoulders (1). Straighten your arms as you raise your upper body off the ground, arching your spine and stretching your abdominal muscles (2).

Back Stretch

Kneel on the floor (1). Drop your buttocks to your feet, and slowly drop the rest of your body forwards. Let your chest relax towards your knees while stretching your arms straight in front of you, palms on the floor (2).

STRENGTH TRAINING

Strengthening exercises are an important part of any runner's conditioning, says De Reuck. 'Runners think, "Oh, I run with my legs . . . I don't need to do anything more." So when they lift weights, they only do upper body and core.'

But De Reuck and many other running coaches *do* recommend leg strengthening. Running is highly repetitive, so the same muscles get stressed in the same way over and over. There is also virtually no lateral, or side-to-side, movement, which you might experience with in-line skating or tennis. Leg strengthening can help address muscle imbalances that might lead to injury. In addition, distance running builds the muscles for endurance, but not necessarily power. More intensive weight strengthening adds power to the legs, which translates to speed.

De Reuck recommends going to the gym twice a week. She advises her serious runners to lift weights on days of hard training, such as intervals. That means the intense training is happening on the same day, allowing the body to truly recover on easy days of jogging. Recreational runners who are jogging several days a week can add the two sessions whenever it's most convenient.

If you're a recreational runner, you can maintain the same strength-training programme year-round. Competitive runners should consider concentrating their strength exercises in the winter or off-season, boosting the frequency to 3 times a week during this base-building phase. As spring and summer approach and the running workouts intensify, it's time to back off from the heavy lifting. Cut the frequency of weight workouts to twice a week so you'll be fresh and sharp on the track and when you race. Your goal at this point is not to build more strength but to maintain what you have. If you do track sessions or other quality workouts, be sure to do drills or weights on these hard training days. Otherwise, you'll be making your easy running days needlessly hard on your muscles.

The programme here is adapted from the one that De Reuck recommends to her runners of all abilities. You don't need to use every machine at the gym or spend an hour a day there to develop strength and stability. Remember, your goal is to complement your running, develop balanced muscle groups and avoid injury – not to chisel yourself into a bodybuilder.

'The important thing is progression,' De Reuck says. 'When something becomes easy, it's time to adapt the exercise so that your muscles keep getting challenged.'

When starting your strength-training programme, keep these tips in mind:

✱ Do each exercise in sets of 15 repetitions.

✱ Choose a weight or resistance that you can complete comfortably but not easily for 15 repetitions. Your last repetition in each set should feel difficult to accomplish, but not so hard that your form deteriorates.

✱ When you can easily complete 15 repetitions of an exercise, it's time to increase the weight or resistance.

✱ Complete 2 or 3 sets of each exercise. If you're a complete novice at the gym, adopt the programme very gradually to avoid intense muscle soreness. That means starting with 1 set of each exercise and building up to 2.

✱ Alternate leg exercises with upper-body exercises. This allows different muscle groups to recover without standing around waiting.

✱ Maintain good form. Be careful to work only the body parts specified, rather than helping them out with the rest of your body. For leg and arm exercises, keep your back in a neutral position, bent neither forwards nor backwards. Consider hiring a personal trainer to check out your form for a session or two at home or at the gym.

Squat

BEGINNER:

Stand with your feet shoulder width apart and your arms stretched out in front of you for balance (1). Bend your knees and lower your buttocks slowly towards the floor. Stop once your thighs are parallel to the floor. Keep your back straight and your head up (2). Return to a standing position and repeat 15 to 20 times.

AS YOU PROGRESS:

Hold a weighted barbell resting gently on your shoulders and perform the same squat. Increase the weight of the bar over time when you can comfortably complete 15 repetitions.

Leg Curl

BEGINNER:

Use a hamstring/leg-curl machine at the gym. Lie face down on the bench, position the cushion on the back of your legs, between ankle and midcalf, as comfort dictates. Raise the weight with both legs, then slowly lower it with one leg only, alternating sides. (This will address strength differences between your two legs and will ensure that the stronger leg won't overcompensate for the weaker one.)

AS YOU PROGRESS:

Lie on your back on the floor and place both legs straight in front of you, with your ankles resting on top of an exercise ball. Raise your bottom off the ground (use your hands on either hip to balance), keeping your body in a straight line. Slowly roll the ball in by bending your legs at the knee. Be sure to keep your hips and back still and straight. Roll the ball back out, and repeat. Looking for something even harder? Hold one leg out to the side and roll the ball in with just the other leg.

Walking Lunges

BEGINNER:

'Walk' slowly across the gym or a flat stretch of ground by lunging with alternate legs: lunge forwards with one leg, then straighten to standing and lunge forwards with the next leg. Be sure your front shin remains perpendicular to the ground; your knee should not extend past your foot.

AS YOU PROGRESS:

Hold a barbell behind your head resting lightly atop your shoulders. For more of a challenge, try this: Each time you lunge, press the barbell up towards the sky, returning it to your shoulders as you straighten to a standing position.

Calf Raise

BEGINNER:

Stand on the edge of a step. Rest a hand on a railing or wall for balance. Let your heels drop slightly (1) and then raise them to a level position (2). Once you can easily do the exercise with both feet, switch to doing it with one foot at a time.

AS YOU PROGRESS:

Use a calf machine at the gym to add resistance weight to this exercise. Rise up on both legs, then lower yourself on one leg.

Press-up

BEGINNER:

Stand at a sofa, table or other stable object at roughly hip height and place your hands flat on the surface. Take a large step back so your legs are extended straight behind you, feet flat on the floor. Bend your arms at the elbows and lean in, keeping your body in a straight line, then extend your arms straight again.

AS YOU PROGRESS:

When you're ready, there's no better exercise for your core and arms than the classic press-up. Lie face down on the floor with your hands resting palms-down beside your shoulders. Keep your back and legs in a straight line as you push your palms into the floor to raise your body. Once your arms are straight, slowly lower yourself back to the starting position.

Triceps Dips

BEGINNER:

Sit on the edge of a heavy, stationary chair or bench. Put your palms on the front edge of the seat, beside your bottom. As you use your arms to support your body weight, bring your buttocks forwards, off the chair (1). Then slowly lower your bottom towards the floor until your arms are bent at a 90-degree angle (2). Push yourself back up and repeat.

AS YOU PROGRESS:

Place a medicine (weighted) ball in your lap to increase the resistance.

Back Extensions

BEGINNER:

Kneel on hands and knees. Raise and extend one arm forwards and the opposite leg (for example, your left leg and right arm) back, lengthening your body in a line. Hold in place for up to a minute, then switch to extend the other arm and leg.

AS YOU PROGRESS:

Lie on your stomach, arms extended straight in front and legs extended straight back. Arch your back slightly, and 'kick' both arms and both legs in a freestyle-swimming motion for up to a minute.

Abductor Walk

Use elastic exercise bands or tubing for this exercise. Stand and place the tubing around both ankles so that your feet feel resistance when they're more than 15–30 cm apart. Walk sideways first in one direction, then the other.

You can also do this exercise walking forwards and then backwards, keeping the resistance around your ankles. (You might need to shorten the tubing for this.)

Adductor Swing

Use elastic exercise bands or tubing for this exercise. Stand with your legs hip width apart. Anchor the tubing low to a solid unmovable object, such as a couch leg or a post. Loop resistance tubing around one leg. Swing the leg with tubing across the supporting leg, pulling it away from the anchored point of resistance. Let it swing gently back and repeat. Switch legs and repeat.

Upper Abdominal Crunch

BEGINNER:

Lie on your back, knees bent and feet flat on the floor. Cross your arms in front of you and rest them lightly on your chest. Keeping the small of your back flat on the floor and your face pointed up towards the ceiling, bring your shoulders off the ground (1). Without letting your shoulders touch the ground, pulse slowly up and down without resting, counting off each pulse for a total of 20. For best results, do 1 set of 20 crunches like this straight up and down, and then twist your trunk slightly to the left and the right for 1 set of 20 total (2).

AS YOU PROGRESS:

Hold a weight to your chest while doing the same exercise.

Lower Abdominal Crunch

Lie on your back, knees bent and feet flat on the floor. Cross your arms in front of you and rest them lightly on your chest. Raise your upper body off the ground to the point at which your shoulder blades no longer touch the floor. Keeping the small of your back flat on the floor, curl several centimetres further forwards (1). Lower yourself by only a few centimetres, not letting your shoulder blades return to the floor. Pulse up and down in this manner by a few centimetres for the first set of 20, then twist your trunk slightly to the left and the right for 1 set of 20 total (2).

AS YOU PROGRESS:
Hold a weight to your chest while performing the same exercise.

More Abdominals

Lie on the floor, with shins resting on an exercise ball. Push arms straight up into the press-up position. Bend your knees and slowly roll the ball by pulling your knees towards your chest. Extend legs to roll the ball back, and repeat.

Running with Dumbbells

This is an excellent strengthener for arms and core that specifically targets the muscles you use during running, and it can even improve your running form. Hold dumbbells of a comfortable weight in each hand. (Most women will want to start with about 2.5 kg in each hand.) Stand in place, with one leg forward, knees slightly bent. Without moving your legs, swing your arms the way they'd move naturally while you run. Count to 50 repetitions, then switch so that your other leg is forward and do 50 more.

Do this exercise in front of the mirror and watch for the following: keep elbows bent at roughly 90 degrees. Your trunk should not rotate. Don't let your shoulders shrug up towards your ears; make sure they stay relaxed. Your hands should not pass an imaginary centre-line in front of your body. By observing these elements, you'll have proper form – and be that much more likely to hold yourself in alignment when training and racing.

Squat Thrusts

Place your hands on the ground in press-up position, and extend one leg behind you, with the other leg bent and tucked under your chest. Keeping hands and arms still, 'run' with your legs, jumping them to switch positions forwards and back, forwards and back. Begin with a comfortable number of repetitions – 10 to 20 – and build up to 50 from there.

DRILLS

Although they sound tough, drills are the same silly hopping, skipping and jumping exercises you knew and loved as a child.

Drills force you to develop both sides of your body equally, calling into play both large and small muscle groups, says Diane Palmason, a world-record holder in the 60-plus age group and former director of a series of women's running camps. Palmason, who coaches women of all abilities, encourages runners to do drills on a regular basis. 'Drills are an exaggeration of the motions you use in the act of running,' she explains. 'They develop strength specific to running patterns, where you transfer weight from one foot to another.'

Although you don't actually hop while you run, a hopping drill can develop your push-off strength. That power will then translate to a longer stride when you run. Other drills develop your buttocks and hamstrings, counteracting what Palmason calls runner's shuffle. 'You see a lot of runners using a very sloppy style, shuffling along and relying on their quads to drag themselves forwards. But if you have strength in the back of your leg, then you can pick up that leg and move it forwards in a more efficient range of motion.' Still other drills develop the muscles along the sides of your legs

Pool Running

To be honest, pool running isn't for the faint-hearted. It's repetitive and monotonous, and unlike running, you don't get a change of scenery to keep you engaged and entertained. But, for serious runners who insist on maintaining fitness when they're injured or want to prevent injury, pool running can be a godsend, saving fitness freaks from losing their hard-won conditioning and falling into outright depression.

Although you can pool run without a flotation device, you'll probably feel more comfortable using a buoyancy vest designed to keep you afloat and in the correct upright position. To find out more about pool running and where to buy the kit, visit www.aqua-running.co.uk.

When running in the water, keep your body erect. Try as hard as you can to approximate your road-running posture. The biggest mistake runners make in the water is leaning forwards from the waist, which results in more of a crawl than a run. When you run correctly in the pool, you don't cover a lot of ground. Rather, you'll move forwards at a very gradual rate.

that tend to absorb the shock of running. 'And,' she adds, 'unlike with weightlifting, you're doing the work in a dynamic way. That means that you develop all the tiny muscles in the foot and ankle.'

For best results, do drills twice a week. If you do them only once a week, you'll be starting from scratch each time. Worse, you'll feel sore after each session because your body will never quite adapt. Start with a few minutes and build up to 10 minutes or so in total, doing each drill for 50 to 100 metres.

Drills are best performed on a smooth surface with some give that will minimize impact. A grassy field is perfect. Palmason encourages you to adapt such exercises, changing the drill session each time. 'Just be sure that whatever you're doing, you're focusing on good form and extension. There's no point in doing sloppy drills. Other than that, do what feels good to wake up those muscles, get that bounce into your step,' she says. Be creative: leap from side to side, jump over low things; think of the things you did as a child. For optimal benefits, mix flexibility exercises into the strength drills to counteract tightening. For example, follow a skipping exercise with a 'rag-doll' run in which you let your arms flop limply at your side. And be sure to stretch gently after the session.

Just as you would on the road, you can vary the intensity of your workout by varying the pumping frequency of your stride. In fact, due to the monotony, you'll probably find pool running most enjoyable when you play around with different 'speeds'. Bear in mind that 'speed' while pool running refers to your stride rate, not to your movement forwards. Some runners do whole interval workouts in the water, with an easy warmup, then a workout alternating hard, fast pumping with rest intervals, and finally a cooldown. Just don't attempt to base your workout on a heart rate: the cooling effect of the water will keep your heart rate slower than on land.

While the resistance of the water gives you an intense strength as well as endurance workout, it can tire you out. The harder and faster you try to stride, the greater the force of the water working against you. Don't be surprised if you tire quickly the first few sessions. Build up gradually as you would with any new activity.

Bounding

Run slowly with a greatly exaggerated stride. Concentrate on the push-off motion with each foot. Try long bounding, where you see how far you can leap with each stride. Then try high bounding, where you try to jump as high as you can with each stride. Speed does not matter. The slower you go, the better your push-off will be. Use your arms in an exaggerated manner, pumping high in front of and behind you.

High-Knee Run

Run quickly with light steps, lifting each knee as high as possible. Don't worry about how much ground you cover.

Buttocks Kick

Run quickly as you try to hit your bottom with your heels. Don't worry about how much ground you cover.

Striding

Run in a slow, exaggerated motion, pumping your arms and leaping from leg to leg to make your stride as long as possible.

Sidewinder

Run sideways, placing your rear leg first in front of and then behind the lead leg. Switch sides and lead with the other leg.

Hopping

Hop on one leg for several steps, then hop on the other. Switch back and forth every 10 steps or so.

CROSS-TRAINING

Cross-training is a term that can mean just about anything. If you run 4 times a week, cycle with your family at the weekend and swim 1 morning with friends, you're cross-training. Used loosely, the term applies to any sport or exercise that supplements your primary sport.

While the term sounds a bit clinical, you don't have to cross-train rigorously or even that formally to get results. That means that when you're engaging in your supplementary sports, you needn't worry about intervals, workouts or scientific terminology. One of the points of cross-training is to offer you a complete rest from the rigours of your primary sport. That means giving both your mind and your body a rest.

Everyone from the recreational fitness jogger to the professional can benefit from some break in the routine of her running programme. This applies to both a micro-level – taking a day off from running to swim – and a macro-level – taking a month off after a marathon or a hard racing season to let tired legs fully recover. Older runners especially swear by mixing other sports in with running to reduce stress on their bodies.

The activities you choose for cross-training ultimately depend on your goals and needs as a runner. Here are some options:

❋ If you want to develop seldom-used muscles, gravitate to sports that focus on lateral (side-to-side) motion and upper-body strength. To develop your inner thighs, arms and trunk, look to activities such as Pilates, in-line skating, tennis, squash, basketball and martial arts.

❋ If you want stress release, look to activities such as swimming and rowing. Both are relaxing and provide a non-weight-bearing break in the routine. They're also quiet, meditative activities that produce a mindset similar to that of running.

❋ If you want to become faster, weight training, drills and activities that are closely related to running, such as cross-country skiing are best. Some runners swear by the benefits of cycling. They say that it's an intense leg strengthener that at the same time allows your joints to rest from running's impact for a day. Other runners feel that cycling further tightens already taut leg muscles. They think that cycling can overdevelop your leg muscles in a way that interferes with your running performance. Most runners who find cycling beneficial are older runners looking to reduce stress on their joints.

The bottom line: choose a sport or activity that you love. 'The main criterion when choosing another activity to supplement running – or any fitness programme – is to pick something you find fun,' Browning says. 'It should make you giggle, feel great when you walk back in the door. It shouldn't be another chore. It's less important to tie it in to running than to be sure that it provides a mental break.'

And that holds true for the jogger and the elite racer alike. In fact, Browning says that while the hard-core runner may obsess about the performance benefits of her cross-training, she's often the one who could most benefit from a mental break in her routine.

TRAINING LOG

Inspired by my multitalented friends, I decided to break one summer's running ennui by racing my first triathlon. *I'm in good shape,* I thought, *How hard could it be?* Here's how hard: after performing well in the running leg (unlike most triathlons, this course put the run first and the swim last), I plodded along with my underdeveloped quads as 500 cyclists swarmed past me. I wasn't in dead last yet. No, that milestone occurred when an 11-year-old boy passed me as I flailed in the water during the swim. While the other competitors ate bananas, I swallowed post-race humble pie.

Running will make you fit, all right, but it's not the only game in town. I faced a decision after that race: do I attempt to branch out and master this triathlon thing or stick to running? For me, the answer was clear. Running was my true love, and I would remain a runner. I resigned myself to the fact that I'd never be breaking the wind for anyone on a bike ride and that my swimming is at best a survival skill. But the race did point out the imbalances in my body. Afterwards, I began to do more strength training and flexibility work to ensure that I was fit in a well-rounded manner.

Not everyone needs to be a multisport athlete. Some personalities like to delve deeply into one area, while others prefer a smattering of different stimuli. Both can be well-rounded. You are a well-rounded runner if you're aware of your body's strengths and weaknesses. You are a well-rounded runner if you work to develop your fitness in a holistic, enjoyable way. You are a well-rounded runner if you're strong yet supple. And if you can complete a triathlon without someone offering you swimming lessons along the course, well, that's just icing on the cake.

If you're a recreational runner, supplement your 3- or 4-day-a-week running programme with 2 or 3 days of other activities. If you're a competitive runner, maintain your 4 to 6 days of running per week. During the off-season, you can let a rigorous cross-training session such as cycling take the place of a quality workout. During a sharpening or racing phase, however, keep cross-training at a lower intensity and substitute it 1 or 2 days a week for an easy run or an off day.

CHAPTER 19

The Pregnant Runner

LAURIE COULDN'T WORK OUT WHY SHE WASN'T RUNNING FASTER. 'Here I was racing at sea level after training at altitude, and I didn't feel any faster,' she recalls. 'I'd just gone for a run with a friend and I was telling her how rubbish I felt: sluggish, heart racing, just tired. She thought she recognized my symptoms. We were at the train station and she made me go straight to the chemist and buy a pregnancy test. We checked it right there in the ladies' room, and sure enough, I was pregnant!'

Other than the part about the train station, Laurie's experience is similar to that of many women runners. Because the sport teaches you to listen to every message from your body, runners often receive the first clues about their pregnant condition from their workouts. Something may simply feel amiss. Your pulse may race, you may breathe more heavily or you may have to work harder to hit the same times. After a few days – or weeks – of wondering what's wrong, all the pieces fall into place when you take a pregnancy test and find out that you're running for two.

Although doctors used to frown upon exercise for pregnant women – especially upon weight-bearing activities such as running – today, many experts consider exercise healthy for both you and your unborn child. A body of research shows that women who exercise through their pregnancies tend to have fewer physical complaints and fears, feel more positive about their pregnancies, retain a better self-image, be more prepared for labour, have a decreased incidence of Caesareans and recover more quickly after delivery.

The physical benefits of running include a reduction in the discomforts associated with pregnancy, including backache, bloating, constipation and swelling. One study shows that women who exercise during pregnancy are 35 per cent less likely to suffer pre-eclampsia (dangerously high blood pressure).

Of course, a woman who exercises during her pregnancy will also retain more muscle mass, so her trip back to fitness after childbirth should be faster and easier. In addition, it's believed that exercise can translate into a more consistently upbeat mood, better sleep and an increase in energy levels – all challenges during pregnancy.

Dr Douglas Hall, an obstetrician who specializes in developing workout programmes for expectant mothers, explains that because exercise can counteract some of the debilitating effects of pregnancy, it results in a better experience in terms of the bigger picture of giving birth. 'Women who work out during their pregnancy overall have a better, more positive pregnancy experience,' he says. 'They take control of the process instead of the pregnancy controlling them.'

Gina, a recreational runner who competes in 5-Ks and 10-Ks for fun, attests to the positive results. After having experienced some rough going in her first trimester, she forced herself out for a brisk walk or jog, even though it seemed counterintuitive. 'Exercising was like a miracle drug for me,' she says. 'It got my digestive system moving and helped relieve the painful wind I was suffering from. It took the edge off the nausea (although it didn't cure it) and it helped me sleep better each night.'

Because of the tremendous number of variables that go into each pregnancy, it's harder to measure the impact of exercise on the foetus. Experts agree, however, that no research indicates that moderate exercise is harmful to a developing foetus, provided that you don't exercise to exhaustion and that you heed any warning signs from your body. Indeed, babies born to mothers who exercise can reap the benefits of a mum who took the time to care for herself. 'A woman who exercises through her pregnancy tends to take an active role overall in her health, instead of taking the attitude, *I'm just trying to get through this.* And that can make a difference to the child,' Dr Hall says. 'Babies don't come out a blank canvas. They reflect what their mothers have put into the pregnancy already.'

Even with a go-ahead from the medical community, you'd be correct to have countless questions and concerns: how much is too much? Will my body temperature or breathlessness harm the foetus? How do I know if I'm hurting my baby?

The first answer to all of those questions is to relax. Your body has an amazing array of adaptations that protect your growing child against harm. The second answer: listen to your body during pregnancy. Listen constantly and listen carefully. Although your body gives off warning signals during exercise to ensure the safety of the foetus, it's up to you to heed the messages that are being sent.

INITIAL REACTION

If you've been trying to conceive, discovering that you're pregnant is joyous news indeed. But for some women, especially serious runners, the first reaction might not be so clear-cut. After years of enjoying the fringe benefits of running – time to themselves or time socializing, improving fitness and a trim figure – it's no wonder some women are ambivalent when they find out they're pregnant.

The Mother's Safety

While your primary focus at this time is naturally on the health of your growing baby, be aware that the changes in your body have implications for you as a runner as well:

⮞ Hormones produced during pregnancy to prepare the pelvis for delivery serve to relax the body's connective tissue. The result is a temporary hypermobility in the joints.

⮞ The pregnant woman's blossoming belly shifts the body's centre of gravity, affecting balance and stability.

⮞ Added weight stresses the back, as well as muscles and joints in general.

Does this mean you're at a greater risk of injury if running during pregnancy? A British study that reviewed research on the matter did not find any increase in joint injuries or falls among pregnant runners. It did conclude nevertheless that loss of balance and joint stability do warrant a greater degree of caution. Be aware and run with focus, especially if you're running on a trail or other uneven surface.

Laurie, who became pregnant at the age of 28, had the reaction of a runner who dearly loved competing. 'I'd just been getting back into good racing shape. In fact, I'd just travelled to go on a racing circuit, and I was really fit at the time,' she recalls. 'So to be honest, my first reaction was, I can't believe this is happening! I was shocked. I wasn't unhappy; I just didn't know how to feel. After a short while, I was thrilled, but my first reaction was definitely, *I don't know how to react!*'

She's not alone. The value placed on career, independence and even thinness in our culture mean that pregnancy can be a loaded emotional issue. For athletic women, questions can be compounded. Because those feelings of ambivalence can be a great source of guilt, it can be comforting to realize you're not alone. Above all, don't berate yourself if you find that your first reaction is one of fear, uncertainty or disappointment. Take comfort in the fact that – provided that other variables in your life are favourable – such extrinsic reservations about the pregnancy typically disappear within a few weeks.

'I had been working very hard to get in shape when I found out that I was pregnant,' says Mya, who was 29 when she had her first child. 'But I couldn't be disappointed. I knew that I could still run well later. You look at other women and see that they regain their old fitness and even more.'

A SHIFT IN PRIORITIES

When you become pregnant, your running goals should change overnight. If weight control or faster times were a priority before, they shouldn't be anymore. You might have been pushing yourself to the limits of fitness before, but now you simply want to pamper yourself for optimal health, well-being and relaxation.

'The women who have a hard time are those who retain the idea that they must be as fit as possible,' says Dr Hall. 'During pregnancy, you want to be as strong as *necessary* but not as strong as *possible*. It can be hard for an athletic woman to change her goals suddenly, because she won't feel like she is doing enough. But it's a very important distinction.'

Here are some ways to help you change focus.

Pamper yourself. Instead of dreading the weight gain, fitness loss and discomforts of pregnancy, look on the bright side. You have a good excuse to indulge completely in your well-being. Appreciate it while it lasts. In fact, these 9 months can be a time to develop good health habits that you can carry beyond pregnancy. With your baby's health foremost in your mind, you might, for instance, begin eating correctly and getting enough sleep for the first time in your life. 'When you are pregnant, you take such good care of yourself,' says Nadia Prasad, an Olympian and 1995 French national 10,000-metre champion who has run through 3 pregnancies. 'Your runs then become such times of celebration and joy.'

Just get out there. Symptoms during the first trimester can make exercise sound less than joyous for some women. Nausea, exhaustion and dizziness make it tough to function, let alone run. Most women say that running during the first few months of pregnancy is even more difficult than running during the final months before delivery. But they all agree that mustering the wherewithal to get out the door – even if it's for only a little bit of exercise – is just the thing to boost your energy.

'I was lucky; I didn't have many symptoms. The only thing that affected my running was that I was so tired,' Mya says. 'But running helped that because it gave me a burst of energy. If you're running before you become pregnant, don't stop. It will help give you energy and let you feel more in control.'

Give your training diary a rest. Ah, control. You'll quickly learn to go with the flow. Planning workouts, especially in the first trimester, can be a lesson in futility. One day can differ from the next dramatically in terms of energy levels and other factors that affect running, such as heart rate, blood pressure, breathlessness and dizziness. It's hard to ignore the demands of the little one growing inside you, and in fact, you shouldn't try. Consider those symptoms to be signals telling you to take it easy.

'For some women, the experience can be frustrating because they can no longer run at the level they desire,' says Judy Mahle Lutter, co-author of *The Bodywise Woman*. 'But it's time to listen to your body and be wise.'

Lutter's own daughter was disappointed because discomforts kept her from exercising to the extent that she wished during pregnancy. 'As with so many women, she found that she needed to stay active because that's who she is. Working out was a stress reliever.' It's easier to continue, Lutter says, when you understand that the usual rules don't apply. 'Understand that things will happen – you'll get a backache or something else that a run might ordinarily help – and now the run is making it worse. If things don't feel good, that's probably reason to stop for the time. But that doesn't mean that you have to give up on exercise entirely.'

LISTEN TO YOUR BODY

What's an appropriate level of effort for running during pregnancy? When you're running for two, it's helpful not to look at this as a matter of miles or pace. Instead, here's your new goal: you don't want your developing baby to have to compete with your exercising body. Not for adequate blood flow, not for oxygen delivery, not for fuel. That means moderation is your new guide.

Amazingly, your pregnant body will help you, as its natural adaptations lessen the possibility of training to the point of risk. Several studies have shown that most pregnant women will naturally stop or slow down in a workout before they reach a point of dangerous intensity. Since your core temperature rises during pregnancy, for example, you'll feel overheated and uncomfortable earlier in your workout, making you more likely to back off. Likewise, the elevated heart rate of early pregnancy will force you to run more slowly.

Follow these guidelines to keep your baby safe.

Stay at a moderate level of exercise. Let your perceived level of exertion be your guide. Don't run to the point of breathlessness or overheating. When in doubt about the intensity level of your running workouts, err on the side of caution. Keep in mind, however, that most of the medical community thinks that exercise at a moderate intensity poses no risk to your baby if you are already used to such workouts. And while moderation is clearly well advised, much of the counsel offered to pregnant women in this regard is rooted in common sense as opposed to science. For example, according to the Royal College of Obstetricians and Gynaecologists, exercise is safe for both mother and foetus during pregnancy and studies support initiating or continuing exercise in most pregnancies to derive health benefits associated with activity.

Don't worry about past actions. If you, upon discovering that you are pregnant, remember with horror an intense speed workout or long run that you did unintentionally beforehand, relax. Just like those one or two glasses of wine you might have had before you realized that you were pregnant, a few harder workouts shouldn't have hurt you. Once again, your body is likely to have signalled you to slow down before allowing you to hit a level that could be damaging to the foetus.

Nadia's experience with her second daughter should be of some comfort if you're worried that you trained too hard early in your pregnancy. 'I had been doing 100 miles a week, all my hard workouts, everything,' she recalls. 'I had just run my best time yet in the 10-K, a 33:40. What finally made me realize that something was wrong was that I was getting more and more tired on my long runs. And at the end of workouts, I felt like throwing up. I got tested and realized that I was 5 months pregnant.'

At that point, she hadn't yet gained any weight. She dropped her mileage, cut back her intensity, and began doing some of her workouts in the pool. Four months later, she gave birth to healthy, happy Anita. This story *isn't* meant as licence to go out and put the pedal to the metal, though. Remember, your first priority is the baby. It's likely, however, that your body and your baby are a good bit more resilient than was once thought.

Postpone major running challenges. Save the marathon or personal-best attempt for another time. You should not be doing training that extends you to your limits, and trying to run fast or far will do just that. If you've been training to run a marathon, it's best to cancel your race plans. Even if you were to run the race slowly, you'd still be exerting yourself for several hours.

Put away the heart-rate monitor. The increase in maternal heart rate renders general heart-rate formulas invalid for pregnant women. The Royal College of Obstetricians and Gynaecologists issued guidelines on exercise in pregnancy in 2006. For pregnant women under 20 years, heart rate should not exceed 155 beats per minute. For women aged 20 to 29, the maximum is 150 beats per minute. For 30- to 39-year olds heart rate should not exceed 145 beats per minute, and for pregnant women 40 and over, heart rate should not exceed 140 beats per minute.

Alter your workout for comfort when necessary. Partly because of the jostling involved in activities such as running, doctors used to tell women to rely primarily on non-weight-bearing exercise during pregnancy. Today, it's generally considered safe for women who are already running to continue to do so as long as they remain comfortable. How long to continue is a judgment call, and one that's different for every woman. Nadia reports stopping at around 7 months with all of her 3 pregnancies, because the manner in which she was carrying felt awkward. Mya, on the other hand, was still running up to 4 miles at a stretch 2 weeks *past* her due date! When running no longer feels comfortable, consider walking, running in a pool or swimming in order to maintain fitness. If you go through a setback that stops you from running early in your pregnancy, don't count yourself out for the duration: you might be able to pick it up again at a later stage. Consult your doctor or midwife first, though.

Let your previous fitness steer you. The level of fitness you enter your pregnancy with will directly affect the amount of running your pregnant body can handle. In uncomplicated pregnancies, it's been shown that competitive women runners can safely retain a quite high level of training. You should probably use this information to put your mind at ease – to reassure yourself that you're not likely to harm your foetus by running – rather than taking this as licence to continue your exercise programme with no changes.

Risk Factors

Most women can continue to exercise at a mild to moderate level during pregnancy. For some women, however, the additional stress of exercise might put them at higher risk of suffering some negative consequences for themselves or their babies. Women with the following conditions are generally advised to refrain from exercising:

➔ Pregnancy-induced hypertension

➔ Pre-term rupture of membranes

➔ Pre-term labour during a previous or current pregnancy

➔ A cervix that dilates prematurely

➔ Persistent second- or third-trimester bleeding

➔ Inadequate foetal growth

Although some doctors discourage exercise for women with a history of premature labour, 3 or more miscarriages, or multiple-birth pregnancy, others feel that there is no evidence proving that exercise is indeed harmful in these cases.

Remember, shifting priorities . . . . Unless you're earning a living with your racing – and even then! – you can probably afford to let go of your lofty fitness ideals for a few months.

Back off at high altitudes. Pregnant women are advised to avoid running – or any strenuous exertion – at altitudes above 6,000 feet (or 1,800 metres). If you're exercising at altitude, watch for any early signs of altitude sickness, which include nausea, headache and shortness of breath. And follow the same rules you would at sea level, which means don't run to exhaustion.

Eating for Two – And Then Some

As a pregnant woman, you need about 300 extra calories per day – slightly less in the first trimester and slightly more in the second and third. If you run throughout your pregnancy, your calorie requirements will be higher than those of a sedentary woman. And if you've been denying yourself pancakes and pasta, here's a reason to indulge: in addition to needing more fuel,

In addition, Dr Roger Henderson, a runner and GP, advises you to carefully monitor your body's reactions while exercising. Consider any of the following as signs to discontinue exercising and consult a doctor before resuming:

- Bloody discharge from the vagina
- Any gush of fluid from the vagina
- Sudden swelling of the ankles, hands or face
- Persistent, severe headaches or a visual disturbance
- Swelling, pain, and redness in the calf of one leg
- Elevation of pulse rate or blood pressure that persists after exercise
- Excessive fatigue or any palpitations or chest pains
- Persistent contractions (they may suggest the onset of premature labour)
- Unexplained abdominal pain
- Insufficient weight gain

your pregnant body processes food differently, relying more heavily on carbohydrates during both rest and exercise.

Between pregnancy and exercise, you'll want to be vigilant about meeting your energy needs. That can be tough if nausea is interfering with your appetite. Here are some ways to solve the problem.

Graze. If you're experiencing nausea, food aversions or a loss of appetite, eating several smaller meals a day can be more comfortable than 3 large meals.

Separate liquids from solids. Drink liquids separately from meals – at least half an hour before or after – and don't have liquid items such as soup with meals. In some women, the combination of liquids and solids strains the digestive system.

Never run when you're hungry. An hour before your run, try something plain, such as a piece of toast or some crackers.

Always have breakfast, lunch and dinner. You should never skip meals, especially if you're exercising. This is not a time to worry about keeping your trim runner's figure, or a time to try to 'bank' weight loss as a hedge against the inevitable gains coming a few months down the road. You should gain between 12 and 14 kg. Some runners who start their pregnancies in an extremely thin state report their weight shooting up almost instantly as their bodies attempt to pile on the appropriate reserves.

'It was a struggle at first, thinking of gaining all that weight,' says Laurie. 'I've never been more than 2.5 kg over my racing weight in my life. Then, immediately, in the first 3 weeks, I put on 5 kg. It was as if my body was saying, *You need the extra weight.* That was a shocker – I thought that I was going to gain 40 kg at that rate! But it levelled off. It worried me a little at first, but I wasn't going to let it take control of my emotions and the baby's health. I kept eating extra like I was supposed to.'

Smart Tips

Take these precautions to keep you running comfortably through your pregnancy:

➡ Drink plenty of fluids to counteract the dehydrating effects of exercise.

➡ Dress in comfortable layers to ensure adequate ventilation. You might overheat more quickly than you are used to.

➡ Consider running smaller loops and staying close to home. That way, if fatigue strikes early, you can easily walk home.

➡ Wear sunblock. Sun exposure can exacerbate the 'mask of pregnancy', a skin darkening that affects many women during pregnancy.

➡ Try using a special maternity belt once you begin to put on weight in your midsection; some women find the extra support beneficial. These are available in most maternity stores.

The Royal College of Obstetricians and Gynaecologists issues guidelines on exercise during pregnancy. To find out more visit www.rcog.org.uk.

Relax. Some women runners who continue to train throughout their pregnancies report difficulty maintaining the proper weight during the final few months. 'At 7 months, I'd put on 15 kg, but then I started losing weight,' says Shirley. 'Sienna was 4 kg when she was born, so she was taking a lot of energy inside there. My body fat was actually disappearing in the last few months. I ate and ate and ate but didn't gain.'

After gaining all that weight early on, Laurie was having a similar experience at 8 months. 'I made myself eat then, even when I wasn't hungry, because I'd stopped gaining,' she said. 'It felt like the extra energy requirement with running had slimmed down my hips and legs, and all the food I was taking in was going straight to the baby.' Although experts advise you to shoot for regular and consistent weight gain over the course of the pregnancy, such fluctuations are not cause for alarm. You should continue to ensure that your overall weight gain is sufficient and that your caloric needs are being met.

DISCOURAGEMENT FROM LOVED ONES

Although books, doctors and magazines might all be telling you to go for it, you can bet that someone in your family or circle of friends won't be so enthusiastic about your running. Old attitudes die hard. And, from that other person's perspective, it can be awfully hard to watch the pregnant woman you love take on tiring pursuits.

'People did try to talk me out of my running,' Shirley says. 'My husband was annoyed that I would consider joining a team to do the running portions of a quadrathlon. He was appalled. He'd seen me dissolve into tears because I was so tired, so he condemned me for adding to the stress with running. He was just concerned for the child and for me. And it was, in fact, a hard time because I was so tired. But I needed to continue to run for myself. When he saw that in the second trimester I had more energy, he was fine with my running.'

If people you love are discouraging you from running, ease your mind by:

Remembering that they mean well. After all, you know how worried you are about ensuring the optimal health of your baby.

Reassuring your concerned loved ones. Let your husband or mother know that you *are* keeping your child's best interests at heart. Explain to them the health benefits for both the child and you. Finally, make sure they know how important your fitness is to you, both physically and emotionally.

Being a good listener. Sometimes it takes an outside observer to see things clearly. Pregnant women who are pushing themselves to accomplish everything at their pre-pregnancy rate risk overdoing it. If you've been running yourself down, your mum, your partner or whoever it is could be right: it might be time to take a day off from running, housework and everything else, and just take a nap.

ON THE COMEBACK TRAIL

Running might be the last thing on your mind immediately after giving birth, but don't ignore your body altogether at this time. A growing body of research supports the idea that exercise is a useful treatment for – and might actually help to prevent – postpartum depression.

'Exercise is a good component of any recovery programme from depression at any time,' says psychiatrist Dr Nada Stotland, who specializes in obstetrics and women's mental health issues. 'Women are particularly vulnerable to depression who have been running and who had to stop more or less against their will, due to pregnancy and delivery. People need to find a way to get back into an exercise routine . . . especially if it was something that was very important to them before.'

That's not to say that a woman with no background in running who is suffering from severe depression can be magically cured. However, regaining one's sense of self – including feelings about one's body – can only help in retaining a feeling of control after childbirth has turned things upside down.

It's not as easy as slipping on your running shoes and heading out the door. Many of the same physiological factors that limit your ability to run during pregnancy persist for several weeks after you give birth. What's more, your body has been through a fairly traumatic event, generally with a variety of accompanying physical repercussions.

For a healthy, successful return to running, keep these guidelines in mind:

Beware of setting expectations. Don't create a time frame in which you'll return to your former self. This could force you to overdo it or to be disappointed if you fall short of your planned schedule. You'll notice that there's no training schedule in this chapter for returning to running. That's because of the great variety in experiences women have after giving birth.

Start gradually. Let your body decide when it's ready to go for a spin around the block. Your first sessions should be short, easy walks. Don't

The Myth of Pregnancy and Performance

Rumours abound about the performance-enhancing effects of pregnancy. And in fact, women have run personal bests during and after their pregnancies. Although reputable research on this subject is scanty, a number of possible explanations have been put forth, including hormonal shifts, increased aerobic capacity and a higher pain threshold due to childbirth. Reports have even circulated that coaches in Eastern Bloc countries in the 1980s – a period tainted by admissions of improper drug use – tried to capitalize on such 'pregnancy effects', encouraging their female athletes to become impregnated and then abort the foetuses.

'There is no solid research about performance improving after pregnancy,' says Judy Mahle Lutter, co-author of *The Bodywise Woman*. 'It's a case-by-case basis. Most of the reports of improvement come from elite athletes. But for women on a more recreational level, it's hit or miss. Some say that they become stronger, and plenty of others say that they never quite get back to their former strength or stride. While improvement is a physical possibility, it shouldn't be expected. And it is even less likely for non-professional runners because they suddenly have the added responsibility of a child, meaning less time to train and a shift in priorities.'

set goals for time or pace. When you can complete these sessions with no trouble, gradually increase your time and work in brief periods of slow jogging. Follow the rules for beginning runners, gradually working up to half an hour or so of walk/runs. Only when you can comfortably jog again for at least half an hour 4 or 5 times a week should you consider picking up the pace. If you experience complications such as heavy bleeding at any time, lay off the running for at least several days before trying again.

Remember that you're different from other women. Lutter points out that women vary dramatically in their post-pregnancy experiences and that measuring yourself against others can be a setup for disappointment. Although some literature says that you can return to your former fitness in 6 weeks, 'for plenty of women, it's more like 6 months,' she says. 'Their babies are still up all night, the women are supertired and it's not realistic.

It's better for a woman to assume that the process will last at least 6 months. Then, if she happens to be back in 2 months, that's great.'

Listen to your body. Just as women have different experiences returning to running after childbirth, the same woman can have different experiences from one pregnancy and delivery to another. Resist comparing yourself with where you think you should be or with where you were in a previous pregnancy. Just as in training during pregnancy, listen to your body and proceed at a pace that feels comfortable.

Mya was able to begin running 3 weeks after she had a Caesarean. After a few weeks of training, she felt up to entering a race. She ran it as 6-week-old Michael watched from the sidelines. Shirley's experience was more challenging. 'I tried to start running 6 weeks after giving birth, but my breasts hurt too much from breastfeeding. So I stopped and waited until about 10 weeks. I ran a race shortly thereafter, and I didn't feel very strong, but I felt very light. Between breastfeeding and running, I was burning a lot of energy.'

Breastfeeding Concerns

Whether you breastfeed or not might impact the rate at which your body returns to 'running normalcy' after giving birth. But that means different things for different women, and it's impossible to predict the manner in which your body will respond. Some women claim that the caloric requirements of breastfeeding help them drop extra weight in a jiffy. Others believe that breastfeeding encourages their bodies to hang on to extra adipose tissue. As with most other factors surrounding your pregnancy, this is a decision you should make with the baby's best interest in mind. If you do choose to return to your running programme while you are breastfeeding, monitor your baby's weight gain. Insufficient gains could be a sign to cut back on exercise. To ensure adequate milk production, be sure to consume enough calories from healthy sources, and don't drop weight too quickly.

Some research indicates that your post-exercise breast milk may contain lactic acid. Although this won't harm your baby, some babies get fussy about the different taste. If your baby doesn't like your post-exercise milk, simply use a breast pump to express some milk before your run. Or just wait it out: your lactic acid levels will return to normal within an hour after your run.

TRAINING LOG

Never let it be said that I don't research my subject matter thoroughly. Over the course of writing this book, I learned that I was pregnant. My life, my work and my running would never be the same.

I admit that my initial thoughts were not exactly lofty: what will happen to my body? What will happen to my time alone to run? And what of my quest for the Olympic Trials?

A week passed. I saw my baby on an ultrasound, a blurry pulse vibrating in my womb. It might as well have been a lifetime. My life and my running had already been inexorably changed, and the questions of only a week ago no longer seemed important. I was no longer concerned about muscle tone; my body instead became a source of nurturing. I ate 5, 6 times a day, as hunger dictated. My 'training' had become exercise for the health of the baby and myself. I ran as my body told me. When my heart raced, I stopped. When I felt good, I would walk and jog for up to an hour. When I felt bad, I would skip it altogether.

And the Olympic Trials? Somehow the idea of whipping my body into shape after giving birth seemed not only stressful, but rather beside the point. My dreams had become consumed with other priorities, of health and fitness not only for myself, but also for my child.

Pregnancy gave me a gift I never could have expected. I'm left with sheer wonderment at and respect for the other things my body is capable of. My running, always a celebration of movement and strength, now is also a celebration of life.

Nadia experienced both extremes. She began running a mere 1 week after her first and second pregnancies. (Six weeks after the birth of her second daughter, she managed to click off a half-marathon in 1 hour and 11 minutes.) But the birth of daughter number 3, Nyla, was a more difficult affair, and Nadia's comeback was significantly slowed. 'I made things worse by trying to meet the expectations of the previous pregnancies and by not listening to my body,' she says.

Most of the women I interviewed for this book reported a change in focus after the birth of their children. Even the most serious competitors who planned racing comebacks acknowledged that baby now came first. The general consensus was that if the running came around to its former level, great, but it was no longer necessary. Recreational runners began to focus less on bodily perfection. For most women, moderation seems to be the key after a baby enters the picture. This means neither pushing all-out in runs nor sacrificing your workouts to all the other demands that compete for your time. Just because your pregnancy is over, you needn't forget everything you've learned about taking care of yourself. Your children will be relying on you for years to come, and a healthy, happy mother will be better able to meet their needs.

'When I had my baby, I thought, *I want to return to my running career, but mostly I want my kids to be happy.* That comes first,' says Nadia. She sums it up with the love of a woman who is clearly inspired by both her children and her running: 'Every time you come back from your run and you see your baby, it's like the sun in the house. It gives you energy. Life becomes more full, more grounded. You no longer run just for yourself; you run for your baby, you run for your family. You feel as if you can do anything.' Marathon world-record holder Paula Radcliffe agrees. 'Motherhood is great. I don't know how I would have coped with training some weeks before my daughter Isla was born: I've been trying to fit in so many things but playing with her gives me balance and perspective.'

CHAPTER 20

The Younger Runner

WHEN IT COMES TO RAISING YOUNG RUNNERS, ENJOYMENT IS THE KEY. Keeping athletics fun, encouraging a child in all areas and staying involved as she grows up are important aspects of support echoed over and over again by experts in youth fitness.

Dr Jack Daniels, author of *Daniels' Running Formula*, is one of the many coaches to advocate this fun approach, mixing running with other sports, when it comes to training for children. 'To me, there are two major advantages to this approach,' says Daniels. 'Firstly, children have a chance to see what sport they really enjoy and are good at. Secondly, this more general fitness approach prepares a youngster for a great variety of sports. If a specific sport becomes a bore or is not well suited to the individual, another sport is still within reach.'

The psychology of how you approach a youngster's training is important too. 'Start easily and make every day of training a success in the minds of the runners,' explains Daniels. 'Training at an early age should not be about becoming faster – any training will accomplish that, so there's no need to make a point of it.'

If you have a teenager who dreams of winning a gold medal at the 2012 Olympic Games in London, the key to success is balance as well as enjoyment. Former Commonwealth 5,000-metre champion Rob Denmark, who works as a Talent development Manager with UK Athletics, believes that youngsters who have a balance of physical ability, concentration, mental strength and dedication will go far.

Setting a great example is one of the ways you can encourage your daughter to enjoy exercise, a philosophy reflected in the training policies of one of the UK's most enlightened running clubs, Trent Park Running Club in North London. 'The club's young athletes, just like their senior counterparts, put the emphasis on enjoying sport,' says Ian Turner, the club's junior secretary. The club welcomes runners of all standards and varies training activities throughout the year, putting the emphasis on games and relays. 'Our coaches are very aware that the sessions must be fun, and that good practices will form the habits of the juniors' future sporting lives,' Turner says.

GROWING UP HEALTHY

What children learn from watching adults is, in fact, crucial. But what a lot of them are seeing clearly isn't good: in a recent government survey, 3 in 10 boys and 4 in 10 girls under 15 in the UK are not doing the amount of physical activity recommended by the Chief Medical Officer.

Childhood today is simply less conducive than ever to physical activity. Computer games, the Internet and, of course, television keep children's bottoms glued to their seats during their recreational hours. Schools have cut budgets that funded physical education programmes. Cars have become the normal way to get around; bicycles and walking, the exception. Households in which both parents work have become typical, so children are more likely to spend their time indoors in a day-care setting. Neighbourhoods where people don't know one another and a general fear of crime and violence mean that children are less likely than ever to be outdoors when they're at home – even in the best neighbourhoods.

The result is a generation of children growing up unfit and overweight. 'In our part of the world, obesity is the number one chronic health problem,' says Dr Oded Bar-Or, author of *The Child and Adolescent Athlete: The Encyclopaedia of Sports Medicine*. In fact, in the UK, the current trend suggests that 50 per cent of children will be obese by 2020.

Dr Bar-Or points out that exercise is the simplest solution to that growing problem: the more physically active a child is, the less likely it is that she'll become overweight. That's no small thing. In fact, the direction a child takes early on can have lifelong implications. Heart disease, which remains the leading cause of death in the United Kingdom, has been shown to begin in childhood. And on the positive side, introducing children as young as

2 years old to healthy exercise and nutrition habits has been shown to have lasting effects into adulthood.

Beyond the obvious physical impact, girls in particular benefit from physical activity in ways that can affect them for the rest of their lives. According to research conducted by the Women's Sports Foundation (www.womenssportsfoundation.org), girls who participate in athletics are:

* less likely to become involved with drugs
* less likely to engage in sexual activity
* less likely to get pregnant
* more likely to graduate from high school and college
* more likely to have higher than average grades

'Girls who do sport are able to look at their bodies in a different way,' says Lynn Jaffee, co-author of *The Bodywise Woman* and a specialist in girls' and women's health. 'Instead of viewing it as a question of *How thin am I?* or *How pretty am I?* it's, *How strong am I? How fast am I?* They view the body as a competent thing rather than only as an object of attractiveness.'

Those benefits continue beyond the teen years. The women who participate in sports as girls demonstrate higher than average confidence, self-esteem and pride in their physical appearance. They are also less likely to suffer from depression.

THE RIGHT START

When should you encourage your child to become active? The earlier the better. A 1989 study showed that if a girl doesn't participate in sport by the time she's 10 years old, there's only a 10 per cent chance that she'll be active in athletics when she's 25. This may be changing slowly with the greater numbers of women discovering sport and the greater acceptance of older women in sport. But clearly, the earlier your daughter becomes active, the better off she is physically, mentally and emotionally.

That doesn't mean that you should take your child to the track and start timing her as soon as she can walk. In fact, forget 'running' altogether, at first. For youngsters, being active is the goal, not being competitive. Going to extremes and pushing too early can have a counterproductive effect. It's been shown that children who specialize in a particular sport early are more likely to become injured. And rather than getting a head start on athletic glory, many find their later athletic careers become truncated due to physical or emotional burnout.

So ditch the stopwatch and focus on fun. 'We need to find ways to encourage girls to exercise with their friends,' says double Olympic gold medallist Dame Kelly Holmes. Physical activity for children needn't be – shouldn't be – structured until they are at least in secondary school. Instead, sports should remain play. That way, it becomes a regular part of daily life. Here are some ways to incorporate healthy pastimes into your child's routine as she grows.

The Pre-school Years

Play outdoors. It's important to get your child into this habit early on. Setting this pattern early might help avoid a video-game habit later.

Be creative with activity. Playing catch, doing somersaults and jumping in leaf piles are examples of fun pastimes that build coordination.

Primary School

Encourage natural child's play. Child's play is, after all, pretty much running around. 'When I was brought up, my mother would shove us out the door and we'd run around the fields,' recalls Priscilla Welch, whose world-best 2:26:51 marathon as a masters runner ranks among the sport's greatest performances. 'But it was playtime, not hard miles on the roads.'

Kim Jones recalls a similar experience. 'I grew up in a household of 11, and we had to share one bike,' she says. 'If we wanted to go to the beach, which was a mile or so away, we would just run. It wasn't training – it was all natural.'

Engage in low-key contests. A garden can be the perfect training ground for building lifelong active habits and sportsmanship. Races, tag, ball games – just about any outdoor activity that entails moving around is all the running a young child needs. 'The goal shouldn't be fitness at a young age but rather to have fun,' says Susan Kalish, author of *Your Child's Fitness: Practical Advice for Parents*. 'If they always have fun with it, they'll always do it. You don't want young children to think of exercise as work or to have the upsetting connotations of not meeting performance goals.' Welch concurs: 'When you take children by the collar and structure them seriously, that's how you lose them.'

Play with your children. Ask them to teach you the outdoor games they play in school. Invite their friends over to kick a football around or play rounders in the summer.

Be a good role model. Experts say that one of the best ways you can ensure that your children get exercise is by setting a good example. At this age, children are sponges, witnessing and mirroring your actions and values.

Now's the time to show them your health is a priority to you. Seeing you include running, cycling or walking in your day will help your children think of physical activity as the norm.

Turn family outings into active fun. Take your child on walks, hikes and bike rides; all are great family activities at this age. Be sure to let your child set the pace. 'I started running with my daughters while they were on their bikes,' Kalish says. 'Then they started running when they wanted to. We go

A Note on the Marathon

As the marathon has grown in popularity, some children have shown interest in running the event. Plenty of parents, even those who have completed such a race themselves, aren't sure what to make of this. If a child shows the interest, discipline and ability to train for a marathon, is that a good thing? Well, not entirely.

Just because a youngster shows abilities that might make her capable of running a marathon, it's still not recommended. Children under the age of 18 simply should not run a marathon, says an advisory statement issued by the International Marathon Medical Directors Association. Physical concerns include a great risk of stress fractures and other overuse injuries at the level of training required for a marathon. Shorter strides mean the sheer number of steps youngsters take to train the same distance is far greater than that of adults. In addition, cartilage that is not fully formed is more susceptible to injury. Also, children have less ability to disperse heat from their bodies and therefore are at greater risk of heat stress.

The position paper also points out emotional concerns: 'Emotional burnout is a real phenomenon that can have the exact opposite effect of that intended by participation. Children may develop feelings of failure and frustration when the demands, both physical and cognitive, exceed their internal resources.'

Ultimately, even the most goal-oriented children need guidance. Perhaps a child who is precocious enough to consider a marathon is particularly in need of good counsel. Parents would do well to steer such a child towards age-appropriate challenges and encourage her to save the marathon for later.

Running and Growth

You might have heard that running can stunt a child's growth. Not true, say experts in youth fitness. 'The source of that notion seems to come from dated observations, in which active children were thought to grow at a slower rate than those who were sedentary,' says Dr Oded Bar-Or, author of *The Child and Adolescent Athlete: The Encyclopaedia of Sports Medicine*. 'At least one reason for that turned out to be simple: the children who did well in sports and thus were studied were already more mature than those who were less active. They had already gone through their growth spurt, while the sedentary children had their growth spurt yet to come – thus the perception of unequal growth. More recent studies confirm that running and other sports do not stunt growth one bit.'

In fact, recent studies suggest the opposite: that running as a child can translate to better bone health in later life. A 2007 study at the University of Southampton compared the average amount of physical activity of 200 4-year-olds with the strength of their bones and found that the children who were more physically active had stronger skeletons. Dr Nick Harvey, who managed the study says: 'Evidence suggests that the better your bones are when you are young, the better they will be when you are older, and so more physical activity as a child could potentially mean stronger

---

as long and hard as they want, and we play a lot of games. We might race to the stream. But if they want to stop and catch tadpoles, then we stop. I'm very careful not to push them. And I let them take the lead, literally going in front of me. That way, they stop when they want to.'

Expose children to different sports and activities. Now is the time to think broad instead of deep: try a dance class in the winter, football in the spring, tennis in the summer. This will help your daughter develop a range of skills and movements while encouraging overall activity. The added bonus is that she'll be exposed to a variety of things. Since you can never know what her particular love or talent will be, it's a gift to encourage a wide range at this age, when chances are greater that she'll be open to it.

Begin lessons if your child wishes. Let your children participate in organized sport or lessons if they wish, but don't force them. If they feel

bones in old age.' Activities such as running 3 days per week or more, 10 to 20 minutes at a time, will augment bone mineral accrual in children and adolescents. That's significant, since the peak bone mass developed during childhood and early adult years determines risk of osteoporosis later in life.

The process of growth during puberty and adolescence can impact on running performance. That's because, during growth spurts, bones grow at a rate far exceeding that of muscle. The result can be a decline in athletic performance during periods of growth, when the body is literally out of balance. 'The anecdotal observation that running performance can suffer during these "awkward phases" – when the limbs are lanky and seem to go all over the place – is probably due to a mismatch of growth between the bones, muscles and tendons,' Dr Bar-Or explains. 'For girls, muscular development catches up to the bones at the very end of a growth spurt. For boys, it can take even longer – up to a year – for the muscular development to catch up.' Although it's perfectly safe to run during these times, these growth spurts are yet another reason to keep any training light during the pre-teen and teen years. Young bodies should be expending the lion's share of their energy on proper growth, not training for a marathon.

passionate about something, there's nothing wrong with them developing skills and learning concentration. Most important at this age is that they learn and enjoy, not that they turn into Junior Olympians.

Secondary School

Find active weekend and holiday pursuits. Your child will be spending more time away at school and with friends. Make good use of family time by planning healthy activities. Hiking and cycling can be combined with camping trips.

Enter a race together. Walk together in a 5-K. Not only is it great exercise, but you'll be exposing your child to the festivity of a race environment.

Consider organized sports. By now, your child may express an interest in team sports or even in more regimented training for an individual sport

Staying Healthy

Injuries are, unfortunately, a significant risk for girls starting a running programme. Research has found that the highest rate of injury among high school sports is in girls' cross-country. This is partially because untrained girls come off their summer breaks and immediately start logging miles in the autumn. The results can be shinsplints and stress fractures.

Girls can avoid injury by following the same smart training principles that apply to any beginning runner: never increase mileage or speed too quickly, do some running on soft surfaces and be sure to wear appropriate shoes and insoles. Most important for youngsters is to do some preliminary running over the summer so that they don't enter the autumn programme on 'cold' legs and abruptly increase their mileage. Running a few miles three or four times a week over the summer might be all it takes to avoid a debilitating injury in the autumn.

---

such as running. That's fine, as long as the impetus comes from your child and not from you or a coach. Forcing a programme on your child at this stage could turn him or her off the sport for good.

Combine sports with charity work. Encourage your child to walk a race for charity, earning money from sponsors in your neighbourhood.

Continue to encourage healthy pastimes. Fight the video habit with active family recreation. Teens enjoy fun activities such as swimming and throwing a Frisbee without even realizing that they're getting exercise.

Let your child join a sports club or team. A team atmosphere will help to develop cooperation and sportsmanship. At this age, children are old enough to handle greater training structure and competition.

Get a health check for your budding competitive runner. Cardiologists suggest that competitive secondary school runners be screened before starting more serious training. Congenital heart problems can exist unbeknown to parents. While the incidence is low and the risk rare, it's a safe bet to pre-screen children before they enter a competitive training situation.

In addition to encouraging your children to be active, there are things you can do to make sure they get off to the right start. Here are some tips to ensure that your own behaviour is supportive of physical activity:

Provide positive feedback. Negative criticism can turn your child off sports altogether. Always offer positive feedback when training or a race has gone well, but also when something goes wrong. By focusing on the positive, your child will have the confidence to keep trying their best.

By providing a supportive environment, you'll be encouraging your child to take chances and learn.

Be aware and involved. Listen to your child. If he or she is feeling pressured, take action by talking to the coach, switching to a club with a different emphasis, trying a new sport or making sure you're available to offer support and guidance. Anita Bean, author of *The Complete Guide to Sports Nutrition*, encourages her daughters Chloe and Lucy to understand the importance of proper nutrition and the importance of breaks and recovery for long-term fitness. 'Active kids need more calories than non-sporty kids but may also need more vitamins to convert the food into energy, minerals and protein to repair muscles after bruising,' explains Bean. 'But once they have met their daily targets for fruit, vegetables, grains and protein- and calcium-rich foods, it's fine to have one or two treats.' The result is athletic success but also two strong, well-adjusted young ladies.

THE SHIFT TO COMPETITION

There is no magic age when your child can or should start focusing exclusively on training for one sport. Most experts, however, recommend that you keep your children involved in a variety of activities for as long as possible. This keeps things fun and prevents boredom. It also helps children develop a variety of skills at an age when they're most easily able to learn. Runners especially, Dr Bar-Or points out, can be 'born' at any age. Unlike gymnastics and figure skating, which require specific skill development at an early age, running does not need to be mastered early and does not require early specialization for later success.

Secondary school traditionally has been the time when kids make the transition from playing to training. But community and out-of-school time programmes are increasingly available for younger children who wish to engage in competitive running. 'Organized groups can be a good way to take running from the fun, family stage to something more goal-oriented,' says Roy Benson, an esteemed coach and heart-rate-training expert who has had 4 decades of experience working with runners of all ages and ability levels. He adds, however, that parents should make sure that the programme has the right emphasis.

'These programmes are good if they teach some of life's valuable lessons, for example, about the relationship between hard work and rewards. Or if they enhance self-image through accomplishment,' Benson says. 'But they can be bad if self-image is damaged because the child does not measure up to somebody else's definition of success. The worst thing is when children experience this type of unexplained failure and lose their love of running or competition because they are told that they aren't tough or good enough.'

If your child wishes to concentrate solely on running – or on another sport – follow these guidelines to ensure that she'll have a positive experience.

Get her involved in numerous athletic events. Most coaches agree that, even if your child shows talent, you shouldn't focus exclusively on running too early on. Standout runners of all ages have 'disappeared' after promising school or university careers, quitting the sport altogether or never living up to early expectations. The syndrome is referred to as burnout, and it's all too common in an intense sport such as running. What has happened to these promising youngsters? They have exhausted themselves prematurely – sometimes physically, sometimes mentally, often both.

Make sure that she doesn't get too serious too soon. 'Except for the truly elite talents, most young runners have a window of 4 to 6 years in which they can give it their all,' says Benson. 'The elite runners can run just fast enough to win – they don't have to go into the depths of their psychic wells – and so they can prolong their running careers. But all the others, the kids *striving* to excel, must give an enormous psychological and physical effort. If a youngster is going to be good at this, he or she has to give up a lot. After giving 100 per cent every day, and in every race, and basically giving up being a normal kid or teenager, eventually he or she will need to say, *That's enough.* So if you start them at age 10, their career might be over at 16.'

Keep the training light. Benson and other coaches agree that it's preferable to undertrain a young runner than to overtrain her. After all, the most important aspect of training a school runner is ensuring that she sticks around for the years to come, whether competitively or recreationally. Keeping training miles light in her early years can prolong a young girl's career. She will be fresher mentally should she decide to continue competing, and she'll be less likely to suffer injuries.

Proper mileage will be different for every young girl, but Benson does offer some rough guidelines. In the first few years of secondary school, young runners – even those who demonstrate natural ability – should go very easy on mileage to avoid injury and allow bones, muscles and tendons to slowly adapt to the repetitive stress of running. Although every girl is different, 15 to 20 miles a week is considered a conservative, low-risk estimate for a runner beginning her training. When she reaches sixth form, an athlete's body should have adapted, and she should be comfortable with this level of training. At this point, Benson recommends, girls can move up to 30 or 40 miles a week, as their natural ability allows.

Fuelling Small Engines

When it comes to hydration and nutrition, children don't respond just like miniature grown-ups. Although it seems as if kids can keep going and going without tiring, in fact, children are more prone to dehydration and overheating than adults. 'When it comes to dissipating heat from the body, children are at a disadvantage,' says Dr Oded Bar-Or. 'Children don't sweat as much as adults; they produce more body heat; and they take in more heat from the environment, since their ratio of surface area to volume is greater than that of an adult.' That triple whammy adds up to a greater risk of rapidly rising body temperature during prolonged exercise such as running.

To protect against such a rise in temperature, make sure your children drink before and after exercise. If they're active for a long period of time, encourage them to take breaks to drink every 15 minutes or so. This can be tricky, since many children turn up their noses at water. Because they are likely to drink greater amounts of a flavoured drink, a sports drink or diluted juice might be preferable.

For optimal nutrition, don't feed your children as you would yourself. Your low-fat, heart-healthy diet isn't appropriate for growing bodies. That doesn't mean you should let them load up on junk food and unhealthy saturated fats. Instead, include healthy protein- and calcium-rich foods – peanut butter, cheese, milk, meat – in most of their meals without trying to cut fat at every corner. The standard mandate to load up on fresh fruits and veggies still holds; most children take in far too few of these nutrient boosters. Finally, though it may seem impossible, try to limit sweets as much as possible to avoid development of a sweet tooth and its ensuing dental difficulties.

THE COACHING RELATIONSHIP

Training, as it turns out, is just one part – and maybe the simplest part – of the equation for coaching youngsters. Developing the mind and building the positive attributes that can come with running should be the priority at this stage. These are the things that a young runner can take with her and apply later in life to anything from work to relationships.

'For secondary-school athletes, coaching should be more about direction than workouts,' says Ann Boyd, an elite runner and coach. 'It's the coach's job to give young runners the tools, with instruction and mental and emotional support. Proper coaching for young girls is not a matter of yelling, "Faster, faster!"'

Parents and children must be on guard for coaches who try to wring every ounce of talent out of a young runner for the sake of the school or for personal gratification. 'The best thing a coach can do is pass a runner on as a malleable prospect,' Benson says.

If your son or daughter feels that he or she is not getting proper coaching, talk to the coach or athletic director about your concerns. You don't have to be an expert on training to know good coaching from bad coaching. If your son or daughter feels put down or pressured or is chronically exhausted or injured, the coach needs a talking-to. If the coach disagrees or fails to change his or her slant, you might want to get your child involved in a different running programme or change running clubs. 'If you don't get it right, your child's potential could be significantly reduced,' says UK Athletics Talent Development Manager Rob Denmark.

BODY IMAGE

Eating disorders and body image issues can plague girls well before their teens. 'Kids are talking about being fat when they're 5 and 6 and 7 years old now,' says Dr Nada Stotland, a psychiatrist who specializes in women and eating disorders. Research suggests that a dramatic number of very young girls are presenting with an obsessive concern about health and fitness, severe food restriction, significant weight loss and even arrest of growth and development.

But early detection can make a significant difference in recovery: there is strong evidence that the longer the duration of illness, the harder it is to achieve recovery. Parents should be diligent in looking for warning signs and shouldn't be afraid to get help at their first suspicion of a body image issue.

'Look for warning signs such as refusal to eat food, or hiding how much they're eating,' Stotland says. Other warning signs include, 'saying "I'll eat in my room", or "I'll eat somewhere else".'

Whether athletics exacerbates or improves body image and eating issues is unclear, and it probably varies highly from case to case. While some research suggests that eating disorders are more prevalent among athletic girls than among non-athletes, no causal relationship has been proven. Meanwhile, another broad study of athletes actually found a lower incidence of eating problems among non-elite secondary-school athletes and lower levels of body dissatisfaction among athletes overall than in the general population.

TRAINING LOG

My daughter was born to run. At least that's what everyone tells me. Her father is a five-time world record holder. A two-time Olympian. My running world was nothing like that, but I suppose I was better than average.

So when people see Bianca, all skinny arms and legs, light on her little feet, they inevitably ask: 'So, is she running yet?'

Um, no.

Bianca is 6. She loves gymnastics, likes dancing, rides her bike around the neighbourhood and runs when she plays in the park. When the local races hold kids' fun runs, sometimes she joins in. More often she doesn't, saying she doesn't want to. I'm not about to force her.

I had a parent who decided that I was going to be a runner. I wasn't given much say in the matter, and I was racing before I started senior school. After some rather miserable years at school when I didn't even want to compete but was forced to, I stopped running altogether. Luckily I overcame my dad's influence and found my way back to the sport as an adult.

Did my dad introduce me to the sport that's defined my life? Yes. Could it have been a more enjoyable path, one that wasn't so fraught with anxiety? Yes again.

My goal for my daughter is to expose her to the *idea* of running. We'll have silly little races in the park. She sees her father and me run on most days. She goes to the races and cheers on her friends' mums.

If the day comes when she decides to run, she'll know it's an option. Maybe she'll be good at it; maybe she'll even be great. Mostly, I hope she finds something that keeps her fit and happy as she develops into adulthood. Meanwhile, I'll happily keep buying her leotards.

In other words, there's no evidence that sport itself results in a greater risk of disordered eating. Rather, many experts believe that girls with certain body types or personality types are more likely to become athletes and that these girls already were more at risk for eating disorders.

You can contribute to your daughter's healthy attitude about food and her body by doing the following:

- **Set a good example.** Eat healthily yourself, and don't express extreme dissatisfaction with your own body.
- **Stay away from inappropriate comments about weight.** Don't criticize her weight or give her ultimatums to lose weight. Negative remarks about weight at a young age can have a devastating effect on a girl.
- **Ensure that she knows about proper nutrition.** If your young runner is concerned with her performance, you can have a big influence by impressing upon her the long-term training benefits of proper nutrition.
- **Limit exposure to television.** Research has actually demonstrated a causal relationship between television and increased eating disorder symptoms in school children.

Anita Bean, author of *The Complete Guide to Sports Nutrition*, recognizes the importance of providing a positive influence for her two daughters. 'Children of any age are more likely to copy what you do than what you say,' Bean says. 'We share mealtimes as often as possible and between meals I encourage them to eat healthy snacks to keep their energy levels topped up. I link healthy food to something that matters to them: better running, faster times, more energy.'

If your daughter exhibits signs of an eating disorder, seek professional help. For more on eating disorders, see chapter 15.

CHAPTER 21

The Older Runner

Diane Palmason has a supple, youthful figure that's more limber and fit than most 30-year-olds'. When she tells people her age, she says, 'They actually doubt me.' Palmason is 69, and she has held world age-group records in numerous distances. She credits running, which she took up at the age of 38, with helping her age with energy and grace.

'To a great extent, running has helped to keep me free of all the things that make someone *look* and *feel* [old],' she says. 'My overall energy, wellness, strength and posture are better. Running has, essentially, slowed the ageing process. I wouldn't give it up for anything.'

Running can't stop time, but it certainly can soften the blows. The typical sedentary woman can expect her fitness to decline over the decades. The process typically starts as early as age 30, with gradually decreasing aerobic capacity, muscle mass, bone density, metabolic rate and immunity.

Several studies have shown that aerobic and weight-bearing exercise such as running slow these and other natural effects of ageing. In addition to these physical benefits, studies also show that, as fit women age, they have better psychological health. In fact, women who engage in regular aerobic exercise programmes, such as running, are less likely to suffer from:

✽ dementia
✽ cardiovascular disease

* diabetes

* high blood pressure

* breast cancer

* stroke

* symptoms of menopause

* obesity

* mood disturbances

And the good news isn't limited to those who, like Palmason, have been training since they were middle-aged or younger. 'Women can reap these benefits at any age,' says Lynn Jaffee, co-author of *The Bodywise Woman*.

Start with a Check-up

Many women overlook the fact that they might be at risk of heart disease, especially in light of heavy media focus on breast cancer. Heart disease remains the number one killer in the United Kingdom and kills more women each year than breast cancer.

Women who are beginning a running programme at any age should have their health checked by a GP. For women over the age of 40, that's even more important. Undiagnosed heart disease is the primary concern for anyone who's about to begin an aerobic exercise regimen, says Dr Lisa Callahan, author of the best-selling book *The Fitness Factor: Every Woman's Key to a Lifetime of Health and Well-being*.

Recognizing and treating the disease is key: you can run with heart disease if you maintain proper treatment. It's those who have an undiagnosed problem – and those who know they have a problem but ignore it – who are at risk of making the problem worse with exercise. In fact, they put themselves at a much higher risk of having a heart attack while running.

'The person who gets into trouble is the person who has disease and doesn't know it or has disease and doesn't deal with it . . . the person who has a heart condition and gets it properly identified and treated and then exercises within the appropriate recommendations of their doctor can do very well,' says Dr Steven Van Camp, a sports cardiologist and

Even if you've been sedentary throughout your life, you'll still reap positive effects from running, whether you start running in your 40s or in your 70s.

Indeed, many women who start running later in life report feeling healthier and more vigorous than they did when they were years younger. 'If everyone were physically active, we'd have entirely different standards of what is normal for any age,' says Palmason.

IT'S NEVER TOO LATE

At the age of 64, Mary Kirsling had never run before. One day, she decided to watch some of her family members take part in a marathon. Her granddaughter, then 8 years old, offered a challenge: 'Grandma, I'll run the 5-K

co-author of *Manual of Sports Medicine*. 'People can have a covert problem. Exercise doesn't confer immunity.'

Even if you don't have risk factors but are starting a new running routine, it's a good idea to see your doctor or cardiologist first. Van Camp particularly recommends that you see your doctor if you have risk factors such as a family history of heart disease, or if you yourself have high cholesterol, high blood pressure or diabetes. And even if you're an experienced runner, if you experience any symptoms such as chest pain (that goes beyond the subtle lung-burn that many runners feel), shortness of breath or dizziness, it's wise to pay a visit to your GP.

While heart disease is of primary concern during an exam at this age, a GP will also want to look for other underlying medical conditions, such as hypertension or diabetes, and for anatomical warning signs, such as musculoskeletal problems, stiff joints or arthritis. None of these factors will necessarily stop you from running. 'But if they are addressed up front, it's far more likely that the woman will enjoy and succeed in her training programme,' says Dr Callahan, a former competitive runner who now trains recreationally. 'If not addressed, these are the types of problems that can cause injury or discouragement and a premature end to the fitness programme.'

next year if you do.' 'Well,' recalls Kirsling, 'I thought, *I'd better start tomorrow!*' So she did. She began, as she puts it, 'telephone pole to telephone pole'.

'For my first few runs, I put on an old pair of sneakers and I ran down to the end of the block,' she says. 'I quickly realized that that wouldn't do, so I went out and bought my first pair of Nikes.' Kirsling divided her 12-month window into a gradually increasing schedule, working out how far she'd need to progress each month in order to complete the 3.1-mile course the following year. She surprised herself by hitting the milestone with 2 months to spare. As she promised, Kirsling then ran alongside her granddaughter in her first 5-K. When it was over, she was shocked to learn that she'd finished second in her age group.

Since that day, Mary has completed more than a dozen half-marathons and competed in the National Senior Olympic Games. When she turned 80, she was nationally ranked in her age group. Now in her mid-80s, she still trains regularly, including long runs and various quality workouts on the track. She travels far and wide to compete, counting her blessings as she counts the miles.

'Working as a nurse, I'd seen so many unhealthy people for so many years,' she says. 'I'd see some people in their 70s who were planted in their rocking chairs, and I knew I didn't want to be like that. It was wonderful when I started going to the races and seeing so many older, healthy, active people. I know it's made a big difference to my health. I recover faster when I am ill, I have more energy. Some folks in their 60s come up to me and say, "Well, I'd be out there running too, except for . . . " and they'll mention this and that excuse. And I say, "Well, give it a try. I did!"'

TRAINING FOR A LIFETIME

The best part about running is that you can keep going and going. 'With what we've seen women accomplish now, I can say with confidence, "I can be a marathon runner at 85,"' says Susan Kalish, author of *Your Child's Fitness: Practical Advice for Parents.* 'I love football, too, but it's a contact sport, and I know that sooner or later I'm going to have to stop because I'm going to break some bones. But I can roll with most any punch in running. Granted, my pace might be a little different, but I can be out there.'

Not only can women keep running into old age, but as it turns out, their pace may not have to drop as fast or as precipitously as we might imagine. A 2004 study in the *British Journal of Sports Medicine* found that the performances of older top finishers in the New York City Marathon have significantly improved over the past few decades. Their performances improved at a rate better than that of younger runners, and that held true particularly for females.

Just because you hit 40 – or 60 – doesn't mean that you have to revamp your training programme. You do have to be more careful about following the training rules that apply to all runners. 'People talked about hitting 40 like I was headed for a cliff and about to fall off,' says Lorraine Moller with a laugh. Moller, 52, is a four-time Olympic marathon runner who won the bronze medal in the 1992 Olympic Games. She now coaches and runs recreationally. 'Women age at different rates,' she says, 'and there is not a line or a point at which they must change their training.'

The training principles you'll follow at age 40, 50, or 60 are the same you followed at age 20 or 30. The older you are, however, the smarter you have to train, explains Dr Lisa Callahan, author of *The Fitness Factor: Every Woman's Key to a Lifetime of Health and Well-Being*. Over the years, your muscles stiffen. That makes you more likely to get injured. Plus, if you do get injured at age 50 or 60, your body may take up to twice as long to heal.

'The principles remain the same for all ages, but acting on them is more crucial,' says Dr Callahan. Masters competitors attest to the extra attention needed for the less obvious points of running. 'You can definitely get away with things earlier that you can't do when you are older,' says Jane Welzel, a five-time Olympic Marathon Trials qualifier and a masters runner standout with more than 50 marathons under her belt. In her mid-40s, Welzel was still able to compete with runners half her age, often placing in the top race spots. Welzel says that she hasn't changed her routine much over the years, but that's because she always performed strength and flexibility work as part of her workouts. 'If you don't already have the discipline of good nutrition, stretching and everything else, now it will catch up to you,' she says.

Here are 7 good running habits to consider adopting to ensure your optimal health:

❶ **Always warm up.** A proper warmup will loosen muscles and make your workout less of a stress on your body. You'll be less likely to pull a muscle or otherwise hurt yourself.

❷ **Focus on recovery.** The most noticeable impact of ageing upon training is the need for more recovery time between workouts. If you're a competitive runner, this might mean a greater number of easy running days between hard workouts; if you're a recreational runner, this might mean fewer actual running days per week. Your total training volume and miles will be likely to drop. 'You might have done 3 hard workouts a week before, and now it's 5 every 2 weeks,' says Palmason, who has coached hundreds of women over the years.

Don't let numbers guide you, though. Getting the proper recovery is the important thing, and that's more a matter of feel than anything else. If you ignore your body's request for rest, you could find yourself injured or chronically tired. 'Part of running is always paying attention to the signals you are

Nutritional Concerns

As women age, retaining muscle mass and bone density becomes a greater challenge, as both naturally diminish with age. To make matters worse, we have less muscle and bone mass than men to begin with. But fighting the clock on this front is time well spent; it pays off not only in terms of running performance, but also in overall health and vitality.

For older women, strength training becomes more important than ever. Weight training can slow the natural process of muscle atrophy and also contribute to bone remodelling, both of which will keep you in healthy running form, not to mention active in all your other endeavours.

Running itself is a weight-bearing activity that helps to maintain bone mineral density. However, those women who begin running prior to menopause experience the greatest benefit. Running post-menopause will not build additional bone mass, but will help you hold on to what you have. It will also maintain your muscle strength, which reduces the risk of falling and fracturing a bone later in life.

Older women are also advised to cut back on their cola intake. Research has shown a connection between cola consumption and reduced bone density in post-menopausal women. (From the 'life's not fair' department: no such correlation was found in men.) The lower bone density was found whether the women drank caffeinated or decaf, sugar-filled or diet drinks.

Finally, the multivitamin that was optional when you were younger is probably a better idea now. As we age, our bodies absorb nutrients less efficiently than they once did. And women have even higher needs for bone-protecting calcium as they age. To ensure that you're getting the proper vitamins and minerals, take a daily supplement. Drink plenty of water and watch your intake of diuretic drinks such as cola and coffee.

getting,' Palmason says. 'By the time we're 55 or 60, we should definitely have learned to do that!'

③ Take easier days off. Now that you're taking more days off, make sure that they actually give your body a break. A strenuous hike on a day that you don't run, for example, might not allow you to recover. If you want to stay active, do something that is not weight-bearing, such as swimming or cycling. This type of activity will allow your running muscles and joints to rest while developing other parts of your body.

④ Always stretch after your runs. Counteracting the tightening effects of running becomes more important with age. Stretch gently, without bouncing, in order to avoid injury.

⑤ Don't run in a worn-out pair of shoes. Replace your shoes about every 400 miles to make sure that they're offering the proper support and cushioning.

⑥ Try to run on a variety of surfaces. Give your legs a break from asphalt by running on dirt roads or in grassy parks, which will cushion the blow to your legs. If you have to run on pavement or concrete because of where you live, try to drive to a course with a softer surface at least once a week. Be mindful of your balance on challenging and rocky trails.

⑦ Keep challenging yourself. As you age, the pace of your steady runs and speedwork will eventually slow. But that doesn't mean you can't still challenge yourself. Be creative in the way you test yourself. For example, you might hit 'reset' on your personal bests each year, and aim for the season's best time, instead of comparing your times to previous years.

PERFORMANCE CHANGES

Runners can slow down the ageing process, but they can't fool it altogether. Sooner or later, all of us will be looking back on our record times instead of setting new ones.

Women distance runners typically hit their years of peak performance before the age of 40. Runners who start training later in life, however, can expect years of improvement, no matter what their age. Mary Kirsling, for example, continued to get faster well into her 70s after starting at age 64; Diane Palmason experienced 8 years of improvement after beginning to run at the age of 38. In general, from the day you start running, you can expect 8 to 10 years of improvement before your times begin to slow.

Slowing times might be inevitable, but that doesn't make them any easier to accept. You may feel frustrated. You may look for excuses: is it just an off year? 'For so long, it's about getting better, getting faster. Then suddenly there's a realization that you won't,' says Welzel. 'But if you're running because you enjoy it, you will find a way to continue. There are always other things to achieve and other reasons to be running – so much more that you can get from the sport. It's better to focus on those things rather than wishing that you could still do the other stuff.'

Here are some alternative focuses for runners who are no longer getting faster.

Change your goals with your changing age. As you get older, you can challenge yourself by focusing on your 'new personal bests', trying to run your best time since turning 50 or 60, for example. 'I look forward to getting older and entering a new age group,' says Ros Tabor, a runner from London. Tabor typifies the struggle that comes with changes due to ageing. 'It's great to be able to compete against runners of a similar age, thanks to each 5-year age category. It has certainly kept me motivated. I compete regularly against my local rivals and look forward to regional and national events where the competition is even higher.'

Race organizers, recognizing the influx of older runners into the sport, have responded by adding more age groups. 'When I started racing (in the 1980s) there very rarely were any age groups for older runners – it was just "60 and up",' recalls Kirsling. 'And because there were so few women out there to begin with, I was often racing against myself.' Thanks to the greater number of older runners now in the sport, 5- or 10-year age groups can be found up into the 80s and sometimes beyond. (The breakdown typically depends on the size of the race.) Naturally, the 'youngsters' in each bracket will have an advantage; thus the sweet irony of looking forward to growing older in order to enter a new age group.

Run a different type of race. If you're used to focusing on your time in a 5-K or 10-K, choose a challenge that you can't compare with those. Try a trail race, a relay race with friends or a duathlon, which combines running and cycling.

Run for your health. Instead of trying to lower your times, try to lower your blood pressure or your cholesterol level.

Run for someone else. More running events now focus on charity. Consider using your running to raise money for an organization by entering one of these races. Or dedicate a race to the memory of a loved one. Or encourage a daughter or granddaughter – or grandson – to start running with you.

Run to see the world. Many younger runners don't have time to travel to races. Pick a major race in a city you've wanted to see and create a holiday around it.

MENOPAUSE

Few studies have looked at the relationship between running and menopause. Research has generated intriguing theories but little in the way of definitive answers. 'Until recently,' as Palmason puts it, 'we have all been experiments of one.'

Evidence does suggest that physical activity can alleviate menopausal symptoms in some women. Several studies report fewer mood disturbances, fewer hot flushes and less sweating among women who are active than among their sedentary counterparts. One study of female runners showed that they were less likely to experience the weight gain that typically follows menopause. And a 1998 survey of 625 women readers of *Runner's World* magazine found that 74 per cent of women runners felt that running improved their overall menopausal and post-menopausal experience.

An interesting finding of the study is that running may make you hit menopause sooner. According to the *Runner's World* survey, the average menopausal age for the runners was 47.6; the national average for all women is 51. Jaffee says that the questionnaire results corroborate anecdotal evidence that women runners have been reporting for years. Until further studies are done, researchers can only theorize as to the reason for such early menopause, but they believe it might be related to the typically lower hormone levels in active women.

Whether women experience an accelerated decrease in performance during menopause has also yet to be proved. 'Some women do complain that their pace drops dramatically while they are going through menopause,' Jaffee says. 'While everybody's pace drops eventually due to ageing, it seems that women experience a more pronounced impact than men.' However, it's still unknown whether slowing in women runners is due more to the effects of ageing or to the effects of menopause. If it's menopause, then those performance fluctuations might reverse themselves when menopause is complete, as many runners report.

The impact of hormone replacement therapy (HRT) on running performance is also uncertain. Anecdotal evidence suggests that the therapy can go either way: some women find that it helps and others believe it hampers their performance. A *Runner's World* questionnaire found that of women taking HRT, 22 per cent felt that taking the hormones made a difference in their running. About a quarter reported a reduction in symptoms that made running difficult, 21 per cent reported an increase in energy and 17 per cent said they could run longer and faster. Nineteen per cent, however, said that HRT had a negative impact on their running.

It should be stressed that experts agree that the primary basis for deciding whether to undergo HRT should be your personal and family medical history. While HRT was once liberally prescribed for its protective effects against osteoporosis and relief of symptoms of menopause, it

TRAINING LOG

When people ask me who my running inspiration is, one woman comes to mind: Mary Kirsling. When I met Mary, she was 73 years old. She was training on the track once a week in the same group that included her 2 daughters and her grandson. As Mary would complete her 400s and 800s, the rest of the group would shout encouragement with whichever familiar moniker seemed most appropriate given their own age: 'Go, Mum!' Or, 'Go, Grandma!' Mary, it seems, had become every runner's adopted matriarch.

Over the years, Mary has become a minor celebrity of sorts. Runners one-third her age stop her on the cycling path to talk. They tell her what an inspiration she is to them, how they hope to be as fit and strong and confident and happy as she is when they reach her age. And I have told her the same thing.

Several years ago, Mary and I were both in a group of runners that had gone to the mountains for a combined camping trip and training retreat. During the weekend, I caught a glimpse of Mary running by herself, several miles out from the campsite, and heading up the steep mountain road that pointed the way back. I marvelled: how many women her age would be on that camping trip? How many women her age would even be walking in those mountains, much less running? How many Marys will it take before this scene seems ordinary?

Women traditionally have more fears than men do about growing old. We live longer; thus, the statistics say, we're more likely to be left alone or to be left in ill health. To see Mary – or to see any of her ever-growing number of female cohorts – on that mountain road, on that track, on that cycling path, is to see the realm of possibility that each of our futures holds. Thanks to Mary and the others, the future is looking good.

is no longer widely recommended because of its associated risks of cancer, heart disease and stroke. It's recommended that women who do take HRT take the lowest dose necessary for the shortest time possible. Some types of HRT are more risky than others, so discuss the decision with your doctor.

Index

Boldface page references indicate photographs.

Underscored references indicate boxed text.

child-care issues, 136–37
commitment and, 135–36
compulsion to run and, 139
partner's objection, 134–35
reasons for overcoming, 133–34
scheduling running time, 135–36
Training Log, 140
Child-care issues, 136–37
Chondromalacia patella, 211
Chronographs, 14
Clinics, running, 57
Clothing. See also Shoes
    for cold weather, 13–14, 24
    CoolMax, 13–14, 199
    Frequently Asked Questions, 24–25
    hats, 24, 213, 221
    for hot weather, 24
    jackets, 13–14, 221
    during marathon, 107
    after marathon, 115
    for rainy weather, 13–14
    shorts, 12–13
    socks, 10, 14
    sports bras, 6, 11–12, 24–25
    tips for finding right, 19
    tops, 12–13
    vests, 24
Clubs, runners', 57, 124, 125, 129
Coaches
    in advanced training programme, 76
    benefits of, 125–26
    compulsive runners and, 141
    Internet, 129
    selecting, 129
    working with, 126–27
    young runner and, 297–98
Coffee, 24, 160–62
Colds and flu, 199
Cold-weather clothing and gear, 13–14,
    24
Commitment, 64–65, 135–36
Competition. See 5-K races; Half-
    marathon; Marathon; Racing;
    10-K races
Compulsion to run and exercise, 139–41,
    182
Concentration, 51–52, 99–100
Confidence from running, 25, 33, 149
Consistency and training, 37, 65
Cooldown, 44. See also Stretching
CoolMax clothing, 13–14, 199
CoQ$_{10}$, 156

Core exercise, 232, **232**
Corns, 199–200
Cramps
    heat, 203
    menstrual, 207
    muscle, 208
Cross-training
    in caring for body, 192
    definition of, 268
    importance of, 268
    in injury prevention, 192
    in intermediate training programme,
        57
    options, 268–69
    timing of, 270
    Training Log, 269
Cushioned insoles, 17
Cushions, metatarsal, 17

D

Dairy products, 165
Dehydration, 138, 200–201, 203
Diarrhoea, 201
Diet. See also specific foods
    for active woman, 153
    in advanced training programme, 77
    balanced, 153–55
    in beginner training programme, 44
    business travel and, 138
    calcium in, 162–66
    carbohydrate-loading and, 158–59
    carbohydrates in, 158–59, 164
    changes to, 161
    coffee and caffeine in, 160–62
    cupboard and, stocking, 161
    dairy products in, 165
    eating habits and, 161, 172–77
    energy and, 177
    energy bars and gels in, 164–65
    evaluating, 77
    fat in, 44, 157–60
    food choices in, making wise, 175
    Frequently Asked Questions, 23–24
    glycogen stores and, 162, 167
    grazing, 279
    hydration and, 168–70
    importance of healthy, 107
    indulgences and, 175–77
    information on, 152–53
    iron in, 166
    90/10 rule and, 176–77

distance in, 52
Fartlek in, 54–55
'hard–easy' approach in, 53
hills and, 55
improving running and, 49–50
intensity in, 53–55
long run in, 53–54
next step and, 56, 59
pushing to new limits and, 50–52
16-week plan, 55–56, 60–61
strength training in, 57
time in, 53
tips for, 57
variety in, 53–55
Internet coaching, 129
Interval training, 67
iPod, 28
Iron, 166
IUDs, 196–97

J

Jackets, 13–14, 221
Jet lag, 138
Jogging, 46
Juice, 170, 201

L

Lactate threshold, 67
Lactate threshold run, 72–73
Legs
  in running form, 41
  strengthening exercises, 240, **240**,
    241, **241**, 242, **242**, 243, **243**,
    253, **253**
  stretching exercises, 228, **228**, 229,
    229, 230, **230**, 234, **234**
Libido, 192
Lightning safety issues, 223
Listening to body
  in beginner training programme,
    43–44
  in caring for body, 188–89
  in injury prevention, 188–89
  in marathon training, 109
  pregnant runner and, 271, 275–78,
    284–86
  racing and, 87, 100
  successful training programme and,
    33
Liverpool Women's 10-K, 94

Long run
  in advanced training programme,
    71–72
  fast, 72
  in intermediate training programme,
    53–54
  in marathon training, 104–5, 112–13
Loving body, 179

M

Marathon. *See also specific name*
  bath after, cold, 115
  checklist, 110–11
  choosing race and, 107–8
  clothing after, 115
  clothing during, 106–7
  considerations about, 108
  day before, 110–11
  drinking during, 113
  form during, 113
  Greek legend of, 102
  hydration after, 115
  morning of, 11
  pace in, 113–14, 113
  recovery after, 115
  rest after, 115
  shoes for, 106–7
  tips, 106–7, 113, 115
  training
    advanced, 118–20
    beginner, 116–17
    distance in, 105
    eating and drinking on run, 106–7
    flexibility and, 106, 115
    goals for finishing, 104–9
    goals for racing, 109–15
    listening to body, 109
    long run in, 104–5, 112–13
    pace in, 114–15
    partners and, 107, 107
    rest in, 106–7
    time for, 108–9
    time in, 105
    tips, 106–7
  Training Log, 121
  women and, 102–4
  younger runner and, 291
'Mask of pregnancy', 280
Massage, 77, 190–91
Maternity belt, 280
Maximum oxygen uptake (VO$_2$), 67

Medical examinations, 23, 294, <u>302–3</u>
Medication
  pain, 191
  side effects, 205
Men, running with, 130–32, <u>130–31</u>
Menopause, 206, 309–11
Menstrual issues, 205–8
Mental aspects of running
  health benefits of running and, 149–51
  mental fitness, 146–47
  motivation, 142–44
  perspective, 145–46
  positive attitude, 144–46
  self-discovery and, <u>148</u>
  Training Log, <u>150</u>
Mental edge, 69
Mental fitness, 146–47
Mental readiness in racing, 86–87, 95
Metatarsal cushions, <u>17</u>
Mileage. *See* Distance
Minerals. *See specific type*; Supplements
Minimal training for optimal results, 34
Moisturizers, 213
Monounsaturated fats, 160, <u>163</u>
Motivation, 51, <u>84</u>, 142–44, 181–82
Multivitamins, <u>107</u>, <u>306</u>
Muscle cell adaptation, 66
Muscle cramps, 208
Muscle soreness, <u>163</u>
Music players, 28
Myths of running, debunking, 28–30

N

National Eating Disorders Association, <u>184</u>
National Institutes of Health Office of Dietary Supplements, 168
National Register of Personal Trainers, 128
Negative thinking, 87
Neutral feet, 9–10
New limits, pushing, 50–52
Nike, 18
90/10 rule, 176–77
Nutrition. *See* Diet

O

Objection to running by partner, 134–35, <u>284</u>
Older runner
  age variances and, 303–4

diet for, <u>306</u>
health check and, <u>392–93</u>
menopause and, 309–11
performance changes and, 307–9
recovery and, 305–7
research on, 301–3
stretching for, 307
tips, 305–7
training for, 304–7
Training Log, <u>310</u>
Olympic Games 2012, 287
Omega-3 fatty acids, 160
Optimal results from minimal training, 34
Orthotics, <u>17</u>
Osteoporosis, 208–9
Overhydration, 169–70, 203
Overpronation, 9–10, 211
Overtraining, 68, <u>74–75</u>, 208
Ovulation, 205–8

P

Pace
  in beginner training programme, 42–45
  building, 67
  change in, 65
  Frequently Asked Questions, 26
  in marathon, 113–14, <u>113</u>
  in marathon training, 114–15
  racing and, 95–99
  surges and, 72
  tempo run and, 72–73
Pain. *See also* Cramps
  Achilles tendon, 193–94
  back, 195–96
  in beginner training programme, 44
  bone bruises, 198, 211–12
  Frequently Asked Questions, 27–30
  iliotibial band syndrome, 204
  medication, 191
  myth of running and, 28–30
  plantar fasciitis, 209–10
  runner's knee, 211
  shinsplints, 211–12
  shoes and, 27
  side stitches, 212
  as warning sign, 27
Painkillers, 191
Parks, running in, 137
Partners, running, <u>76</u>, 107, <u>107</u>, 123–25, 144

Reinjury, avoiding, 189
Relaxation and running, 42, 87, 100
Replacement insoles, 17
Research on women's running, 5, 271–72
Rest
    in advanced training programme, 69
    in beginner training programme, 44
    business travel and, 138
    after marathon, 115
    in marathon training, 106–7
    training and, 34–35
Reverse discrimination, 130
Reynaud's disease, 202
Rice, 163
Role model, being a good, 290
Role of running, changing, 138–39
Royal College of Obstetricians and
        Gynaecologists, 280
Routes, running, 25–26, 57, 138
Runners' clubs, 57, 124, 125, 129
Runner's knee, 211
Runner's World website, 128
Running boom, women's, 2–5
Running camps, 57, 128
Running clinics, 57
Running store, 19
Running buggies, 136
Running tracks, 73–77, 137

S

Safety issues
    animals, 220
    attackers, 216–19
    business travel and running routes,
        138
    cars, 220–21
    precautions, 217–19
    pregnant runner, 273
    terrain, 221, 307
    Training Log, 222
    weather, 221–23
Salads, 163
Saturated fats, 160
Scheduling challenges to running, 135–36
Sciatic nerve, 195
Segments, 72
Self-confidence from running, 25, 33, 149
Self-consciousness about running, 25, 29
Self-discovery and running, 148
Self-talk, 100, 145
Sex drive, 192

Sexual performance and running, 192
Sharpening, 67
Shinsplints, 211–12
Shoes
    arch types and, 9–10, 16–17
    importance of right, 6
    inserts for, 16–17
    for marathon, 106–7
    motion control and, 10
    neutral, 10
    pain and, 27
    racing, 77, 107
    second pair of training, 106
    selecting, 7–11
    stability and, 10
    testing, 10, 107
    women's, 11
Shorts, 12–13
Side stitches, 212
16-week plan, 55–56, 60–61. *See also*
        Intermediate training programme
Skin problems
    acne, 194–95
    blisters, 197–98
    calluses, 199–200
    chafing, 199
    corns, 199–200
    heat rash, 204
    razor bumps, 210–11
    sun damage, 212–13
    wrinkles, 212–13
Sleep, 77, 107
SmartWool socks, 14
Snacks, 167, 177
Social running
    camps, 128
    clubs, 124, 125
    with men, 130–32, 130–31
    partners, 123–25, 144
Socks, 10, 14
Soft drinks, 162, 306
Solo running, 122–23
Soya products, 163
Speed. *See* Pace
Sports bras, 6, 11–12, 24–25
Sports massage, 77, 190–91
Sports watches, 14
Starvation tactics in weight loss,
        avoiding, 174
Stomach upset, 213
Strength training
    in advanced training programme, 66–67

in beginner training programme, <u>44</u>
exercises
  Abductor Walk, 247, **247**
  Adductor Swing, 248, **248**
  Back Extensions, 246, **246**
  Calf Raise, 243, **243**
  Leg Curl, 241, **241**
  Lower Abdominal Crunch, 250, **250**
  other abdominal, 251, **251**
  Press-up, 244, **244**
  Running with Dumbbells, 252, **252**
  Squat, 240, **240**
  Squat Thrusts, 253, **253**
  Triceps Dips, 245, **245**
  Upper Abdominal Crunch, 249, **249**
  Walking Lunges, 242, **242**
importance of, 238
in intermediate training programme,
  <u>57</u>
as supplement to running, 177
tips, 238–39
in training for running, 66–67
weight loss and, 177
Stress fracture, 189, 213–15
Stretching
exercises
  Abdominal Stretch, 236, **236**
  Back Stretch, 237, **237**
  Buttocks and Lower-back Stretch,
    233, **233**
  Calf Stretch, 228, **228**
  Hamstring Stretch, 229, **229**
  Hip and Buttocks Stretch, 231, **231**
  Hip and Core Stretch, 232, **232**
  Hip and Waist Stretch, 235, **235**
  Inner Leg and Groin Stretch, 234, **234**
  Thigh Stretch, 230, **230**
importance of, 226
in injury prevention, 190–91, 227
for older runner, 307
Stride, 27, 41
Style. *See* Form, running
Sun exposure and damage, 212–13, <u>280</u>
Sunglasses, 19–20
Sunscreen, 212, <u>280</u>
Superstitions, avoiding, 93
Supination, 9–10
Supplements, <u>156–57</u>, 166–68
Support team, building positive, 145
Surges, 72
Sweating, 170

T

Tapering, 67–68, 89–91
Tea, 162
Teflon socks, 14
Tempo run, 72–73, 115
10-K races, 66, 73, 77–78, 90
Terrain safety issues, 221, 307
Testosterone, <u>157</u>, <u>192</u>
Thigh-stretching exercise, 230, **230**
Time, 53, 105
Toast, 24, <u>163</u>
Toenails, black, 197
Tofu, <u>163</u>
Tops, 12–13
Tracking devices, 18–19
Tracks, running, 73–77, 114, 137
Track sessions, 73–77
Tradition, starting a running, <u>57</u>
Training. *See also* Advanced training
      programme; Beginner training
      programme; Intermediate training
      programme; Marathon
  advanced competitor, 78, <u>80–81</u>
  base building in, 66
  beginner competitor, 77–78, <u>78–79</u>
  consistency and, 37, 65
  energy, 68
  genetics and, 32–33
  goals, 31–32, <u>36</u>
  half-marathon, <u>82–83</u>
  hill, 51, 55
  intensity of, 53–55
  interval, 67
  listening to body and successful,
    33
  minimal, for optimal results, 34
  for older runner, 304–7
  optimizing, 68
  patience and, 37
  peaks and plateaus, 35, 37
  personal trainers and, 127–28
  principles and rules, 34–39
  rest and, 34–35
  resuming, after injury, 192–93
  shoes, <u>106</u>
  smart, 190
  strength training and, 66–67
  Training Log, <u>38</u>
  variety in, 53–55
  weight loss and, 173–74
  whole body, 37, 39